DO NOT REMOVE
CARDS FROM POCKET

10/14/93

How TO HELP YOUR CHILD LAND THE RIGHT JOB (without being a pain in the neck)

HOW TO HELP YOUR CHILD LAND THE RIGHT JOB (without being a pain in the neck)

Nella Barkley

WORKMAN PUBLISHING, NEW YORK

Library of Congress
Cataloging-in-Publication Data
Barkley, Nella.
    How to help your child land the right
    job (without being a pain in the neck) /
    by Nella Barkley.
        p.   cm.
    Includes index.
ISBN 1-56305-512-0 ISBN 1-56305-152-4 (pbk.)
        1. Job hunting. 2. College graduates—
Employment. 3. Vocational guidance—Parent
participation. I. Title. HF5382.7.B36 1993
650.14—dc20 92-50929 CIP

Cover Illustration: Fred Winkowski
Author Photo: J. Henry Fair

Workman Publishing Company, Inc.
708 Broadway
New York, NY 10003

Manufactured in the United States of America

First printing May 1993
10 9 8 7 6 5 4 3 2 1

This book is dedicated to my mother, who died at age 93 after years of telling me, "There's no such word as 'can't' in the dictionary."

Acknowledgments

Writing this book has been much more of an adventure for me than I expected. I knew I would someday get around to the business of creating books and other products based on the Crystal-Barkley Life/Work Design process. That day, for books, would have been much farther off were it not for the remarkable talents of Josleen Wilson, an accomplished writer in her own name. She has helped me shape this book from concept to completion. Her willingness to immerse herself in the Crystal-Barkley process personally as well as professionally has enabled me to express myself with what I am certain is much more clarity and balance than would otherwise have been possible. Besides, she made the venture fun.

I am indebted to my agent, Barbara Lowenstein, for introducing Josleen to me and for proposing the idea for a book for parents of job seekers (only to discover we at the Crystal-Barkley Corporation had long wanted to write it!). It was a remarkable incidence of serendipity. Barbara agreed to support me in what were not always orthodox procedures, because I was determined they would work. With her help, they did.

Producing this book has been a collaborative effort in every sense. My colleagues at Crystal-Barkley's New York City office contributed long hours of thought, brainstorming, and practical suggestion: Marjorie Long, as wise a parent as she is a consultant; Grace Broad, who invariably brings that special needed insight gleaned from her relationship with clients; and Clifford Oblinger, who never fails to look at an issue with fresh eyes. Many members of the staff contributed their perspective and their stories: Elizabeth Erbach, Gary Wertheimer, and Giselle Liberatore. Linda Yan was steadily on hand to provide judicious support.

Outside of the company, I received outstanding help from two talented young writers, Lee Randall and Jeffrey Felshman, who listened to and interpreted dozens of hours of tape-recorded creative sessions among the Crystal-Barkley staff. Special thanks are owed to Shelagh Masline, who did a remarkable job of researching and organizing the unique, multifaceted information that comprises the resource section at the end of the book.

Eric Sandburg, Crystal-Barkley's partner in Career Design software is also due mention, for the long years of working with him to develop that project gave us ideas for this one.

Judith Bobrow, of Bobrow and Hollingsworth, who is Crystal-Barkley's public relations representative, has been a steadfast friend, offering helpful points of view throughout.

I would like to thank Suzanne Rafer, my editor at Workman Publishing, and her associate, Margot Herrera, for the absolutely exhaustive attention given to the manuscript. The work profited greatly from it.

In a category all its own is my family. My children, Nella, Miles, and Rufus, were kind but always truthful editors, a lovely combination. My husband, Rufus, filled whatever role I seemed to need him to and, because he has devoted his life to helping the rest of us live satisfying lives, applauded the prospect of this book.

All together, these people have made it possible for me to run a business while writing a book. No mean feat! And I love them for it.

And lastly, I acknowledge for myself and for you, the reader, a huge debt of gratitude to John Crystal, who began all of this in his own life and work. He was unorthodox only because he had a knack for seeing things as they are, and he taught me how to look through his eyes.

Contents

PART II: SPECIAL SITUATIONS

PART III: RESOURCES

ON THE THRESHOLD

How often have you heard someone—yourself included—ask a child, "What do you want to be when you grow up?" We're only half serious when we ask this of a five-year-old, fully expecting a response like "cowboy," or "ballerina," "fireman," or "president." Nevertheless, this innocent question plants the idea that grown-up people are defined by their job titles.

In this book, we are going to turn that notion on its ear. You will help your young adult-child discover himself, or herself, so that he or she can define a job, rather than be defined by it.

While most young adults are a bit beyond "What do you want to be when you grow up?" most are still wrestling with its implications. And so are we, their parents. How quickly our bright expectations turn to worry and frustration as we watch these newly minted grown-ups standing frozen on the threshold of their lives. I know because I have been there as a parent; and as a professional whose business it is to help people figure out what to do with their working lives, I've had to learn how to solve this dilemma. In this book I want to share proven strategies developed by the Crystal-Barkley Corporation with other parents wondering where to turn for help.

Whether your child is a new job seeker sporting a fresh college degree or already working and unhappy on the job, you can get him or her moving in the "right" direction by following the steps outlined in this handbook. You can vastly increase the chances of your offspring's achieving a satisfying life (to say nothing of your own peace of mind) by learning how to become a partner in your child's quest for fulfilling work.

This book is partly in response to requests from parents who, contemplating mid-life career changes themselves, participated in Crystal-Barkley Life/Work Design programs. Having discovered how to redirect their own work lives, they wanted to pass on the benefits to their children, too. But there is nothing more frustrating than trying to give advice to a grown child. How, they asked, could they translate the Crystal-Barkley process for their kids?

The anxiety these parents were feeling finally impelled me to lay out the blueprint for them as well as for other parents. Many of their stories appear here, but names and sometimes the locations have been changed to protect their privacy. Be assured that the stories are true in every other respect.

Linda, the mother of a recent college graduate with a degree in English literature, told me, "Every time I ask Jennifer what she wants to do, she just shrugs and says, 'I don't know.' I want to shake her."

Many of us find ourselves in Linda's uncomfortable position as our kids graduate from college, to the tune of $70,000, with few ideas about how to make their way in the world or even about what they want to do. Little wonder that they are approaching job hunting in a fog.

Jennifer belongs to the next twentysomething generation—48 million young Americans walking in the shadow of the famous baby boomers—trying to be adults, facing a world profoundly changed and profoundly confusing.

It's a harsher world than we remember, even those of us only 20-plus years older than our kids. Young people tell us they feel helpless in the face of social problems—a deteriorating environment, drugs, illiteracy, poverty, racial discrimination, homelessness. They tell us they would like to help solve this litany of ills, but feel inadequate to such a huge task.

Above all, they worry about the amount of money they need to live independently. An unstable economy looms like a stubborn beast between them and their futures. Our kids realize the stakes are high in the working world, and when we talk about job security, they know better. Today, no job or industry can be counted on to be either secure or lucrative.

Larry, the 24-year-old son of another client, moved back home after losing his first job. He wants to get back on the career ladder but says it feels more like a greased pole. In the meantime he's camped out in his old room, which his dad had converted to an office for himself. Suddenly Larry's parents find themselves parenting all over again.

Young people are often urged by teachers and career counselors to analyze the "growth" industries and make premature "career" choices. Many, under mounting pressure, knuckle under to the first job that promises a steady paycheck. Or, caught in the thicket of their desires, expectations, and worries, they fall into a kind of crippling passivity and lack of commitment, afraid to try anything or loathing everything they do try.

Tony insisted his daughter Sharon major in accounting so she could "always make a living." After graduation,

Sharon randomly applied for entry-level corporate jobs, her eye on the starting salary. She hopped from job to job, and finally wound up working for a national chain of nutrition centers, with her salary tied to a small commission. Six months later, she was exhausted and stressed out. "She's so unhappy," her father says. "I want to tell her to chuck it, but she hasn't liked any job. And in this economy she's lucky to have a job at all."

The truth is, Sharon owns a piece of information about herself that she doesn't even realize exists. Systematic questioning revealed that Sharon has a multitude of interests but didn't know how to relate any of them to the marketplace. She loves rock music and entertained fantasies of being a rock star. She also loves clothes and fashion—she spent all of her money on the latest styles. She had never once explored the many ways these interests could be shaped into a career.

Any enthusiasm or ambition can be turned into employment. Even if her father is right that Sharon "can't sing a lick," there are many other ways for her to connect with her passions. In and around the fashion and recording businesses, dozens of careers might combine her primary interests with her training in business and accounting—if she decides she wants to capitalize on these skills. Sharon has *hundreds* of other skills that she hasn't even begun to uncover, however. Who knows? Maybe she'll be the greatest agent in the music business.

Work doesn't have to be the opposite of play. Twenty-six-year-old Lindsay recently visited her college roommate, who now works as a designer in a book-packaging company. There she discovered four adults stretched out on the floor, amid sketches and layouts, discussing the best cover design for a new edition of *The Wizard of Oz*. Surprised, Lindsay said, "You people get *paid* for this?"

At their parents' urging, Jennifer, Larry, Sharon, and Lindsay all came to Crystal-Barkley looking for answers to the same question: "What can I do with my life that will fulfill my dreams for fascinating work *and* allow me to live the way I want to?" It is the same question asked by the thousands of people of all ages who attend our courses every year.

On the satisfaction scale, lowest marks go to a job that just pays the bills. At the most satisfying end is work we enjoy, that enriches our lives at every level. To move toward that "best" end means discovering inner passions big enough to encompass all our talents and dreams. That's what this book is all about.

Surprising as it may sound, the first step for every young person looking to make the right career choices in a fiercely demanding job market is to develop a systematic way to tap into inner desires and define interests, goals, and values. Within each of us lies the secret formula to a successful future, and it is tremendously difficult to capture the attention of potential employers without this knowledge.

We All Have True Callings

Over the ages great thinkers have advised us to look within for direction, but most people don't listen. We get little social reinforcement for doing the things we really want to do. We usually get approval only for doing what others— including our teachers, parents, and peers — expect of us.

Many of us think it's impossible to accomplish what we really want. We relegate our fantasies to the realm of "if only." If we pass this way of thinking on to our children, we will rob them of their greatest advantage in today's job market. In the face of a tight economy, nothing is more practical than living one's dream, because the energy that comes from desire and well-placed skills is very appealing to employers.

Even if your son or daughter chooses a job that is not immediately lucrative, or a field in which there are not a lot of jobs at the moment, he or she can still make it work.

THE DISCOVERY PROCESS

Here are the steps to discovering those callings in your job seeker:

Step 1: Systematically uncover what he or she deep down inside *wants* to do.

Step 2: Figure out what aptitude he or she has for it.

Step 3: Learn how to translate this information into a job.

Every child has definite, specific callings for which he or she can feel passion, even if they have never been expressed. It's not only the toddler mathematician who multiplies fractions at the dinner table or the adolescent who studies the heavens with dreams of space exploration who can live richly directed work lives. Everybody has at least one calling, and most people have several. Ultimately, following his dreams is the most practical step your child can take. Give him the chance to be irresistible to employers—he will be a refreshing alternative to apathetic job seekers who are frightened and tentative.

A Parent's Place

How can we parents help our kids take hold of their lives and step into the job market? Whether kids are 18, 22, 30, or 40, parents remain their primary role models and most-ardent cheering section. Because of our own hard lessons learned, battles lost and won, we are the most logical career coaches for our adult children—if only we knew how.

To my knowledge, this is the first book to show parents a

proven method to help kids get jobs and shape careers. It is a method used successfully with thousands of adults who attend week-long Crystal-Barkley courses, which are combined with personal one-on-one consultations.

Every course is led by a consultant I have trained personally. He or she coaches each client through the dozens of exercises and activities that reveal hidden talents and desires, values and interests. Then, in personal one-on-one consultations, each client plans how to fit this lively bundle of attributes to the needs of the contemporary workplace.

This handbook shows you how to assume the vital role of coach to guide your child through this same process. No one knows your child as intimately as you do, and no one cares as deeply.

Assuming a Role

As parents, of course, we have a couple of factors making it difficult to help our kids: preconceived notions about the working world that are reinforced by our own experience, and our kids' natural reluctance to listen to anything we have to say. This handbook gives you ways to overcome both problems.

The first step is to get on an equal footing with your child. By assuming the role of coach, you automatically remove much of the psychological tension which is natural to the parent-child equation. View your child as your "client," a respected equal for whom you can provide a valuable service. The term "client" may sound oddly impersonal to you at first; however, thinking of your son or daughter in this way conveys a feeling of respect which will make a significant impression on your child. I guarantee you will find it fascinating to see how a simple change in language creates a new dimension in your relationship and also helps you avoid overly parental reactions during the process.

Looking Inside

The Crystal-Barkley method is the only job-hunting method of which I am aware rooted firmly in a set of principles. First among them is that solving the job problem—regardless of a person's age—begins with knowing the inner self. Understanding the person inside and matching this to the field in which he or she wants to work are the keys to gaining a satisfying life.

To do this we start by asking questions:

"Who am I?"
Answering this question involves discovering talents, skills, and aptitudes—what your client will bring to a work relationship or any relationship.

"Where am I going?"
Discovering dreams and desires, even passions, is so powerful that your client will feel a magnetic pull toward specific work.

"How do I get there?"
Revealing the how-to's of the Crystal-Barkley process equips kids with techniques to approach job hunting in a way that makes sense both to them and prospective employers. Your client will be able to market her or his skills so effectively that employers will be convinced their needs will be met.

These three questions form the heart of the Crystal-Barkley process. Each will be explored and answered by using information you and your client have available right now. You don't need elaborate tests or training. What you do require is a personal way to access this information, and I intend to show you the way.

THE JOHN CRYSTAL STORY

Since 1981, the Crystal-Barkley Corporation has been offering professional counsel to individuals and organizations on how to manage their most valuable assets: themselves and their workers. We happen to believe that the best work is done when people are happy, and to this end continue to research, develop, and expand our unique and proprietary methods whereby enterprises thrive and individuals live satisfying lives. The process was pioneered by my partner, the late John C. Crystal, more than 40 years ago. It is actually a product of his own life experience.

Against all odds (he had very poor eyesight), John became a U.S. Intelligence officer during World War II, and his imaginative and unorthodox methods of survival in enemy territory led to an illustrious, highly decorated career.

At war's end, however, this master spy was out of a job. One would think that American industry would have been quick to seize upon his unique skills, but John's resume confounded his first post-war interviewers: "We appreciate your exceptional training, Mr. Crystal, but we're not hiring any spies today!"

Undaunted, John applied the same field strategy that he had used behind enemy lines to looking for a job. First he asked himself, "What do I most want to accomplish with my life?" Put in those terms, John most wanted to help war-ravaged Europe acquire the goods and services necessary to rebuild.

He next measured his own skills and aptitudes to discover the best way he could make a contribution

Continued

to this goal. He knew it was not enough just to zero in on what he wanted. He had to be able to convince an employer that he needed what John had to offer. But which employer? The next vital question John asked himself was, "Who shares my desire to do this?"

John began to research American businesses—a part of the process we now call "surveying"—to find out who had the goods and services Europe needed. When he had a list of major corporations, he picked his top choices and began to formulate a practical business proposal, showing how his skills could help sell their products abroad. John chose the Sears Roebuck Company, which had an excellent management-training program as well as the kind of products and services he thought could best help European countries. With training, he became Sears's first Manager of Operations for Europe and the Middle East.

Later John refined the method that had led to his own success and began to counsel others. John's pioneering ideas were first popularized when he contributed the fundamentals to the best-selling *What Color Is Your Parachute?* by Richard N. Bolles. John and Dick Bolles later coauthored a workbook for job counselors and students, *Where Do I Go From Here With My Life?*

When I first met John, he had a private consulting practice, and I was a strategic-planning consultant for profit and nonprofit organizations. I had become aware that many of the people I worked with were unable to use their management skills on their own behalf. Time and again high-level executives complained to me that they were unhappy in their jobs, or felt they were stuck in the wrong jobs. I became fascinated with these problems and decided that what I most wanted was to help people solve these dilemmas and have fulfilling work lives. I felt there had to be a systematic way to do this.

In 1981, John and I formed Crystal-Barkley Corporation, bringing together the work each of us had been doing in different ways—John for 40 years and I for 20—to enable individuals and organizations to make maximum progress toward their goals through skilled decision making. Our idea was to extend John's revolutionary concepts on career strategy to a wide audience of individuals and organizations.

Together, John and I, with the help of a growing cadre of colleagues, embellished his already remarkable process to produce the Life/Work Design program, a new way for individuals to apply proven management techniques to control the direction of their lives and work.

Each year, hundreds of people participate in Crystal-Barkley programs in New York, Chicago, and Los Angeles; several thousand more learn about these methods through workshops and speeches in such cities as Denver, San Diego, Washington, D.C., Atlanta, and Boston. In addition, Crystal-Barkley offers special programs to organizations such as the World Bank, General Motors, and the U.S. State Department, teaching managers how to appraise, hire, and promote talented individuals. We have now also developed Career Design software, for coaching via personal computer, to reach those who cannot reach us. (See Part III, Resources.)

Since our doors first opened, more than 20,000 people have benefited from the Crystal-Barkley method.

How to Use This Handbook

This handbook is your coach's guide, whether your client is seeking a great new job, making a decision whether or where to go to college, trying to get out of an unsatisfying job, or simply trying to make a propitious next step. You can consult a single chapter and see results in a few hours or spend several weeks taking your client through the complete process. You will probably refer back to certain chapters repeatedly as your child's job search evolves and new issues change and old ones need fine-tuning.

Chapters will lead you through potentially hazardous forks in the road of any young adult's life, moments when choices must be made. Each chapter concentrates on a real-life trouble spot. You will learn how to help your offspring solve a short-term problem while keeping an eye on the long-term effect.

You may wish to jump right in to the chapter which pinpoints your client's present dilemma. This is fine; however, the chapters are linked sequentially. Reading each one in order will reveal the total Crystal-Barkley process. If you do choose to start in the middle, you may want to back up to earlier chapters so that your client can assemble all the information he or she needs to make a propitious move. I ask you to have patience with this and follow along, even when the title of a given chapter may not seem relevant. This is a systematic process and, as is the case in any system, if any part is missing, the process may not work as a whole.

Each chapter ends with a series of activities and exercises adapted from the successful work accomplished by thousands of Crystal-Barkley clients. These exercises have been designed to help you help your client find the answers to the three central questions: Who am I? Where am I going? How do I get there? You will also have a good time doing them together, and will likely establish a new way of relating to each other which I hope you will continue to enjoy throughout your lives.

When it comes time to do the exercises, the best approach for parents is to:

- Keep it light.
- Avoid the "big talk," that endless harangue during which everything is supposed to get settled and nothing does.
- Boost conversation to adult level and speak to your client as you would to a close friend.
- Ask, "How would this work best for you?" "What do you think is the best way for us to start this process?"
- Remember that timing is everything. You don't have to grab *every* opportunity to work on the process.

You will notice that the exercises are developed in an unusual way. At the first pass, you will learn a little about the topic. The exercises in later chapters build on and refine that information. Each time you return to a subject, you look at it in a different way and a deeper level is uncovered.

In Chapter 4, for example, you begin to match your client's skills with his interests. In later chapters, you look at skills on a much more sophisticated level, pinpointing where and how each is best used. This is a process first of discovery, followed by refinement, then followed by deeper discoveries and more refinement.

In Part II, four chapters deal with situations in which some parents and children may be currently embroiled: deciding on a college or a major, handling a bad-job situation, and coping with being fired. Even if your child is not immediately dealing with these particular problems, it's still interesting to see how they might have affected him in the past or might affect him in the future.

The Crystal-Barkley method is a tool for personal decision making and action. It is not psychotherapeutically based; any results similar to those gained from therapy may be real, but are coincidental.

At the end of the book you will find highly selective listings of resources, including counselors, books and other reference material, computer software, and audiovisual programs invaluable to modern job seekers. Each resource has been thoroughly reviewed and only those which I feel make a genuinely positive contribution to the job search are included. Organized by topic, the information evaluates the most current resources available to job seekers and tells you how to locate them.

The purpose of this handbook is to help you and your client fashion an individualized road map by which he can navigate through the working world at his own speed, ultimately traveling the route to where he wants to be.

With these new tools at hand, it is never too late to provide support and practical counsel. Whether your client is 22 or 42, you can turn the plaint "I don't know what to do!" into "Guess what? I just got a great job!"

Note: If you wish to use The Handbook for your own purposes, simply ask a friend to act as your coach. Or, perhaps, you will have the pleasure one day in the future of having your client become your coach.

PART I

THE JOB
SEARCH

Chapter One

GETTING STARTED

E ven in their late teens and early twenties, our "kids," in our minds, are still the babies we nurtured. The habit of guiding them, of being ready to catch them if they fall, may still be in force. This "parental" attitude won't help your child find a job, however. Parent-child relationships are usually too fraught with parental authority and childish rebellion to be effective in an adult task such as job seeking.

So as outrageous as the thought may seem, forget about being "the parent." Your role in this process is to act as a trusted counselor and friend. Your aim is to treat your child with the same respect as you would your friends, which usually means elevating the "child" to your own level. This is why I ask you to turn your child into your "client."

Benefits of Coaching

There are four important ways you personally benefit from stepping down from the parent pedestal and becoming a coach to your child-client.

• As a coach, you are not expected to have all the answers.
• Customary parent-child tension is reduced.

- You are relieved of the pressure to "fix things."
- Being a coach to your kids is more relaxing and a lot more fun than being "the parent."

There is a fifth benefit: Assuming the role of coach introduces a subtle but powerful change in mind-set that may form the foundation of your future adult-to-adult relationship.

The Importance of Being Equals

Establishing equality depends greatly on the current relationship between you and your child. It won't be the same for every family, or for every child within a family. To start the process, it helps to look at what your pattern has been. Are you trapped in the old act-react mechanism—they act, you react? They return the car on empty, you shout "Not again!" just like you did when they spilled the milk. The pattern reinforces itself over the years. Like a lot of parents, you may have inadvertently become entrenched in a situation in which your children tell you as little as possible about their actions for fear of your disapproval or for fear of having their missteps observed by the authority figure in their lives. Sensing this hazard, you may have stepped back only to have your hands-off attitude interpreted as indifference.

For example, Beth says, "My parents always bend over backwards to stay neutral, let me make my own choices. I appreciate that trust, but it sometimes seems like what I do isn't very important to them—unless something goes wrong. Then they're sure to remark on it. They never come out and say, 'We're proud of you.' 'Wow, good for you!' They never acknowledge the productive things I do."

If you're too extreme in either direction—too protective or too indifferent—you can readjust the balance. It is possible to experiment with being more or less involved in your child's life. To do so, you may have to ask for a readout on your parenting style. It takes a little courage, but sometimes the other parent involved can give you an accurate assessment of how you are perceived by a child. If asking your spouse doesn't appeal to you, perhaps another child or family member can do the same. (Grandparents, for example, are often sounding boards for children on their relationships with their parents.) If you are sincere, you can probably secure candid commentary on how your child perceives your style.

Becoming an equal is a big shift for your child as well. Some kids will be uncertain about how to adapt to even a welcome change. While some may embrace it with open arms, others may react with suspicion, wondering what's going on. Remember that changing a relationship's dynamic doesn't happen overnight. Stick with it. The benefits will last long after your child lands the right job.

A Change in Vocabulary

Often a simple change in vocabulary can quickly break down barriers and help create a new kind of equality between you.

Hal's son, Johnny, says that he wants to work in advertising. He stands before his dad in cutoff jeans, with long hair and three small earrings in one ear.

Hal thinks, "What you *should do* is cut your hair and get yourself cleaned up." Instead, Hal says, "Maybe you want to ask Mac Nelson down the street if you could spend some time with him in his office downtown. He runs a successful agency. It would give you a feel for the atmosphere and see the different kinds of people who work there." He then adds, "You *might also want* to take a look at the way people in the advertising field are dressed. Do you think you want to conform to that world? For instance, how would you feel about dressing like Mac?"

Sometimes in our eagerness to help a child solve a problem, we look for shortcuts: "Do it this way, and get on with

WHICH PARENT MAKES THE BEST JOB-SEARCH COACH?

One-on-one? Two-on-one? Either or both parents can successfully act as coach. Dynamics are different in different families, and with different children in the same family. Both parents can coach together, but, personally, I believe that one parent is most effective. One-on-one helps create parity between you and your client. Gender is irrelevant.

Generally the best choice is whichever parent the child is most comfortable talking with, given the subject matter. Most young people prefer to work with the less judgmental, more listening-oriented parent.

Parents can also take turns working with different parts of the process. Go with *your* strengths. There will be occasions when two-parent conversations are natural. Dinner-table talk will probably gravitate toward the issue your son or daughter is dealing with at the time and these conversations can be productive. As Jim says, "I'm talking to my parents about starting my own business. They both bring up good points because they have different opinions. I get good feedback from them together, because they interact with each other and I listen." But in these conversations, be careful not to gang up or let others gang up on your client.

In certain situations a close friend may be a more effective coach than either parent. Most of the time, however, parents make resoundingly good coaches because the depth of their caring is unsurpassed.

it." But if a friend should come to you with the same problem, you'd listen, think, and ask questions before offering help. That's exactly what Hal did with Johnny. Hal's method took longer, but it got results, because Johnny could "hear" his dad, and because the choice of action was left up to Johnny. Hal's approach also relieved a lot of tension.

In another father and son situation, Arthur and his son James are very different personality types. Arthur, a very successful businessman, has a low-key, introspective personality. James, who wants to start his own business, is an enthusiastic, high-flying type. Arthur feels that James is too reckless and too quick to make decisions. He tries to balance James's quick reactions, but his efforts often translate into disapproval. "You need to" and "you ought to" permeate Arthur's conversations with his son.

Arthur made a deliberate effort to change his language. Instead of dictating "the truth according to Dad," Arthur let James talk and then engaged in a dialogue to explore the possibilities. He got on James's team as a player, instead of acting as its captain. Rather than "You should do some research before you decide," he said, "Have you thought about asking somebody else for input?"

When Arthur stepped away from his long-standing authoritative attitude, James was able to listen to him—and, for the first time, benefit from his father's opinions.

Not all parents are as savvy as Hal, or as willing to change as Arthur. Parents who are recognized achievers in their own work are likely to see themselves as experts in everything else, too. Like a lot of people who have earned their stripes, they tend to be especially dogmatic about their particular area of expertise.

One well-known entertainment lawyer considered himself the last word in theatrical know-how. If the subject had to do with music, acting, production, directing, writing, Ben

LISTENING—YOUR NUMBER ONE SKILL

With our method, kids talk, parents listen. Effective listening is an active process. It goes like this: You listen to your client, then respond by restating what you've heard or by asking a question that helps clarify the meaning. The trick is to avoid getting defensive. Kim's mom fell into this trap.

KIM: "You complain about me not doing anything about this job hunt. But you don't ever have time to sit down and talk with me."

MOM: "What? I ask you all the time how I can help. I called Uncle Joe the other day and made an appointment for you, but you never followed through. I've done a lot. I put myself out for you."

KIM: "You told me about the appointment at the last minute. I had a research paper due, so I couldn't go."

MOM: "You didn't say you couldn't go."

KIM: "But I didn't find out in time. You make such an issue out of everything. I can't talk to you. I'm leaving."

knew. His son Larry wanted to start a rock band. When he told his father about his hopes of forming a band and taking it on tour, Ben scoffed. "That isn't the way music careers are made," he said.

Larry protested, "Dad, things are different in rock music."

Replay

: "You never have time to sit down and talk."

: "I didn't realize you felt bad about this."

: "Let's find a way to make time together."

: "How can you do that?"

: "Maybe I get so wrapped up in the job and the commuting—but when it comes down to it, I always have the time."

: "What are you doing tomorrow night? Can you get off work on time?"

: "Absolutely. Are you going to be at home?"

: "Not only will I be here, I'll get dinner started for us so we'll have more time."

Who's the parent and who's the child in the second exchange? When the speakers are equals, it's hard to tell. The replay proceeded differently because Mom listened well from the very first. Then, instead of being defensive, she asked a question to clarify. She listened intently to the response, which enabled her to make an understanding comment.

Ben countered, "I've been dealing with the music business for thirty years. Do you think I don't know what I'm talking about?"

Parents express their opinions as facts all the time, yet they can be as wrong as anyone. Even if Ben were right, his information is still filtered through his own values and experience. When he blatantly expounded on "the way things are," Larry's ears turned to stone.

Instead, Ben could have asked his son dozens of intriguing questions: "Tell me about it. How do you go about forming a band? How do you get rehearsal space? How do you go about booking a band on a road tour? Do you make your own arrangements? What kind of technical people do you need for something like that? Do record companies send out scouts to hear new bands? What does it take to get started?" These are the questions that would show interest and would also help Larry think more clearly about his dreams.

But Ben didn't ask. Larry felt his father neither understood nor respected him. He reacted by cutting himself off from his family and pursuing his dream on his own. Larry may be successful one day and "show" his father. But even if the rift between them heals, the scar will remain.

Your New Role

Begin seeing yourself as a supporter, listener, and coach. Coaching makes your life easier, and also allows your child— now your client—to be more receptive to your help.

As coach, you will have plenty of opportunity to express your ideas in anecdotal form ("I can tell you what happened when your uncle Harry was in a similar situation"). Telling stories removes all the "ought to's" and the "should's" and lets your client arrive at his own conclusions.

It's hard to accept, but you can't save your child from making mistakes. What you can do is act as a sounding board when things go wrong. Experiment with revealing your feelings and experiences, including your own mistakes, successes, and defeats. You might say something like, "Yes, I felt just that way, and I worried terribly when I was starting

PHRASES THAT MAKE YOUNG PEOPLE SHUT DOWN

It's common to protect our kids by sounding negative alarms: "Watch out!" For older kids this sometimes translates to "You can't do that." "You'd better not try that." In our roles as guardians and caretakers we can become fear-mongers without meaning to.

We want our kids to be safe, to be realistic, to avoid making mistakes. As a result, we often say don't, don't, don't, when instead we should be giving careful encouragement.

Phrases that slam shut an invisible door between parent and child:

- "You never . . . ."
- "You always . . . ."
- "You behaved like this when you were fifteen, and you're still doing it."
- "When are you going to grow up and . . . [start dressing properly, get married, get a job, etc.]."
- "Your sister [or brother or cousin or neighbor] always [or never] does . . . ."

my career in nursing that it might be the wrong thing. As it turns out, I wish I had looked at other possibilities."

Often our ideas about what our kids should do with their lives are strongly influenced by what we ourselves wanted and were denied.

Ian wanted to go to school in Southern California. His mother, Suzanne, thought, "All he's going to do is surf. This is the real world. He should be getting serious about things."

Suzanne's sister, Belle, commented: "This is probably the

best time of life for Ian to explore a place that fascinates him and makes him feel independent. He'll enjoy his leisure time and that will give him more energy for school. Suzanne, just because you never got to go away to school doesn't mean Ian should stay home."

Suzanne realized she was trying to make Ian walk in her tired footsteps. Although no one had ever given her such a wonderful option, she could give it to her son. Suzanne did something very unusual: She told Ian what she was feeling.

"Ian's situation brought back so many memories. I went to a streetcar college—commuted between my parents' home and the campus every day. I had no friends, no campus life, no fun, just four years of drudgery. I told Ian that. I admitted that I envied him. I also told him that I loved him and wanted to help him explore his own life and pursue happiness. But I had to come to terms with my own past before I could happily endorse his plan."

If you are unhappy with your own life choices, there's no point in trying to hide it. The greatest gift you can give is honesty. When older adults are willing to share their own difficulties, kids are relieved to learn that other people—successful people whom they admire—also have sometimes failed. What if you think that your child doesn't respect you, or you don't feel successful, or you feel you missed the boat? Whatever the case, I can guarantee you that the relationship between you and your child will be warmer for your candor. Don't go on about your doubts at length; be brief and open, and then move on to your child/client's issues.

Setting Your Child Free

Your most important and valuable contribution to the job search is to bolster your child's self-esteem, and this will be your primary role throughout the process. Your goal as

TWELVE PHRASES THAT ENSURE COOPERATION

Your client needs your love, trust, and faith. If you believe good will come of his efforts, your client will sense this and dare to try. Repeated positive encouragement has an inevitable beneficial effect over time.

"I love you."

"I trust you."

"I believe you can do it."

"I'm always on your side."

"I have complete confidence in you."

"You can always come to me."

"I have felt that way, too."

"Everybody makes mistakes."

"Every success has its share of failures and doubts."

"Follow your heart."

"It takes time."

"I'm proud of you."

coach is to help your child make his own decisions with confidence and then implement them, a task people wrestle with most of their adult lives.

Lou and Anne Kopel, both lawyers, had three young-adult sons. One Saturday afternoon, their son David, a second-year law student at the University of Southern California, announced that he wanted to drop out of school and become a chef. Lou and Anne were dumbstruck. David had always loved to eat, but, as far as they knew, he had never even peeled a hard-boiled egg.

RED FLAGS

Here are two words to eliminate from your coaching vocabulary:
1. "Should"
2. "Can't"

They refrained from launching into a laundry list of reasons why David was unsuited for a career as a chef. Lou was about to say, "What kind of a job is that for a man?" but instinct prompted him to hold his tongue. In a relaxed and casual manner, Lou and Anne managed to begin asking some questions —one at a time, giving David plenty of time to think and answer in between: What made him think of cooking as a profession? What sort of cooking was he interested in? What sort of job did he expect to have? Did he expect to work in a restaurant? What kind of restaurant? What skills did he possess that might fit in with cooking? What kind of training would he need? How intense a period of study would he commit to?

The Kopels listened closely to David's answers, often repeating them to be sure that they understood what David actually meant. They focused on David's issues and avoided displaying their own worries. They took plenty of time. When it became clear that David was serious about pursuing cooking as a career, they asked him about the kind of lifestyle he wanted. Then they helped him begin to gather concrete information on how to get started.

Today David is a successful caterer in Los Angeles. He is married to a singer. They often visit Lou and Anne and put on wonderful parties for them—David cooks, and his wife sings to entertain the guests. David works long, hard hours, and he loves every minute of it. He is convinced that life is one big party.

On first hearing of David's surprising goals, the Kopels mustered a positive attitude and remained open and easy in their approach. "I had always dreamed of building a family law firm," Lou said, "with me at the head, and all my sons beside me in the courtroom. I had to give up that particular dream. The firm won't be as big, but we'll have a great chef."

The Kopels' approach played an important role in helping David get started. By acting as coaches, they helped their son define his talents and measure the degree of his commitment. They also helped him figure out how to get the appropriate training and experience to fulfill his dream.

In the end, we win when we say "go, do." We have to accept that our aspirations for our kids may not be the same as their aspirations for themselves. And we have to believe that they know something about themselves that even we as parents can't possibly know. It's a matter of trust, of believing that we have helped create an individual who can stand on his own.

Exercises and Activities

Both you and your client will want to keep a three-ring binder or a notebook, with dividing tabs for each chapter, for recording activities.

Exercises in this chapter probe questions that reveal old patterns and illuminate a new approach. If an exercise makes you feel uncomfortable, put it aside to think about later and move on to the next one.

Things to Think on Alone

To put yourself in the role of coach, ask yourself these questions:

1. Do I feel my client can make a good decision about work? Am I willing to leave the decision to him—no matter what it is?

2. Do I feel a vested interest in the outcome? How does my client's occupation reflect on me?

3. How recently have I spent an uninterrupted period of time with my client?

4. When was the last time I praised something my client did?

5. How happy do I think my client is? What do I think would make him or her happy—honestly?

Things to Do Alone

6. Make a list of your client's skills and talents. Make a list of all the things you find attractive in him. Find time, at least twice a week, to tell him about them.

Things to Do Together

7. Select a series of occasions during which you can have a quiet time alone with your client to comfortably discuss future work aspirations. Keep it casual—a walk together, an errand that requires driving time, events you might attend which afford time to talk.

During these talks, if your client asks you questions, be honest about your own feelings. If you have negative feelings about your work, tell your client that you'd like to help her travel a different route. *Listen* to her responses.

8. Each of you write down your "fantasies" about work and life in general. Fantasies are dreams of what would be wonderful—even ideal. Talk about them together.

9. Expectations: This is a verbal exercise to help both of you arrive at an understanding of what you expect from the coaching experience.

Begin by asking your client what he expects from you in the way of emotional and financial support during this period. Try to listen without reacting. You may have to take a deep breath and resist a quick negative reaction if the expectations are out of line with your own ideas.

Ask questions whenever you feel a need to clarify. Try restating what you hear to be sure you have understood it: "In other words, you would like me to set aside some regular time every week to be a sounding board for some of the things you are discovering?" Or, "You feel if I can cover tuition, you can take care of your incidental living expenses?"

Only when you have a good understanding of your client's expectations is it your turn to speak: "Let me tell you what I had in mind." Be honest about what you were thinking *before* this conversation and be honest if the conversation has changed your thinking.

You might say, "I never dreamed you would value a regular sit-down talk on what you're doing. I'm flattered. Let's plan it."

Or you might remark, "In truth, I feel I can swing about half your tuition. Let's talk about what we can do."

Solve the discrepancies together. This adult-to-adult collaboration sets the tone for the future. You can also make room for the other parent: "Your mother has had more experience with the commercial real estate market than I. Why don't you see what she thinks?" Or, "See if you can go along on Dad's next fishing weekend. It would be a terrific time for you to have some uninterrupted talks."

10. Breaking the Mind-Set: Ask your client to imagine that he is a journalist writing a feature on how you found your way in life. This is a one-way interview—your client interviews you as if you were the subject of a magazine profile. You are no longer Mom or Pop but Jeanne Smith or Jack Jones, a person with a first and last name.

For example, your client may ask you:

- What did you want to do when you were 15 or 16?
- How did your parents influence your choice of work?

- What work did you dream of doing when you were a child?
- How did you choose the work you do? What was right about that choice?
- What would you do differently if you had it to do again?

   11. Discuss how both you and your client might use this handbook.

The hardest part is done—you've started. From here on, the challenge is to continue the activities in each chapter on a regular schedule. Think of this as a standard Wednesday lunch (or whatever time you choose) with a good friend—something you get together and do for both pleasure and profit.

   Later, if you feel stuck as you progress in your mutual exploration, review your responses to the activities in this chapter and you may discover what's holding you back.

Chapter Two

MYTHS:
THE COACH'S
ALBATROSS

Back in the 1920s, Frank Hubbard, a sagacious mid-western newspaperman famous for his wit, wrote, "T'ain't what a man don't know that hurts him. It's what he knows for a fact that just ain't so." Hubbard was Will Rogers's favorite comedian, and it's obvious that the two men shared a sardonic turn of mind.

Those "facts" are the myths that as children we ingested with our mother's milk. There are probably a few parents somewhere in the world who don't dispense bromides, homilies, and pithy nuggets of advice to their offspring. Where they are, goodness only knows, because there is scarcely an adult around today who doesn't remember hearing favorite words of wisdom constantly repeated throughout childhood.

Very often this advice was a truism of grand triteness, on the order of "the early bird gets the worm." After a number of these reminders, boredom and irritation take over—along with rolled eyes and sighs of "I've heard that one before." Yet somehow the bromides stick. As adults we find ourselves trotting them out in various situations, and sometimes they even prove useful. When it comes to myths about work, however, we are in danger of unwittingly passing on to our offspring facts that "just ain't so," as though they were X and Y chromosomes. While it's hard to escape our genetic destinies, we are not locked into perpetuating these particular myths through still another generation. Now, as we are getting started on the process of helping our children find satisfying work, is the time to examine what power these myths might have over our thinking.

Myths We Believe

MYTH 1

PARENTS HAVE ALL THE ANSWERS. Many of us think we're supposed to have life's answers. We think that parents ought to know best, and after all, we *are* parents. The truth is, even if we had the answers, it isn't our job to present kids with ready-made lives. Only your child can uncover his or her deepest dreams and values. Our job is to give them a way to self-determine—to make their own choices and their own commitments. Nobody has all the answers, but it is possible as parents and coaches to help our sons and daughters discover the questions that will lead to the answers.

MYTH 2

A JOB THAT PAYS WELL WILL MAKE YOU HAPPY. Generations later, there are still repercussions from the Great Depression. We transmit anxiety about financial security to our offspring. Some of us also get caught up in the desirability of status and image.

Happiness is a debatable notion. Is it money? Stability? Security? What does a well-paying job mean to the worker who hates it? To the person who isn't treated with respect?

Stand this myth alongside the old saw "Money can't buy happiness," and let them duke it out. What a well-paying job does is alleviate financial stress—provided that people live within their incomes. Naturally we want our children to be financially secure. We want them to learn to handle money well and stand on their own two feet but we don't want them to be so security conscious that they flee from their hearts' desires.

MYTH
3

OTHER PEOPLE ARE IN CHARGE. When we're kids, our parents are in charge; in school, we obey our teachers and copy our peers. By the time we hit higher education we've "learned" that academia owns all the wisdom. It's easy to move right into thinking the corporation knows best.

Yet throughout history those who successfully charted and fulfilled their unique destinies carried their own sense of authority: Marie Curie, who challenged conventional bio-medical wisdom; Albert Einstein, who aroused great concern in his parents for blooming so late (could he have been thinking all the while?); or Arthur Fry and Spencer Silver, who kept hammering away until the 3-M Corporation agreed to market their silly little yellow stick-on notes.

Acknowledging that we determine our own futures is a profound turning point. It's convenient for young people to blame work problems on others: "My adviser told me to become an engineer." "I went where the jobs were." "I needed the money so I took the highest-paying offer." "My mom always wanted me to become a doctor." Youngsters need to be encouraged to pursue their own unique vision of life. Our challenge is to raise kids capable of making their own decisions and claiming responsibility for those choices—for better or worse.

MYTH
4

THERE IS ONE PERFECT JOB FOR YOU.
Most of us live life as though we could reach some
ideal state, then *be in it*. We dream of the perfect
job, the perfect salary, the perfect home, the
perfect life—as though life were a room we could enter, lock
ourselves in, and inhabit, contentedly, forever. But the truly
successful are always reaching and changing, always moving
toward new experiences.

Rarely is any job absolutely right all of the time. Adam, a
young office manager, enjoyed his working environment, but
his daily responsibilities weren't stimulating. What could he
do to make the job more interesting? A computer enthusiast,
Adam enriched his job—for both himself and his employer—by designing a computer program to access data about
the company's clients. His idea wasn't to become a computer
programmer, but to make his job interesting and make a
worthwhile contribution.

In one way or another everyone reconfigures his job,
either by apathy or by attention. Anyone with initiative can
enhance a job by looking around and matching personal
interests to an organization's needs.

MYTH
5

**IF YOU CHOOSE A STABLE COMPANY, YOU
WILL HAVE A SECURE FUTURE.** What's a
stable company these days? The truly paternalistic
employer has always been a myth. It's certainly
unthinkable in the contemporary economic climate. No job
is forever; everyone is expendable—from the CEO on down.
Our children understand this—it fuels their fears—but many
parents cling to the notion that large corporations will look
after you for life. The myth matches our desire to nurture
our children forever. It's perpetuated because salary levels
in large companies are traditionally higher, and benefits
usually better, than in smaller entrepreneurial companies.

Ray's story, however, is far more typical of the current climate. Ray has spent 25 years as a middle manager for a large southwestern petroleum company. He grew up believing in the "good company" as protector, and managed to survive several corporate restructurings. Recently his company informed Ray that if he wanted to keep his job he'd have to relocate from his hometown in Oklahoma to west Texas, an undesirable move because Ray and his family have strong ties to their community through his aging parents, other family members, friends, schools, and church. At 52, Ray got a startling lesson in economic reality. Even his good company couldn't be depended on for the secure life. This scenario repeats itself endlessly throughout the country. Some people aren't as fortunate as Ray—they can't even consider the option of relocating, since their jobs have simply disappeared.

| MYTH 6 | **YOUR FIRST AND MOST IMPORTANT JOB-SEARCH TOOL IS A RESUME.** Begin unraveling this myth with the words "first" and "important." Resumes are not inherently evil, but |

they are extremely limited. It's wasteful and damaging for a young person to direct massive effort into producing a resume rather than working on enhancing skills.

The extraordinary emphasis placed on resumes encourages passivity. Job seekers often believe that it's enough to mail hundreds of resumes, then sit at home waiting for the phone to ring. But the world does not come calling on those who simply lick stamps and walk to the mailbox. A passive candidate is not an attractive candidate. Unfortunately the cycle is self-perpetuating. It's easy to feel rejected when no one calls, and hard to get motivated when your ego is damaged. If the phone does finally ring, the young job seeker is likely to spring into action without investigating the company in question. Suddenly he must turn on the charm to sell himself without knowing if he is even interested in the job or the company approaching him.

Here's an example of the way resumes don't work. Howard always wanted to live and work in Paris. He got his resume together and sent it with a cover letter explaining his interest in computer-systems development to the human resources department at Euro Disney, Paris. Coincidentally Howard talked to a friend of his uncle's who did systems consulting for Euro Disney from his Houston office. The friend found Howard's enthusiasm and excellent French appealing and he mentioned Howard to his client at Euro Disney. A line manager from the company immediately contacted Howard and invited him to visit on his upcoming trip to France. During their meeting Howard was offered a job on the spot. He was totally amazed—just before leaving home he had received a form letter from the human resources department: "Thank you for your interest, but at present there are no positions open. Your resume has been filed."

MYTH 7

ENTREPRENEURS ARE BORN. The entrepreneurial spirit is not genetically encoded. It is neither a sex-linked characteristic nor an ethnic trait. While certain personal qualities are common to successful entrepreneurs, these traits develop along a fairly long arc. It is true that some people enjoy taking risks and are willing to put money, time, and security on the line to launch an idea, service, or product. Others perform best as part of a team within an existing framework. The extent to which our independence was nurtured in childhood has a big effect on our ability to think and act for ourselves, in any context. Young people are helped toward entrepreneurial thinking when parents applaud their efforts to strike out on their own.

MYTH
8

WORK IS NINE TO FIVE. Once upon a time this myth was true for many Americans, but it doesn't have to be true today. Many organizations now offer flexible hours, and there's an increasing trend toward hiring part-time and contract workers. As technology advances and fields become international, it's common to find people working "unorthodox" hours.

Employees who spend their days watching the clock feel like cogs in a wheel. People who are in love with their jobs, who like their colleagues, and enjoy their work environment often lose track of the extra hours they put in.

MYTH
9

ARTISTS STARVE. True, artists are rarely hired into fast-track entry-level positions—generally because they don't apply for them! Many artists spend years supplementing their endeavors through unrelated jobs (like tending bar and word processing, to name just two).

Artistic people have widely varying needs. Some can tolerate the long, uncertain route of an independent actor, musician, painter, or writer. They willingly endure privation for the freedom to pursue their muse, often living a life-style guaranteed to set a parent's teeth on edge. Others thrive in a structured setting. Some artists find their niche in corporate frameworks—designing books and brochures, writing jingles, designing textiles, animating films, creating office environments.

Money may not hold the same meaning for artists as it does for their parents. My client Ellen wanted to be a movie director, but her family thought her goal was unrealistic. Her father was still smarting because he'd sent Ellen's older sister to study architecture, a profession she abandoned after graduation. Dad pushed Ellen into a post-graduate business school. Midway through her first year, she dropped out and enrolled in New York University's film school.

Ellen's parents withdrew both their financial and emotional support. Ellen moved into a cheap apartment on the Lower East Side of Manhattan, sharing the flat with an affable German shepherd. She attended school by day and tended bar at night; when she left work at 2 A.M., her dog acted as policeman and chaperon.

Everyone at film school must produce a film, but Ellen was unique: She managed to get hers distributed in Europe and shown at an important film festival. Through dogged persistence, she was hired to direct a movie for a Hollywood studio. This was her big break, and now, thanks to her determination, Ellen is well on her way to becoming a successful director. Unfortunately she's not as close to her family as she'd like to be.

Many of us do not have the wherewithal, or the inclination, to support our children financially as they pursue their dreams, but we can still listen to them, admire their determination, take pride in their successes, empathize with their setbacks. It would be dishonest not to share your fears and anxieties, and a frank discussion about your feelings often proves therapeutic.

| MYTH 10 | **WORK HARD AND YOU'LL BE REWARDED.** This goes hand in hand with the myth about job security. Frankly there's no guarantee you'll be commensurately rewarded for your efforts—finan- |

cially or otherwise. People are seldom rewarded just because they work hard—they're rewarded because their work fills others' needs. The individual who is rewarded is responsive to the whole dynamic of the working situation—the fit and rapport with the boss and other employees, use of skills, and use of time.

For instance, a recent workplace study found that those who do the most talking on the telephone "interfacing and networking" with other workers throughout the organization and industry end up getting the most promotions and the highest salaries. Those who stayed glued to their desks "working hard" didn't do as well. Is that fair? To paraphrase Mae West, fairness has nothing to do with it. Reward is seldom in direct ratio to effort. Rather it's usually a consequence of how much value a boss or client *perceives* in your work, not necessarily how valuable it actually is.

| MYTH 11 | **THE RIGHT CREDENTAL WILL GET THE JOB.** A degree won't get the job for your child any more than a resume will. The fact is, thousands of men and women with prestigious law |

degrees, M.B.A.'s, and Ph.D.'s are out of work. No piece of paper acts as a passe-partout, and it's extremely damaging to our children if we encourage them to strive for a degree believing this myth. If, however, your child receives a hard-earned degree in a subject area she's absolutely wild about, it will never be wasted. She will have the double advantage of a well-earned sense of achievement and well-developed enthusiasm. In the end nothing makes someone more attractive to a potential employer than the natural enthusiasm which comes of being in tune with a genuine interest.

Let's Try Some New Principles

FREEDOM OF CHOICE EMPOWERS. Every individual becomes empowered by exercising freedom of choice. We parents are perfectly positioned to demonstrate this principle by loosening our grip and letting our children walk on their own.

Most of us feel we're being judged in many subtle ways by how our kids turn out. Certainly our children represent opportunities for us to earn sweet praise for a job well done. We want the best for them. In a way they represent fresh starts for ourselves. The strength of our hopes, however, puts us in danger of overmanaging the situation. It's easy to slip from normal, healthy concern into overcorrecting, over-controlling behavior.

We often catch ourselves mouthing tired clichés, just like the ones our parents handed out: "I've devoted the best years of my life to preparing you for law school, and now you want to join the Peace Corps?"

"All the Smith men have been pediatricians since your great-grandfather Elmer!"

"English majors are a dime a dozen. Get an M.B.A."

"Stop horsing around and join the real world."

"Travel for a year! Are you nuts? When you get back, all your classmates will be ahead of you in their careers."

"Take the first offer; you may not get another."

Whenever we convey that the "real" world is hard and somber, we fail to reinforce freedom of choice. Propelled by our own fears and disappointments, words leap from our mouths unedited. We meant to say, "Go; experiment." We meant to say, "I have faith in you."

THE TRUTH RESIDES WITHIN OURSELVES. The formula for our lives lies within each of us. No one owns a child's beliefs, values, talents, and passions—not even a parent. When youngsters learn enough about their true natures and put this knowledge to work, the odds of achieving stunning success rise dramatically. Regardless of age and experience, each person can discover that inner truth.

A POSITIVE ATTITUDE GENERATES A POSITIVE RESULT. This should be self-evident, but unfortunately it is not always practiced. Encouraging words and positive support inevitably yield positive results in every area of life. A self-fulfilling prophecy is as true in the workplace as in private life. Naysaying begets poor results.

Yet it's sometimes hard to be positive with our children when we've been listening to negatives all *our* lives. I see people every day who want to make a significant mid-life change but feel it's too late to go after their hearts' desires.

In fact, studies show that people who change their job from one they hate to one they love increase their income as well as their pleasure. This should reassure parents who wonder whether to encourage kids to freely explore their enthusiasms. Why delay? I like to remind clients, "Your hobby is someone else's business. Why not yours?"

Replacing negativity with encouragement may mean revisiting your own past. Do your reactions to your child have a familiar ring? Do you remember receiving similar comments from your parents when you were a child? Do you recall feeling put down by a parent when you expressed your dreams? Can you remember expressing your dreams at all? If not, why not? Are there any negative phrases you are repeating to your child which were said to you years ago? In the course of assisting your child, you may actually free yourself of parental objections that hold you back.

GOOD DECISIONS ARE BASED ON GOOD INFORMATION. Computer hackers live by the acronym GIGO— garbage in, garbage out. Just as the human body runs best on fresh, healthy foods, the best decisions are made by assembling plenty of solid facts. Decisions based on assumptions and vague hopes will get your client nowhere, whereas decisions based on knowing himself and the needs of potential employers ensure survival.

Securing work and succeeding in a particular workplace depend on understanding what makes the workplace the way it is—how each of its characteristics relate to his own unique capabilities and interests. Only when he knows that there is a good match between a job's requirements and his talents, can your client make a sound decision about the job. There are ways of learning about a field of work and a place of work *before* making decisions (see Chapters 5 and 7).

Activities and Exercises

G ive yourself some quiet time to carry out these activities. Go through them systematically, responding fully. If you feel stuck on one activity, go on to the next one but return to it later. Sorting out your own thoughts about what you believe about work lays the groundwork for how you and your client can work together.

You and your client will probably want to refer to your responses to these particular exercises several times in the course of your work together.

Things to Think on Alone

1. How many of the myths discussed in this chapter do you subscribe to?

2. Are you willing to keep an open mind with respect to those myths you believe?

3. Are there times you can remember in your own life when holding on to a myth held you back from achieving what you wanted? What myth was it?

4. How many myths seem to have been passed down to you from your parents? What are they?

5. What do you believe is the right way to look for a job?

Things to Do Alone

6. Write down the steps *you* would take if you were in your client's shoes looking for a job now. If you don't know, say so, at least to yourself.

7. Much of the magic surrounding a person's success comes from the freedom to explore and self-determine. Read a biography or an autobiography of someone successful in an area that interests your client, observing the perhaps unorthodox steps that person took along the way.

8. Make a list of friends and family members who you believe have found satisfying life/work situations. Ask each what he or she considers the most important steps in getting there. Make notes for future reference.

Things to Do Together

9. Talk about each of the myths exposed in this chapter and discuss your feelings about each.

10. Write down any other work-related myths you can think of.

11. Ask your client what he or she believes to be the "right" way to look for work. Compare your client's answer with your own opinion. Talk about it; both of you make a note of what he or she believes.

Chapter Three

Everyone Has Role Models

P ersonal experience may be the best teacher, but it is possible to learn from others' experiences, too. As parents, we are uniquely positioned to be powerful role models for our children. We can especially influence their attitudes toward work because our day-to-day routines convey a surprising amount of information—both good and bad. However, we are often oblivious to the image we present about our work, not realizing that our children draw their impressions of what work is all about from us.

There are undoubtedly several other people in your son's or daughter's life who will profoundly influence his or her future, too. Role models can be inspiring characters discovered in novels or newspapers, or they can be as close as the next room. From Peter Pan to Indira Gandhi, the high school baseball coach to Roseanne Arnold, role models aren't paragons of virtue as much as they're paragons of particular qualities—generosity, courage, self-discipline, humor, wisdom—whose style sets an attractive example for those who watch and emulate them. You can increase the positive effect of role models in your child's life merely by increasing your awareness of your own role as one and acknowledging the contributions of others.

One of the most important things that role models teach is that we have alternatives. Suzy says, "I was the classic 'good girl,' following all the rules, worrying whether everyone approved of me. I frequently resented my younger brother because he broke all the rules, following his own notion of what was right, yet the sky never fell in on him. Eventually he became my role model for loosening up. By his example he got me to stop trying to be what everyone else wanted me to be. I began to discover my own power and how to trust it."

For Steve, "Seeing my mom head back to college at age 45 really inspired me to take risks, too. I was hugely impressed that she had the courage to change and challenge herself. Mom taught me it's never too late to tackle new ventures."

Mary, a college sophomore, says, "Our next door neighbor suddenly took up jogging at the ripe old age of 53, and before you could say 'Gatorade,' Barbara was running marathons all over the country. Her example got me off my sedentary fanny to start exercising. I became intrigued by the changes in my body and the difference certain foods and exercise routines can bring about. I signed up for some nutrition and anatomy courses. Who knows where it will lead?"

Perhaps the most valuable and enduring effect of role models is that they show us different ways of responding— and prevailing—when things go wrong. "My dad and I don't see eye to eye on most things," said Daniel, now 28 years old. "We're as different as night and day. Yet I remember vividly his behavior when his work crashed. My dad's a filmmaker; a television series he had been working on for eight years— a project in which he had invested his time and heart and talent, as well as most of his savings—went belly-up. He was almost sixty years old at the time. It was catastrophic in every imaginable way. He spent a couple of days acting really depressed, not talking, staying in his room. After that, he came back up, a smile on his face, just as vigorous and feisty as he had ever been. He never complained once about it. To professional colleagues he spoke as if his 'flop' was just another roll of the dice, and he'd start talking about his next project. I admired that profoundly; he sure showed me how to behave when disaster strikes."

Parents as Role Models

Some parents provide a negative image of work, some a positive image, and some no image at all. Steve's father adored his career as a sales and customer representative for a pharmaceutical firm. He communicated this enthusiasm, but never explained the day-to-day routines that occupied him. "Dad always came home in a great mood after work. Entertaining was a large part of his job, so every night I asked, 'What restaurant did you go to today?' I always admired his freedom of not being cooped up in an office all day long. But the weird thing is, I still have no idea what it is he actually does for a living, besides eat out."

Patty also grew up without knowing much about her father's work. "My father never discussed his work, and I was in college before I realized he hated his job," she said. "I finally asked him how he chose teaching. Dad admitted that growing up in a Brooklyn slum, he was told there were only three professions for a Jewish boy. One and two were doctor and lawyer, but the schooling was too expensive. The third 'respectable' alternative was teaching. Even though he loved sports, my father felt it was more appropriate to teach history instead of becoming a gym teacher or coach. I saw that he compromised every step of the way."

Like Patty's father, Elizabeth's mother never talked about her work, although she projected a sour and unhappy image when she returned home. She had once dreamed of becoming a ballerina, but she abandoned her dancing when she married. After having three children, she started doing part-time office work and eventually became a full-time executive secretary to a busy judge. She and her husband separated.

"At day's end my Mom was thin-lipped and exhausted, cooking dinner in total silence," Elizabeth remembers. "If we asked about her day, she'd snap at us. We always felt guilty that she had to work so hard to take care of us."

Elizabeth's mother presented work as a necessary evil, something one simply endures.

Beth, on the other hand, got a positive image about work from her father, although at the time she didn't fully appreciate it. "My dad was a precision tool-maker. I remember one day he came running in the front door, carrying special magnifying glasses and two teeny-tiny pieces of metal. He said, 'We have to mold these two pieces together at work. We have to fuse them together by motion. If one speck of dust gets between them, it's ruined.' I was a teenager and couldn't have cared less, but he was so happy and excited showing me what it had taken him months and months to make at work that I enjoyed his sharing it with me."

"My father had a successful printing and engraving business," says Janet, "but he died when I was young and the shop was sold, so I never had a strong sense of what he did. One day when I was still a child, my mother brought out a slim tooled-leather book he had made. Every page was engraved with gorgeous calligraphy and adorned with embossed colored pictures. I could see by the way my mother handled it—like the Dead Sea Scrolls—that this project meant something special to both of them. I saw that my father didn't become a printer just to make a living; he was a craftsman who loved creating beautiful things."

Does this mean you have to love your work 100 percent in order to be a good role model? Not necessarily. The truth is, unfortunately, an overriding majority of working adults dislike their jobs. It is important, however, to share your work experiences and demonstrate that it's possible to fix mistakes and alter decisions. By communicating both positive and negative feelings about work, we provide children with valuable insights.

While Steve had only a vague idea about what his father did as a sales representative, his mother provided a much clearer picture. "Mom worked as manager of credits and col-

---

UNHAPPY AT WORK—
WHAT DO YOU TELL YOUR CLIENT?

Be honest. Try not to mask your feelings, but don't complain continuously. Tell your son or daughter where you think you went wrong.

Come to terms with a child's right to be happy in work, even if you're not.

Get rid of the phrase "Everyone has to pay his dues." Yes, we all learn by applying ourselves with discipline to the task, and this process is enjoyable when in tune with interests and skills.

Tell your child that you would like to learn from his experience and perhaps improve your lot in life.

Think about whether you ended up in a working situation because of pressure from your parents. If that's the case, tell your client you don't want the same thing for her.

Realize that it's *never* too late for you to change some aspects or all of your working situation and discuss with your child how you might approach doing this.

lection for a big corporation. She hated her job because she never got recognition for her hard work. For two years she came home in a miserable mood. Finally, with the family's encouragement, she quit, went back to college, learned how to use computers, and got a new job as an administrative assistant in a company where they value her contribution. She's so much happier!"

Although Steve's mother complained about her accounting job, in expressing her dissatisfaction she painted a vivid picture of what most people would want to avoid in a job. She then proceeded to prove to her children that negative situations can be addressed and positive moves made toward rewarding experiences.

If you don't share your work experiences with your kids, they'll never grasp your capabilities. Certainly the workaholic who *never* stops talking about work gives a skewed view. But if home is a refuge from the job, where all mention of work is off-limits, kids never discover how Mom chaired an important shareholders' meeting or how Dad sold 30 acres of prime commercial land. They grow up without any insight into what work is all about. Doesn't your child deserve to know more about what you do best? When you consider how much time, energy, and creativity we devote to our careers, it makes sense to look for ways to include our kids. Find ways to share your skills: how you handle people, manage money, negotiate contracts, solve problems. Parents can also convey the message that work has ups and downs, but overall, work adds up to something worthwhile.

One of the most readily available ways of helping your client get a realistic picture of what work means to you is to take her on the job with you. Marge said, "Every so often, my mom took me to work with her. She was the receptionist at a huge office right in the thick of things. Everybody knew her and called her by her first name. I thought it was the greatest thing, and that's probably why I never resented that she worked." Marge enjoyed her mom's popularity and appreciated seeing her doing a variety of activities.

Cliff recalls, "When I was four, my father took me to his job at the Air Force purchasing department. He introduced me to everyone and showed me what he did. Another time, my grandfather took me to the New Hope Union Paper Mills, where he was foreman. He took me through the whole paper mill, top to bottom. I felt really proud."

Normally it can be easily arranged to have your child shadow you for a typical day or to give him some small job at your workplace that would permit him to observe you. There will be lots for you two to talk about afterward.

Outside Role Models

By the time youngsters reach high school, exposure to people beyond the family helps them test their values against the larger world. It's not that outsiders are smarter, or that their opinions are better than, or even different from, ours, but in the critical transition to adulthood, young people often feel less inhibited with a listener who has new experience to offer and who does not represent parental authority. Outside role models seem more like equals—they can be friends, teachers, parents of friends, a boss from an after-school job, or other relatives. Young people are attracted to them because they usually don't say "you should." (Even if they do, somehow it's not so offensive coming from them.) More often they say, "You know, this is what it was like for me." Every child should be lucky enough to have outside role models. They can be especially important for the child who feels "different" from his family. For example, a thoughtful, introspective youngster coming of age amid a gregarious family can be helped enormously by a role model with whom he can identify.

TAKING YOUR CHILD/CLIENT ON YOUR JOB

In some highly structured workplaces you may need clearance before bringing your client on the job, so plan ahead.

Ask Your Boss
Discuss with him when it would be appropriate to bring a young person (specify the age of your child) to work. Also ask for suggestions of people to see.

Discuss the Visit With Your Co-workers
It's more helpful for young people to observe several people actually doing their jobs, so organize it when your co-workers are amenable to a visit.

Ask Your Child
Don't bring a child against his will. Do prepare your child to get the most from the visit. Supply the names of some co-workers and describe their jobs. Ask:

• Do any of these sound particularly interesting to you?
• What are you most curious about? Why?
• What do you feel you know about this subject already?
• What else would you like to know about the company?
• If you could have lunch with anyone of your choice during this visit, whom would it be? (He might say "you.")

Previsit Instructions

The instructions you give vary, depending on the age of your client and any limitations set by your employer. In one way or another they should include:

• It's important to stay out of the way of normal work activities. Be sensitive to the times when the person you're visiting is busy or deep in conversation with other people, and simply observe without comment.

• If someone seems harried or frantically busy, say you'd love to come back at another time.

Refrain from handling papers or other materials, unless invited.

• Dress like the people dress at this job.

• Taking notes is great but ask permission first.

• Never tape-record.

Debriefing

An on-the-job visit offers a perfect opportunity for follow-up discussions. Ask:

• How comfortable did you feel?

• What interests would you like to pursue again?

• Were there any surprises?

• What did you like—and not like—about what you saw?

• Would you like to go back? How soon?

• What other places does this suggest you might like to visit?

If the experience is favorable, it could even lead to establishing a new tradition at your workplace, with other employees doing the same for their kids.

INAPPROPRIATE ROLE MODELS

It's normal for young people to test their ideas with a role model outside the family. It's also normal for them to be temporarily in full-throttle hero worship. Often young adults have totally inappropriate (by our standards) role models. Counterculture heroes are usually passing fancies, and the best solution, in my opinion, is to grin and bear it. However, sometimes a role model can really get under your skin and, worse, may even be leading your child in the wrong direction. Fortunately there are some techniques available to help you maintain communication.

Say something positive—acknowledge that the role model has something good to offer.

Maintain an approving—or at least neutral—stance. Ask questions in a conversational manner. Try to understand what your child finds so appealing about the role model. "Rick Jones seems really interesting. What do you like best about him?"

If your client quotes Rick chapter and verse—and

It's not uncommon for young teenagers to go through a period when they view parents as the most stupid humans in captivity, but it *is* just a phase. Though they temporarily deny our good qualities, children generally rediscover our humanity, especially when they enter the workforce and begin tangibly sharing the world we experience every day. If it was hard to believe that we, too, endured puberty and high school, they can now see us hard at work—just as they are—and become aware that we've learned a thing or two.

Smart role models make a friend of you (and vice versa) without violating the sanctity of their private, confidential you totally disagree, don't push it. Instead, say, for example, "Well, that's one way to look at it. I wonder what Bob and Sam would say?"

If your child gets opinions from Rick that differ from your own—whether about clothes, work, lifestyle, ethics, drug use, etc.—suggest that your child explore the issues further by asking other people who have dealt with similar things.

For example, if your child quotes Rick as saying, "I'm against hard drugs, but I don't think marijuana hurts anyone," you might say, "I'm not sure I agree, but I wonder how you can find out? You might learn more about it by talking to people who have had some experience, like a psychologist or a teacher. Also your aunt Jean is head of personnel at a corporation and may have information about workers who have had difficulties with substance abuse."

Even as you downplay your own feelings, you help your client develop sound judgment. Getting your client to ask questions and broaden the inquiry may provide the substitute for actual experimentation.

relationship with your child. Nonetheless, it's normal to feel a little jealous, even resentful, of our child's role models. Particularly when children are older and have less time to spend with parents, it's easy to feel slighted when we see so much discretionary time being spent with others. Whatever the situation, avoid emulating the role model—be yourself. Deidre, now 45, has managed to maintain open communication with her teenage children. She credits her mother's example. "I was different in personality from everyone in my family. All the time I was growing up, I was enthralled by one person or another: a girl ahead of me in school, one of my teachers, a newspaper columnist, a movie star, you name it. My mom never interfered. She continued to express the greatest interest in every aspect of what I did. To this day she always asks what I'm working on and with whom and what it's about and whether I'm enjoying it. She's full of questions and it's rewarding for me to share my work with her. I couldn't do that if she weren't interested. Mom remembers what I tell her, which I notice. It means a lot to me that she understands what's going on in my life. So I try to be the same way with my kids, even though they are in that 'what do *you* know' phase."

Activities and Exercises

Here you can examine the work-related impressions you are making on your child. Take your time, reflect, and remember.

Things to Think on Alone

1. Do you talk much about your work at home? Is it positive or negative?

2. How does your client react? Does she ask questions? Do you answer them, or decline to? If so, why?

3. How glamorously do you try to portray your work? Or, conversely, how negatively?

4. In what ways were your own parents work role models? Do you remember having positive or negative feelings about their work?

5. Identify your own role models, past and present. Think about the qualities that appealed to you, and how they influenced your life.

6. The best way to be a good role model is to pay attention to your own values and discover what *you* need to be happy. Are you happy with the work you do now? Are you expressing these feelings? If you're unhappy, are you afraid to say so because you fear it will have a negative effect on your child?

Things to Do Alone

7. Write a current job description for yourself. If you're not working outside the home, write a job description for what you are doing every day as if it were a job. This is a good way to recall the many tasks you accomplish each day. Highlight those items you're most proud of and most fulfilled by as well as those you dislike the most. How recently have you communicated any of this information at home?

Things to Do Together

8. Ask your client to describe out loud what he or she thinks you do each day. Discuss these impressions. You'll gain tremendous insight into how he perceives your work.

9. Cultural Heroes: To choose rewarding work, it's vital to define internal values. It's also important to accept that your child's values may be different from your own. This exercise is designed to reveal and explore those values.

Each of you write down and later discuss: What public figures do I admire? What specific qualities make them admirable to me? Which of these qualities do I see in myself? Which would I like to nurture in myself?

10. Identify ways in which your child is a role model to you. Share this with him.

For example, when Richard didn't make the football team as a freshman, he embarked on a campaign to improve his physical stamina through exercise and diet. He lifted weights, and packed muscle on his frame. When autumn returned, Richard was in fighting form for tryouts. His father said he admired the way his son viewed failure as an episode, not a conclusion.

In another example, Jeff lost a coveted summer job at a law office because he couldn't type. So he enrolled in a class at the YMCA and practiced until his fingers flew over the keys. His mother admired how Jeff identified an obstacle and overcame it.

11. Take your child to work. (See box "Taking Your Child/Client on Your Job" for discussion suggestions.)

12. Seek your client's counsel. You might say, "I have a situation at the office which I need to talk over with somebody." Not only will your client be flattered, she or he may have some excellent insights.

13. Likes and Dislikes in People: Each of you divide a page of your notebook into two columns. Quickly list as many qualities as you can—in the first column what you like in people, in the second what you dislike in people. For example:

LIKES	DISLIKES
Good listeners	Overly critical
Empathetic	Self-interested
Interested	Dull-witted
Positive	Narrow-minded
Funloving	Bigoted
Intelligent	Self-important
Straightforward	Disloyal
Considerate	
Broad-minded	
Courageous	

Give yourself 10 minutes. When time is up, read your lists out loud to each other. (This is important: there's a powerful difference between reading to yourself and hearing.) Your selections define your values. By comparing lists, you and your client discover where values coincide and where they diverge. You also begin accepting these differences and, listening to each other, you may think of characteristics you wish to add.

Next, star the most important "likes," those qualities you simply couldn't do without; then double-star "dislikes" you find most offensive. Are the qualities you most appreciate found in your co-workers? Or are you surrounded by people whose values you dislike? (If so, you might seriously consider how to alter *your* work environment.)

This exercise is a great way to let your client know what qualities you value most. If you're concerned about your client's role models, this exercise may also clue you in on why one person is favored over another. Pay attention to what turns your client on—and off.

Finally, notice similarities in these lists and the qualities you noted for "Cultural Heroes" (exercise 9). A consistent pattern of values will begin to emerge.

Chapter Four

DISCOVERING THE REAL PERSON

"**I** know him like the back of my hand," you might say. Do you really? Do you know what he used to dream about while lolling in his room, music on full blast? Do you know what he raps with friends about? Do you know what keeps him awake at night? You know your client better than anyone, but do you really know him?

Your client doesn't even know himself nearly as well as you both will a few chapters down the line. The closer you can get to your client's true nature, heartfelt interests, and actual capacities, the better his decisions will be. Understanding one's self is a prerequisite to finding satisfying productive work, but most people undertake the job search with very little of this knowledge.

Premature Decisions

The best career choices are based on lifelong enthusiasms. But it takes time to discover interests deep enough and exciting enough to support a life's work. Making a quick match between your client's interests and a specific career can drain both the pleasure and the reward from the process of career planning. If the two of you are too eager, you may leap to the wrong conclusion. Take time to enjoy the process.

For instance, Katy mentioned that she was interested in the law and immediately her parents were ready to send her to law school. Katy panicked and backed off. When you press too hard too soon, your child, who is now your "client," veers away like a bar of soap popping out of a wet fist. The child, as a defensive measure, will be less inclined to make any kind of commitment for fear of making a wrong choice.

One 50-year-old man I know was never able to commit to anything as a young man because every time he tried something and changed his mind, his father came down on him like a ton of bricks. "You always start these things, Ronald, and you *never* finish them." He never finished them because any time he mentioned even a passing interest, his father would immediately start putting the pressure on: "If you're interested in engineering, let's get you into engineering school." As a result, Ronald learned to keep his head down and his curiosities to himself.

Everyone has his own time frame. One person may recognize a "true calling" in his early twenties, and another may not come to this realization until several years later. Because Ronald needed more time to explore, his father labeled him a flop, making it harder for Ronald to muster the confidence he needed to move forward. Many factors combine to produce a directionless life—Ronald's father didn't need to be adding to them.

Knowing there is a designated "career" is reassuring but also limiting. Your client is a multidimensional, dynamic individual, full of surprises. When *you* begin to see this magic, your client begins to see it, too.

Connecting Education to Jobs

My client Bill told me, "I majored in American history because I loved the colonial era, but whenever I asked my adviser what I'd be qualified to do after college, he'd stammer and say, 'Err, you could always teach.' I began worrying that I'd chosen the wrong major—teaching seemed like a dead-end street for me."

Departmental advisers are terrific sources of information on their own professions, but they may be poor sources of broad information. Most are narrowly schooled in their fields and tend to push their particular specialty.

Bill's dilemma illustrates a common situation in which both adviser and student have limited views of what can be done with a major. For example, Bill could consider writing novels set in eighteenth-century America or putting together tours to historical sites. Some archaeologists and anthropologists focus on this period, as do art collectors and curators. Others trade in rare or specialized books, research and reproduce furnishings and objets d'art, or restore and maintain historical buildings. All Bill had to do was identify his particular aptitudes and think about how they connected to his interests. He then would discover that he had a huge range of job possibilities, all connected to his major.

One problem with choosing a course of study on the basis of the careers it may suggest is that many kids think they want to *be* something, without understanding the many activities that comprise a profession. When Terry was young she dreamed of being a ballerina. "I wanted to wear a puffy net skirt and toe shoes. All I saw was glamour. When I realized dancers endure hours of grueling training each day and that very few become Pavlovas, my dream dissolved. I wasn't enamored with *dancing*; I was captivated by the beautiful little dolls I saw on stage." Still, Terry needn't abandon her dreams entirely. Now that she's isolated the true lure, she can investigate fields such as costume, lighting, or set design, which fuse her love of costumes, theater, and drama. (For more on connecting studies to a career, see Chapter 12.)

Aptitude Testing

Obviously a job should be matched to a client's talents and aptitudes. These are your client's assets. (Forget about weaknesses. It is essential to spend time and energy discovering what your client has going for her rather than trying to correct or fill in the weak areas.) Some of your client's aptitudes will be more developed or prominent than others, but all her skills and talents are useful. Desire goes a long way toward improving poor skill areas, but if you can help your client concentrate on the skills she seems to do effortlessly, she will take quantum leaps ahead of most of her peers.

Often people can scarcely recall learning the skills they're best at because they're associated with pleasure and innate talent. Think of a child who reads for hours on end, who cannot tear himself away from books. Or the dedicated movie buff who recites plots and dialogue verbatim, effortlessly identifying the shots and camera angles. Pay attention to the recreational activities your client has pursued freely. The way he has approached these will reveal secrets of his aptitudes or talents. If your client is intrigued by buildings, architecture is only one route to feed that passion. Other avenues could be urban planning, historic preservation, or writing about building and architecture. The eventual satisfying choice will depend on his natural capacities.

Aptitude and Interest Tests Can Be Misleading

Some parents and kids gravitate toward aptitude or interest testing to help define a career direction. It can provide some help, but doesn't get to know the inner person very well. In our courses we see many people in their forties and fifties who became lawyers or teachers because a test taken in their teens or twenties told them they'd be good at it. "The test said this is what I should do, so I did it. But I'm miserable," they complain.

Typecasting can start in grade school, when kids are first tested for their aptitude in math, languages, manual dexterity and so on; at the same time, they may be given lists of occupations that employ those aptitudes. The occupations offered may be seriously behind the times. To illustrate just how limiting and chancy this system is, back in the 1950s, a girl with mechanical dexterity and good hand/eye coordination would have been considered a prime candidate to become a secretary or a seamstress. Today, we more readily leap to "engineer."

If an aptitude test indicates that your client has great mechanical, math, or language skills, don't rush to premature closure in choosing a career path. For example, if someone is good in math, there are myriad possible applications. Playing the piano is highly mathematical; so is architecture and engineering, and any business, even manufacturing surfboards and making ice cream, hinges on good math skills when you take into account the scheduling, monitoring, and financial aspects of these. Math is a functional area that your client can bring to numerous fields.

Aptitude tests will indicate some directions that would be interesting for your client to explore, but they are not the end of the road. Similarly, if the tests show your client is weak in certain areas, that doesn't mean she should cross related careers off her list. "Lack of aptitude" isn't synonymous for "zero ability." Lesser aptitudes also can be developed and shaped into serviceable skills if the interest is there to drive them.

A Better Way to Uncover Skills

By their very nature, aptitude and interest tests are limited. Even the best of them draw from pre-existing data bases that, by virtue of their design, can't anticipate your client's unique nature. For instance, a typical interest test may ask: What would you prefer to do on a Sunday afternoon: (a) tinker with the car, (b) go hiking, or (c) read a book. See how small the window of possibilities is? No wonder the information garnered is unreliable. Your client's single answer depends largely on how she or he felt that day, even that hour. And the interpretation depends on someone else's subjective analysis.

The best way to learn about what makes your client tick is through her life history. Hiding in her childhood, school days, various work and volunteer experiences, hobbies, and leisure time is abundant information about her skills, values, interests, ambitions, and the environment in which she flourishes. By tapping into these experiences, you will help her answer the question "Who am I?"

To begin, ask her to tell you a story about something she enjoyed doing in the past. Within the story, skills and talents will be revealed. (See exercise 12.)

For example, Don began a story about his soccer team.

> "I went out for soccer because my older brother played and I knew I'd be even better. I'd race out of class to get on the field first. I really worked hard at perfecting my skills—running, kicking, scoping out the field to determine where to place the ball. Eventually I was team captain. I liked psyching up my teammates, getting them ready to fight and win. Which we did."

Through this brief life story Don's skills and attributes began to emerge. Here is what a list of these qualities might look like based on just these few lines of his soccer story:

- Great enthusiasm ("knew I'd be better," "race out of class").
- Persistence in getting the job done ("worked hard at perfecting").
- Organizing schoolwork cleverly to allow extra time for competitive sports (a correct inference if the student continued to do well academically).
- Handling competitive feelings with my brother in a positive way (used challenge as an incentive to own sports excellence rather than blaming brother).
- Balanced in coping with both failure and success (part of keeping teammates psyched).
- Realistically assessing personal athletic skills (he knew he could do it and did).
- Skillfully determining strategy using perspective and knowledge of teammates' ability (team did well as a result).
- Effectively motivating teammates to win (wins occurred).
- Rising naturally to a leadership position among peers (got elected team captain).
- Disciplined in training my body for maximum performance ("worked hard at perfecting").

This way of recording abilities is far more accurate—and enjoyable—than any aptitude test because it draws on experience. It requires precision (from you) in describing each attribute. Simple sketchy stories produce much information and invite you to ask questions that reveal even more skills.

An important note about life stories: They can be about anything your client remembers with pleasure, even something quite small. And they don't have to have a "big" ending. For example, it doesn't matter whether Don's team won or lost, or whether the tomatoes your son or daughter grew last summer won first prize at the state fair. Stories can be retrieved from earliest childhood or from just last week. The same is true for older people, too. Events recalled from the distant past can be especially revealing.

If you do this exercise repeatedly with different stories your client recalls from the past you will accumulate more and more notes on your client's skills and aptitudes. Soon, a complete picture of his "best" capabilities shows up. This is a much more revealing portrait than testing provides because it has greater dimension.

Exercises and Activities

These activities and exercises are the most important ones you and your client will do in discovering his skills and aptitudes as well as his interests. They are designed to open a door to your client's heart and to help you both know the inner person. The equation to keep in mind is: Aptitudes + Interests = Activities *(jobs!)*.

Things to Do Together

1. Make a list of your client's most likable qualities, strongest aptitudes, and demonstrated skills and talents. Ask your client to also make a list of his best qualities.

2. Combine these into one start-up list. If your client likes the idea, you may want to post the list for other family members to add to periodically as a means of positive reinforcement. This list represents a gift of increased self-esteem you can give your client. Believe it or not, our children often don't realize how highly we regard them.

3. Ask, "What do you believe others think your best qualities are?" "How do you feel about that?" "What skills do you wish they knew more about?"

4. Ask your client to write down as many responses as possible to "The things I do best are . . . ."

Examine this list together and identify skills that may point to career paths or areas of study. Add them to your original "skills and aptitudes" list (above). How could they enhance these skills and aptitudes?

5. Making Connections: This exercise is designed to start identifying your client's areas of interest. Divide a page of your notebook into columns. Ask your client to write down three things she enjoys doing during leisure time, three things enjoyed at school, three things enjoyed in her work environment (if she has worked).

Next, brainstorm to identify possible work your client could do now relating to these pleasurable activities. Write down *all* ideas.

6. Double-Standard Quiz: Examine the list of possible occupations you came up with in the previous exercise. How many of the suggestions are gender-specific? Would you have given different responses if this were a daughter (a son)? Does your thinking suggest a double standard?

7. Ask your client, "What do you wish you could have done in school? As a child? With your free time?" (Solitary activities are as valid as clubs or team sports.)

Do these answers suggest activities your client might like to know more about now? What skills are involved? List them.

If your client held back on certain activities because of a real or imagined lack of skill, discuss ways by which he might bolster these skills, whether through education, job experience, or other avenues.

8. Ask your client, "What do you do on a Sunday afternoon when no one is telling you what to do? When you're home alone? When you're away from home alone? When you don't have to work?" She should feel free to come up with several possible activities that she might indulge in.

9. Suggest that your client read biographies of people whose jobs match his own interests.

10. Admirations: Ask you client to write down on a page in her notebook headed "Admirations = Values" who and what she admires—people, art, games, natural objects, even theories. Admirations may be grand or very simple. (One of my own admirations is the humble gilhooley, a small metal device for opening jars that operates on the gear principle. I admire its simplicity and its ingenuity. It improves everyday life for many people.)

Next, ask your client to return to each admiration and write down why.

Nina's list included the entry: "I admire body builder Cory Everson's physique." When I asked why, she said, "I admire the dedication and discipline it takes to sculpt muscles from the raw material of the human body and the daily hard work of staying that way."

By explaining who and what we admire, we begin to see what we value in life. Ask your client to look at her completed list of admirations. What do these people and things have in common?

The next task is to star up to five items on the list which are most important. It's enlightening to compare this list with the "Cultural Heroes" list from Chapter 3 and see how they reinforce each other. Both exercises reveal values and bring them to the forefront of your client's thinking. It's always a surprise to see just how well developed and clear your client's values really are, even though she may never have voiced them before.

11. What Fascinates Me?: Ask your client to make a list of his interests and curiosities—things that intrigue him. You can help with this by reminding him of things you have observed him enjoying. He can add to the list regularly as he thinks of new interests. The longer the list, the better.

He can begin by thinking about what's attracted his attention lately. Encourage your client to clip magazine and newspaper stories that set off a spark of interest. Ask him to keep a notepad for tracking ideas about appealing radio and TV programs, conversations and arguments, favorite books, philosophies, lectures—anything that piques his interests and attracts. When it comes time to make decisions, the list will be a guide. Include:

- Favorite activities or hobbies.
- Books, magazine articles, movies, television programs that particularly appealed to him—and why.
- Favorite courses or workshops or seminars. (What particular aspect of the course attracted him?)
- Jobs that sound interesting.
- Old and new subjects he talks about with friends.
- Trips, real or imaginary.
- Favorite hobbies.
- Charities.
- Sports.

12. Life Stories: Among the exercises you and your client can do together, this one is critical because it reveals your client's skills and aptitudes. Repeat this exercise frequently. The more you do it, the better it gets.

Ask your client to write a story—a few paragraphs or a few pages—about something she's done in her life that she enjoyed, then read it out loud to you.

Listen carefully to the story. Write down all the skills and talents you each identify within the story. Include the interests cited and the positive personality traits.

After you've made your lists, ask your client to tell you what she found on the first pass. Then read what you found —it will be like presenting your client with a gift. The skills you identify are definitely "keepers."

If you and your client carry out these activities with thoughtful attention, you will see some intriguing patterns emerge. Concentrate on one activity at a time so the task doesn't become overwhelming. Repeat exercise 12 many times so that you help your client discover skills from different types of activities.

Chapter Five

DISCOVERING NEW FIELDS

W hen we ask our children "What would you like to be doing?" the answers can range from "I'd like to travel," to "I would like to make a lot of money," or "I want to explore my creativity." It's the rare young adult who either knows himself or what is "out there" well enough to come forth with a more focused answer. Will it be a job? Graduate school? Some combination of the two? The *Dictionary of Occupational Titles*, published by the U.S. Employment Service, lists 12,741 separate job titles over 1,404 pages. How does a young person begin to cope with the overwhelming task of determining what his options are in the working world and how they fit in with his interests, values, skills and aptitudes?

Your client has learned a lot about the "Who am I?" question in earlier chapters. Now, via a process we call surveying, he'll begin to answer the "Where am I going?" and "How do I get there?" parts of the equation. Surveying is similar to doing market research, except in this case the markets your client is researching are her own areas of interest. Because it reveals options, surveying is a foolproof way of gaining control of important life decisions—choosing a field of interest, a college major, a company, a job, a house, a place to live, or even a spouse. As a tool for job seeking, surveying ensures that your client ends up doing what's right for her—work she will enjoy and have the skills to accomplish. Your client won't feel she has to take the first offer that comes along, because surveying will show her the possibility of other choices.

As a first step, your client must narrow her survey topic to exactly what interests her most. Now is the time to review her responses to the exercises in the previous chapters. Whose biographies did she enjoy most? What were the "future" fantasies you discussed? Do particular skills or aptitudes suggest direction? What about the people or products she admires? What subjects hold the most intrigue? How does she spend her leisure time? All of these exercises helped your client identify and expand her list of interests.

Most people are surprised—and delighted—to discover that surveying is quite easy. As one client told us, "Surveying is much more fun than I thought. I started out thinking I was interested in one subject but discovered so many new aspects of this as I went along, my world opened up."

This experience is common—most people find surveying invigorating and rewarding. Surveying is a way to look first, to explore what's out there, without being forced into premature commitment. Think of how you approach buying an appliance—a VCR, for instance. If you buy without knowing the various features of different makes and models, you may get stuck with a purchase that doesn't suit your needs at all. So, usually we ask around among friends and acquaintances or check the consumer rating magazines, and do a little comparison shopping before buying. It's possible to do the same thing with work—comparison shop before getting involved in a job.

Through surveying, people become experts in the field which interests them most, discover what kinds of work may be possible in that field, and learn how to be comfortable in meetings with people who may be key decision makers in their organizations. Most important, when all the information is gathered, they have the ability to make sound decisions about whom to approach for work.

With a little practice your client will begin to relax and enjoy the process. This is fairly easy because he isn't looking for a job, he's gathering information. The surveying technique eliminates the "job interview" pressure from in-person meetings.

Surveying Opens Up Worlds

Any interest may be a subject for surveying, but it makes sense to begin with the most intense interest. It's this genuine curiosity that makes surveys succeed. For instance, one of our clients grew up using every opportunity to fish and camp. When it came time for him to do a survey, he explored his fascination with the design of outdoor-sports equipment. He wound up going to work for a sporting-goods manufacturer testing equipment in the rugged environments he loved.

Another of our clients in his late twenties was fascinated by marine science, particularly as it relates to aquariums, and had always wondered what kinds of jobs existed in the field, how people chose their careers, and what kind of training they had.

He began his survey by determining his objective: to find out how marine science promotes the survival of rare species in captivity. His method was to talk with at least three people who work professionally in aquariums, three people who teach in the field, and two people who do research or underwater fieldwork discovering and capturing species. He gave

THE BENEFITS OF SURVEYING

Surveying helps your client:

- Greatly increase knowledge about a subject of genuine interest.
- Meet key people in organizations which interest her.
- Introduce herself easily and comfortably.
- Create a broad network of contacts who may serve as resources long after the survey is over;
- Make final decisions about how to build a career and advance in it.

himself eight weeks to complete the survey, and because he lived on the Eastern seaboard, he decided to include the state of Florida as part of the geography he would survey.

On his visit to a large tropical marine aquarium in Florida, he engaged a young guide in conversation. In just 10 minutes, he gained a tremendous amount of information: which fish survive in captivity and under what conditions; what the trends were in conservation of rare species; and who was doing the outstanding work in this regard. He also found out where the guide had gone to college and what her course of study had been; what her present job entailed and how she had learned it; what she expected to do in the future; jobs other people held in the aquarium and what qualifications they had.

Our client was stunned at how much he had learned in one brief talk with an individual actively engaged in his field of interest. It prompted him to plan additional surveys to explore other areas of marine science—including underwater exploration, zoology, and aquaculture—once he completed this survey.

Avid interest in a subject tends to generate magnetism. Most people are delighted to talk to someone who is enthusiastic about their own favorite subject or job.

Developing a Survey Plan

Dan, a sophomore in college, had some ideas about what he might want to do in the future, but he had no idea how to prepare for it. As a boy he had helped his father turn an old mill into a highly functional house, which they then leased. Restorations fascinated him, especially when the old and decrepit was turned into the refurbished and useful. He thought he might enjoy buying old houses and fixing them up for resale.

Then, one summer, while he was still in high school, he was able to narrow in even further on his field of interest. At the time, Dan worked in an office which was noisy, impersonal, sterile, and poorly ventilated. The poor working conditions made such an impression on him that he vowed never to get trapped in such an environment again. As time went on, he began noticing the environments in other places. Even in school, he imagined redesigning the classroom— rearranging the furniture, changing the shape and height of desks and doorways, altering window treatments and wall colors. He seemed to have good spatial abilities and was sensitive to the physical relationship between people and the objects they used as well as between people who shared their space.

When he got to college Dan thought he might study work environments and their effect on the people using them. But he was confused about what major would best explore this subject. He also was uncertain if this was really the field to which he wanted to commit his future. He decided to survey people working and studying in the fields of workplace environments, furniture and office design, rehabilitation and restoration of historic buildings to find out what they found most stimulating and satisfying about their jobs.

Before he could ask busy professionals to take time to talk to him even for a few minutes, he knew he needed a clear, specific topic of interest. He couldn't expect people to tell him *everything* they knew.

Getting Focused

Dan identified a general topic of interest: designing work environments. Next, he isolated what specifically interested him about that general topic: design elements which contribute the most to productivity. He refined his topic even further: rehabilitating older buildings to enhance productivity for office workers.

Now he was focused and able to state what we call at Crystal-Barkley a "tight topic." Dan's was: To discover how older buildings have been rehabilitated to provide enjoyable, productive space for office workers, and to determine the best preparation for redesigning such buildings.

Instead of asking people the broad question as to what they found most satisfying about their work, Dan zeroed in on *productivity* in *rehabilitated buildings*. Now he was in a position to learn much more about his exact interest.

Your assistance is crucial in seeing to it that your client gets under the layers of generalities that can mask the heart of his interest. Keep asking "Why is that interesting to you?" "Exactly what aspect draws you to this?" As a result, the people he sees during the survey will know precisely why your client wants to talk to them and information will flow much more readily.

WHAT'S A SURVEY PLAN OF ACTION?

H ere are the elements of a survey plan of action, which should be written down carefully in advance:

- A tight topic of interest.
- The types and numbers of people to see.
- A schedule by which you will carry out and complete off-site and on-site research, by day and week.
- Where to find reading material on the subject.
- People who might know about the subject but are not involved with it.
- People who are involved in the topic of interest.
- Specific questions to ask these people.
- Visits with these people to ask them the specific questions.

As the survey progresses, add:

- Recommendations of other people to talk with.
- Thank-you notes that were written to people visited —with date and a note of any information that was sent to them.
- Notes from debriefings to measure progress.

The survey should continue until your client is satisfied with both the quantity and quality of information gathered. That may mean extending the time limit or intensifying the effort within the same time allotted. Debriefing meetings with you, the coach, are very important to help your client monitor his progress and insure that the survey plan is carried out in a timely manner.

Survey Objective

The tight topic is the centerpiece of the total survey, but every survey must also include a plan of action. Next, Dan wrote down how he planned to explore his tight topic: By talking with at least two people who have designed rehabilitated offices, two who work within these spaces, two professors in the architectural school who concentrate on this area, three full-time students majoring in design of work spaces or historic preservation, two developers specializing in rehab of older buildings, and two buyers or tenants of these spaces.

Where and How Long

Dan gave himself a month to complete the survey; given this time limit, he confined his survey to a 100-mile radius of his home.

He then began to consider how to begin. Here, again, as the coach you will be an enormous aid in keeping your client moving.

Background Research: Off-Site Sources

Your client should start her research with off-site sources, which include publications (books, magazines, newsletters, yellow pages), as well as friends and relatives who know something about the subject. These sources inform but are not directly involved in the topic. They lead to people who *are* involved. Most surveyers find a research librarian enormously helpful at this juncture, especially if they describe exactly what they're seeking. For instance, when Dan first asked the librarian, "Where can I find information about office design?" he was overwhelmed by volumes of information. Life got easier when he specified, "Where can I find information about the rehabilitation of older buildings for offices?"

Other excellent off-site sources are:

• Clubs or associations serving a particular field—these

groups often have their own publications and staff members who know a great deal about the field.
• Course textbooks and recommended reading lists.
• The local newspaper's reference section.

The use of off-site sources is also the way to uncover information that your client might not be able to discover in meetings. For example, your surveyor won't be so brash as to ask direct salary questions of someone holding a job he'd like to have, but he can usually discover the range of salaries paid for similar jobs through his off-site sources.

Off-site sources and knowledgeable strangers are often quite near and easy to reach. For example, Dan noticed that an old building across from the university's administrative offices was under renovation. He dropped into the office of the Vice President for Operations and asked to look at the plans. The names and phone numbers of the architect and builders were right on them. He also had a chance to talk to the vice president's assistant, who referred Dan to the professor who had coordinated the plans for the building. Dan was on his way.

Suppliers to companies, teachers, spokespeople for professional associations, and retired people are generally fairly easy to meet. Even casual contacts such as visitors to trade shows, receptionists, or maintenance people may have valuable information to offer. People love to be asked for their opinions.

Off-site research can lead the surveyor down many trails of clues. To avoid getting overwhelmed, Dan confined his note taking to his tight topic. He was looking for background information about this specific subject—and especially for the names of people to contact for personal meetings.

Here's an important area in which parents can be of real help. When reading about a topic, do certain names of potential interest to your client crop up over and over?

Make a note and pass it on. Ask yourself, "Whom do I know?" "Whom do I know who might know the right people?" "What's my relationship to this person?" Extending the network is a valuable form of help.

When you come up with a name, tell your client as much as possible about the contact—his or her job and organization. Then turn over the name and number to your client and let him follow through. You cannot monitor the ensuing relationship.

Don't do your client's legwork. If you run across someone working in an area of special interest, make a note of the information and pass it on. When your client follows up, she can comfortably say, "Dad told me you met recently at the golf tournament and you might be willing to talk to me about your experience as a pilot." She needn't belabor the connection, but it's a good icebreaker.

Without monitoring contacts directly, how can you keep abreast of your client's progress? You can ask your client to let you know how a meeting goes, and as he fills you in, you have the opportunity to offer counsel on how to proceed with other contacts. Always take a positive and open-ended approach. Ask, "How is it going?" "How is this survey turning out in relation to what you thought it was going to be?" "What sort of new ideas do you have about where you'd like to work? About the product or services?" "What do you think of the values of this company?" These questions leave the door open for more ideas and brainstorming.

Once your client feels he has a good overview of the subject and a variety of people identified to meet with, he needs to develop a list of questions.

Preparing Relevant Questions
Rainer Maria Rilke wrote, "True wisdom lies not in having all the answers, but in knowing the correct questions." Here are some of the questions Dan prepared to ask architects, devel-

TOO LITTLE TIME

Although surveying is easy and enjoyable for most people, some young adults say they have a problem finding enough time to do it. If your client has this problem, suggest she keep a daily log of all her activities for one week. After seven days, she can review the log and cross out all the things she didn't really *have* to do. Those slots become her surveying time in the following weeks. It helps to remember that the busiest and most productive people always seem to know how to organize and make time.

opers, teachers, furniture and interior designers, students, buyers, and tenants.

- What kinds of physical layouts do you feel yield the best productivity in an open-office situation? (architects, teachers, designers, buyers, tenants)
- What sort of accommodations did you make in your design to reflect management's style? (architects, developers, tenants, buyers, designers)
- How did you prepare yourself for this particular work? (architects, developers, designers)
- How might you approach that differently, knowing what you know now? (architects, developers, designers)
- In what way do you feel this course in restoration technique is specifically useful for office design or redesign? (students, teachers)

Dan measured every question against his tight topic. If the question aimed at the topic, it was a good one. If it missed the mark, he let it go or refined it. For instance, one question to students was "Do you feel this school of archi-tecture has prepared you well?" Dan refined the question to focus it more clearly: "Do you feel this school of architecture has prepared you well for adapting older space for office use?"

In addition to increasing the chances of gaining useful information, preparing questions in advance facilitates the in-person meeting. Questions show off the surveyer's knowl-edge and also let the other person do most of the talking. *You can't not learn from a survey.*

Setting Up the Meeting

Armed with a list of questions to ask targeted sources, Dan was ready to set up meetings. No amount of print or com-puter research will ever replace face-to-face meetings with people directly involved in a specific field. These meetings are the heart—and the magic—of surveying.

Dan developed a short opening gambit and tailored it for each of his "cold" calls. In calling one architect, for example, he began with: "My name is Dan Sloan. Your associate Frank Simons is my mother's team member in the United Way drive. He suggested you might be able to give me a few mi-nutes in your office to discuss your recent work on Old Town Office Square. I understand your offices are actually in one of the restored warehouses. As a probable architecture student trying to sort out the best route to effectively use old structures to create productive office environments, I would much appreciate meeting you."

This introduction accomplished several necessary objectives:

• Reassured the busy architect that the meeting would not take too much of his valuable time.
• Acknowledged that Dan is aware of and admires the archi-tect's work.

- Established that genuine interest, not job seeking, is the purpose of the call.
- Demonstrated that Dan is focused.
- Showed that Dan had done some homework.
- Began to establish rapport.

Assure your client that even "cold-calling" during surveying is relatively easy, because people are sympathetic to an inquisitive mind. Even so, anyone calling to introduce himself for the first time needs to remember the other person doesn't have any idea who he is or why he is calling. Consequently, if your client can't reach someone the first time, he shouldn't feel it's his fault. He may simply have hit upon someone who is exceptionally busy. Counsel that it's better not to leave messages; it's inconsiderate and usually unproductive to expect the other person to call back. The best solution is to befriend whoever is answering the phone —friendliness and consideration may win over a secretary who can tell your client the best time to try again.

TELEPHONE TIPS

- Suggest that your client vary the time of day he calls survey sources and avoid hectic business hours. Early morning or late afternoon may be good, especially if a receptionist isn't there to screen the call. But avoid Monday mornings and Friday afternoons.
- He should be aware of the special hours that might be busy for a particular individual: For example, a restaurant manager can't talk at mealtimes, early morning might find a rock musician asleep and would disturb most writers, and afternoons would be impossible for a swimming coach.

Dan found many people were available only when he was in class or at his part-time job. He asked if he might see them for a few minutes after work or on the weekend, even over a cup of coffee in their neighborhood. This did the trick, and he was able to set up appointments with everyone on his list, including one of his primary role models, a renowned architect who had redesigned the Mercantile Building downtown.

During the Meeting

Parents can be especially helpful when it comes to preparing for in-person meetings. Dan's mother and father both role-played a meeting with him, each taking the part of one of

THE ENCOURAGING COACH

There are many points along the course of surveying at which parents play an important role, including helping to devise the survey plan, role-playing meetings, debriefing, and helping to evaluate information. Young people need both guidance and encouragement as they develop their surveying skills.

The first phone calls your client makes can be especially nerve-wracking. She may be calling strangers —they're busy! What if they slam the phone down, cursing your client for wasting their time? What if your client can't, or won't, make the calls out of fear or inertia? That's where you come in as coach. Demonstrate how easy surveying is by suggesting your client survey someone in the family or neighborhood first. Also, try to think of stories of how others have successfully used surveying. Try doing a practice survey yourself, and tell your client about it.

his targeted sources. (See Chapter 11 for information about role playing.) Before each survey meeting, his parents also reminded him that he was *not* looking for a J-O-B. Throughout the survey Dan held this thought in the front of his mind.

The more questions a surveyer asks, the more she learns. But it's equally important to listen and digest the answers. You'd be surprised how often people continue asking an endless array of questions without processing the replies.

Questions grease the conversational wheels, but other mutually intriguing topics will come up naturally in the course of the meeting. This establishes rapport that will make the surveyer welcome back in the future. However, it's easy to get off the track. Just before a survey meeting and near the end of it a good surveyer checks over her list of questions or key phrases to make sure she is achieving her objective, is keeping the talk focused, and isn't overstaying her welcome, no matter how well the meeting is going.

It helps to take notes, either during the meeting or immediately after. If your client wants to take notes during a meeting, she should ask first, but usually the person being visited is flattered and impressed by the serious approach. When reviewed later, notes often reveal seemingly insignificant information that turns out to be important.

A good surveyer will also always ask for the names of other people to contact. After a pleasant conversation, most people will volunteer a referral or provide an introduction even without being asked. A final note: A good surveyer always sends a thank-you note promptly.

Debriefing

The ultimate purpose of any survey is to put the data to work. Throughout the process Dan kept track of his progress in a special notebook. On the first page he wrote:

- The survey objective: tight topic, people to be seen, and the time limit.

   Using a fresh page for each person he met, he entered:

- Name, address, phone numbers.
- Name of secretary or assistant, if applicable.
- Any personal notes about that individual's hobbies or interests outside the job. (One architect Dan visited had an extensive collection of model sailing ships.)
- Anything relevant about the environment, especially as it relates to his desired working conditions.
- What he learned.
- How that information compared with the survey objective.
- Conflicting answers and conclusions among the various people seen.
- Names, terms, places, procedures, or problems which might be useful in the future.
- Whether all of his intended questions had been addressed.
- Any questions he asked which were not on the original survey plan. He might add these to his list for the future.

Evaluating

When he reviewed his notes, after all his visits were made, Dan compared what he learned with the original objective. His father helped him determine whether he felt satisfied with the information by comparing answers with questions and looking for gaps. If a surveyer is dissatisfied, he needs to review the plan. Did he:

- Develop a plan and stick to it?
- Visit most or all of the people and places on his list?
- Did he feel prepared for each meeting, keeping his part of the conversation focused?
- Did he actually ask the questions he had prepared in advance?

DAN'S THANK-YOU NOTE

Daniel K. Sloan
225 West Lawn Drive
Milwaukee, WI 53225
(414) 246-1108

April 10, 1993

Ms. Irene R. Sweeney
Sweeney & Sweeney Associates
4 Old Town Square
Milwaukee, WI 53212

Dear Ms. Sweeney:

The time spent with you in your offices in Old Town Square was tremendously productive for me. I was so glad to have been able to visit you there, where I could get the feel of what you have created.

I was especially interested in the way you situated the skylights to bring so much space and light into such a massive structure. Is that a signature of your designs? I look forward to touring the Bayside Wharf Building you redesigned. Thank you for arranging my meeting with the managing agent.

Enclosed is the article I mentioned on the new type of thermal glass which filters glare. I will let you know what Professor Land thinks about the possibility of my structuring my own study/apprentice program. The idea appeals to me very much.

You can see how helpful you have been to me already. I appreciate your interest more than I can say.

Very best wishes,
[signed]
Daniel K. Sloan

- Did he listen carefully and take good notes (either during the meeting or right after)?
- Did he get additional contacts?
- Is he still interested in the subject and his specific tight topic?

Results

As a result of his survey, Dan discovered a wide variety of recommended courses to take, including:

Art History: for an exposure to architectural designs, and how they contribute to creativity.

Behavioral Science: to better understand motivational needs of workers, and for the history of productivity efforts.

Industrial Design: how working relationships are enhanced or inhibited by various physical layouts.

RULES OF THUMB FOR THANK-YOU LETTERS

- May be in neat longhand or typed.
- Should be on 8½-×-11-inch or slightly smaller paper, which can be easily filed.
- White, off-white, light-gray, or light-blue paper only.
- Name, address, and (optional) phone number (printed or typed at top or bottom)—black, gray, blue, maroon, or dark-green printing.
- Always at least three paragraphs.
- Never begin with "I." Instead: "Thank you for . . . ." Or, "It was so good of you . . . ." Something which places the emphasis on the reader.
- Written promptly—within the week.

BYPASSING THE SALES PITCH

An occasional problem for people surveying the field of sales or in stores is overzealous sales people. For example, if your client is researching a computer system, she may run into high-pressure salespeople. She can tell them up front that she is researching in order to make a decision about a career—not about a purchase. She should be considerate about salespeople's time, especially if they have buying customers waiting. Suggest your surveyer select a time—usually early morning or early afternoon—when buying traffic is slower.

If your client finds helpful salespeople, she can ask them about themselves: how they got involved in selling the product, how they learned so much about it, whether it is a strong interest, how that interest developed, and what they hope to do with it in the future.

Seeing the Survey Through

It's critical for surveyers to fulfill their objectives, and the encouragement parents provide can make a big difference. Frequent debriefing conversations help identify potential trouble spots. One young college graduate trying to survey the broadcast-communications field without benefit of a supportive coach was so put off by her first meeting that she abandoned the survey. "The woman I met with was so stressed out by her job that I thought, 'I'd never want to be in her shoes.' I lost interest in the topic right then. I see now that I made a mistake. How could I possibly learn about the whole broadcasting field from one meeting? I wish someone had reminded me of that."

Even if the survey sometimes seems difficult, your son or daughter will have got an education about his or her topic. That's what's needed for good decision making. Surveying will be a primary tool throughout his or her working life. Eventually surveying itself can be added to your client's updated skills list.

What if your client decides he doesn't like the field he surveyed? That's valuable information that could save him from making a poor work choice. Encourage your client to put the survey aside and to undertake other surveys on other topics to fully explore alternatives.

Parents walk a thin line between interference and indifference when trying to help an adult client, and it's easy to fall over to one side or the other. It's particularly important to keep your balance during any exploration process. For one thing, your client may come up with topics you don't approve of or conclusions you don't agree with. If you can retain the encouraging coaching stance and reserve your judgment, you'll both be way ahead. With surveying, you both will understand more about her goals and pursuits than with any other method you can follow. When you know her decisions are based on solid information, you will worry less about her ultimate choice. Chapter 11, "Helping Your Client: Do's and Don'ts," offers additional insights into how to work with your client for the best results.

Exercises and Activities

Things to Think on Alone

1. Have you ever explored any interests in a manner similar to surveying? If so, how did it work for you? If not, how much does the approach interest you personally? Do you believe it can help your client?

How do you think your feelings about surveying will affect your role as coach?

Things to Do Alone

2. Try a practice "mini" survey yourself, just for fun. Pick any recreational subject you would like to know more about (one client picked "learning to play Ping-Pong in international competition") and go through the steps described in this chapter in an abbreviated form. Speak with people you haven't met before. Then measure your reactions and results. Tell your client about your experience.

One of our adult clients described her first try at surveying: "For years I'd been thinking about teaching an after-school art program for inner-city kids. But I always put off doing anything about it because I thought it would be too complicated. While my son was thinking about his survey, I did a little practice survey myself. I started looking up after-school programs in the library. Then I mentioned the subject to one of my nieces, an elementary-school teacher. She urged me to talk to the principal of her school, and suggested how I might explain my idea. I was off and running before I knew it. It was much easier than I had ever dreamed."

Things to Do Together

3. The Survival Adventure: Ask your client to imagine that he has moved to a strange city, where he knows no one. He's got enough money to last a month, if used frugally. He has just arrived and is in a bus station next to a newspaper stand and a phone booth, where there is, surprisingly, a phone book. He has one suitcase. It's morning. What will he do in the first hour?

4. Survival: Part 2: Your client has been in the strange city for two days now. He's found a place to stay, but no one seems to notice he's around. He's lonely and feeling lost. What does he do for the next five days?

5. Survival: Part 3: Your client now has three different job possibilities. One is a job as a messenger, which requires bicycling around the city, a skill your client is good at. The salary is just enough to make ends meet. The second job is waiting tables in a fancy restaurant. The money's good, but your client is inexperienced and frightened of starting. The third job is in a field that interests him, but it is an internship that doesn't pay. All three jobs have flexible hours, and any one is his for the taking. Given this scenario, which job would he take? Why?

These survival adventures reveal how your client will explore—survey—under conditions of total freedom and exceptional survival pressure. For example, Part 3 indicates how creative—and risk-taking—he might be in order to preserve his closely held interests. All three "imagination" exercises help identify strong interests and also measure the depth of your client's commitment to them.

6. Tight Topics: At the top of a page in her notebook ask your client to write down the most appealing item from her long list of interests. (For instance, classical music broadcasting.)

Identify and write down the most fascinating aspect of that topic. (Radio.)

List the elements of broadcasting classical music over the radio that seem most interesting. (Planning programs; raising money for programs; doing market studies; selling advertising; being an on-air host.)

Pick the most intriguing. (Planning programs for classical music, specifically opera.)

Brainstorm the various ways your client might be able to exercise her skills if she were working in this area. This will help your client refine a very specific and compelling tight topic. This brief exercise gives your client a basic understanding of how to define a tight topic and begin to explore it.

7. Finding People Resources: Whom does your client know who may know about his subject? Whom do you know? Write down their names.

Can't think of anyone? How about friends or relatives who might know informed people. Put their names on the list.

Suggest that your client ask a resource librarian about relevant books and tapes, contact clubs or associations and their publications and ask for names, ask professors or teachers in the field for suggestions of informed people.

Make notes of people mentioned in news or magazine articles on the subject.

The names on this list are the surveyer's "start-with" people. Many will lead to other contacts, who should be added to the list.

8. Debriefing Exercise: After your client has completed a survey meeting or two, ask a series of debriefing questions:

Are you still interested in your chosen subject?

Is your interest stronger than ever?

Did the meeting uncover other appealing aspects of the field?

How well do you feel work in this area matches your skills and personal capacities?

How committed do you think you would feel to this kind of work? For how long?

If you chose this work, would you be challenged, stimulated, or satisfied in other ways important to you?

Do you like the people whom you met?

Chapter Six

WHAT DIRECTION TO FOLLOW

As a young man Richard had wanted to "do politics" behind the scenes, not as an elected official. It was his passion and his love. He was an ardent organizer and volunteer for local party fund-raising and campaigning. But his marginal income meant he often had a tough time paying the rent without tapping his savings. He happened to run across an opportunity to invest his small savings in a printing company while earning out the balance of the ownership. Richard felt it was a sound business deal but wondered how the printing business could complement his interests and values.

Twenty-five years later, Richard is famous in big-city politics as the printer every candidate *has* to use for printed materials—from petitions, to legal documents, to pamphlets and flyers. You name it—if it involves politics, he prints it. But only for the party he supports. He helps his clients by having a lawyer review each candidate's document to see that it meets legal requirements. All of his free time is spent at the political meetings and functions he loves. He never supports one candidate over another—although every candidate believes Richard likes him best—because his underlying goal is to be constantly working to help his party. Richard's work is fully integrated into his life goals.

Pat, on the other hand, was working in public relations and very unhappy. She didn't know what she wanted to do with her life. She decided to get a law degree in order to have more clout in the job market. Three years later she is back where she started—she has no idea whether she wants to work with a large or a small law firm, or to join the legal staff of a corporation. Sadly, she will not come across as an attractive candidate because she has not defined her goals, and has no fire, no ambition.

Goals provide the rationale for our lives, the reason for getting up in the morning. Call them your "mission," the "direction" for your life, or simply say they're where you're headed. By any name, they are crucial to a satisfying and productive life because they give meaning and shape to our lives.

Goals answer a crucial question: "What do I want to accomplish with my life?" There are many different routes to their fulfillment. The person who wishes to preserve and protect the environment could become a teacher, journalist, explorer, lobbyist, EPA inspector, forest ranger, or the vice president of public affairs for a waste-management firm. Yet many people never connect their job prospects to something they care about. That's a surefire route to mediocrity and frustration, as Pat's example illustrates. If Pat attempts to practice law without having a strong sense of the value of her work, she will surely do a pedestrian job, and will probably be job hunting again within a few years.

Unfortunately, many people are so focused on finding something to *be* that they become rigid, fixated on a word like "doctor" or "accountant." Faced with the normal frustrations of daily work, they often break down. We are much more flexible and able to cope when "lawyer" is a means of achieving a goal—such as "defending and promoting the civil rights of children," or "preserving the law and order of my community." You will notice I express goals with "ing" words because when they fit us well they are always ongoing. These are aspirations which drive us to be *doing,* not just to do once.

Goals as Guides

There are dreams inside every young person's head which, when coupled with skills, point out the route to exceptional accomplishment. The idea is to coax out the goals first—and then the various occupations that might fulfill them. Our client Nancy learned this the hard way.

During her freshman year in college, Nancy decided to major in hotel management, which had been described to her as a prerequisite for getting anywhere in the hospitality industry. Her father objected strenuously. Though not in the industry himself, he knew a lot about it and insisted Nancy was not physically or emotionally strong enough to withstand the high-pressure atmosphere. He also felt that the pay didn't compensate for the stress and demanding hours and he feared Nancy was too much of a maverick to conform to the rigid standards of the hotel industry.

Her father's disapproval was just the red flag she needed to charge forward. Nancy countered that the industry required her to be good with people, which she was, and that it offered chances to travel, which she loved. Nancy made a lot of assumptions about the life-style without surveying to discover the truth for herself.

After graduation, Nancy easily found work with a large hotel chain. It wasn't long before she began to hate her job as assistant to the banquet manager. She was pigeon-holed, had little flexibility, and was oppressed by bureaucratic red tape. What an embarrassment! She talked with people in other hotels. The atmosphere seemed to be the same at them, too. She had made the wrong choice—partly because she was a rebel and partly because she hadn't taken a close look at the industry.

Nancy felt foolish for spending four years studying "the wrong thing," and unhappy at the prospect of remaining with the industry. She quit her job. "Now I'm back to square one," she fumed. In reality, the experience had provided Nancy with some valuable information about herself. The process of setting goals would help her recognize and organize this information.

Uncovering Goals

Each person's goals are unique. For instance, saying "I want to be living happily" doesn't resonate until it is flavored with what makes that individual happy. Everyone who "wants to be living happily" must knit his own values, interests, and skills into his goal statement. For example, one young man with excellent math skills wanted to make lots of money but also enjoyed helping older people and working as a volunteer for certain charities. His version of "living happily" came out like this: "I am using my superior math capacities to design new investment products for older, retired people and philanthropic groups, while ensuring my own financial comfort." This specific statement is much more real and personal than saying, "I want to be a financial planner" or an "asset manager," which would always raise the question "Why?"

Nancy started to find her goals by reexamining her likes and dislikes, which are equivalent to values. Then we asked her to look back on her college years and recall any specific moment when she felt gratified and happy. She quickly responded, "The best time I ever had was when I single-handedly formed a new sorority on campus." Nancy said she

spent hours on the phone to national chapters, months acting as a go-between from the administration to her classmates. Her task consumed her, and it brought to light
many of her talents: dedication to the task at hand, initiative, a flair for management, and the ability to inspire others
towards a common goal.

Her skills reminded me of a national survey in *Recruiting Trends Report,* by Patrick Scheetz of Michigan State
University's Career Planning and Placement Office, in which
employers were invited to rate desirable qualities in new college graduates. Most important to employers were: depend-
ability, honesty and integrity, the ability to get things done,
a willingness to accept responsibility, and intelligence. Ranked
next, and almost as important, were common sense, problem-
solving skills, and interpersonal skills. This episode in
Nancy's life story displayed virtually all of these highly
valued skills.

Nancy remembered the celebration marking the sorority's opening. With more than 300 people crowding the
auditorium, she was pushed up on stage to make an im-
promptu speech. She came through with flying colors. The
next day some of her friends asked if she had ever considered
an acting career.

Thinking back on this prompted Nancy to consider acting—but this time she did a survey. She spoke with several
young actors and acting coaches, all of them very enthusiastic about their business. Next, she talked to older actors with
more experience. She also met with a playwright and two
experienced directors. Unlike the acting coaches and young
students, who tended to romanticize the profession, these
individuals gave Nancy a no-frills picture of life in the theater. She started getting a fuller picture of the commitment
a theatrical career demands from even minor players. Nancy
realized it was far more complicated than standing up in

front of her peers and talking extemporaneously, and she didn't feel a real drive for it.

"Where does this leave me?" she wondered. A teacher suggested theatrical or film production. Planning, diligence, enthusiasm, people skills, and persuasiveness are all useful and desirable qualities in the production end of things.

Nancy considered her interests and reviewed her skills and aptitudes again, thinking about which she enjoyed most. She recognized that she's a doer, good at organizing and managing programs and arranging unusual events for large groups. She's excited by the entertainment business and wants to be in the thick of things—but not *the star*. Knowing this, Nancy began to formulate a goal statement and it soon became clear that she wanted to *"shine as the impresario* who is known for creating special events which live in the memories of both observers and participants."

She started working again at an entry-level job, as a receptionist in a talent agency. Entry-level jobs can be wonderful stepping-stones for the person who has a direction; without direction, these jobs are often dead ends. Nancy began a new survey. Through the agency she learned the names of people in special-events production on the West Coast, and saved for a trip to California. She wrote in advance and used her telephone skills to set up meetings with her contacts. She met with a producer of rock concerts, a director of special events at a large resort, and one of the producers of the Emmy-awards show. Her natural enthusiasm and growing knowledge of the field encouraged the people she met to recommend her to others, and the trip proved invaluable both for the information gleaned and the friendships and contacts she forged.

With her goal clear in her mind, the picture of a perfect job began to evolve: producer/director of special events in the entertainment world. She knew she might have several different jobs in the future but felt certain that each would be consistent with her goal.

As Nancy's goal statement below illustrates, fully formed goals include more than the work we choose; goals also include things that delight us in our leisure time: family, friends, causes, hobbies, sports, health. Goals are lifelong desires that are multidimensional and evolving. They affect the relationships we choose and how we spend our time. Goals always sound superlative, because anything less will fail to excite the imagination and inspire dedication.

We may play many different roles as we pursue our goals. I have been a management consultant, parent, initiator of housing-rehabilitation programs, wife, community volunteer, and head of my own company. What goal underlies these roles? I am enabling individuals—including my family and myself—to live fulfilling, productive lives. I can tell you that without the goal structure providing my raison d'être, I might have thrown in the towel a number of times.

NANCY'S GOAL STATEMENT

"**I** am shining as an impresario, communicating my zest for life, making the most of my capacities to think fast and organize diverse elements in producing events that put style and glamour in the lives of all who participate in or watch them, reaching out to the world, living in clear fresh air, loving and tending children, nurturing mind and body for maximum performance, infusing home and close relationships with the inner excitement I feel, and, above all, making this extraordinary gift of life a fun experience for myself and others."

Do Goals Ever Change?

Goals continue to evolve and be refined as a person learns and grows, but once they are revealed, the heart of them remains constant. What do change regularly are the demands of the workplace. In fact, the world is changing so rapidly that many traditional careers will be outmoded or radically altered in the next 20 years. Yet if a young adult knows *why* a particular career beckons, she can move ahead of events—be they changes in her own life or those in the marketplace.

Take the case of our client Denise. Denise was an exceptionally talented dancer. At age 20 she was chosen for the American Ballet Theatre's summer program, one of the world's premier testing grounds for new talent. Then, two weeks before the program began, Denise was in an automobile accident that smashed her left knee.

Denise had spent so many years dedicated to the idea of being a dancer that she was convinced there was no other road for her. She embarked on a strenuous physical therapy program designed to bring the knee back to perfection. Through her own ordeal she acquired so much knowledge about physical training that she became something of an expert. She had a gift for figuring out which muscles contributed to specific aches and pains and during her long months working out at the gym, she helped and advised other people trying to develop their muscles. Although her own knee could progress only so far, her therapeutic techniques translated into magic for others' conditioning.

Despite her efforts, Denise had to face the truth: she would never be the dancer she wanted to be. At first, she assumed she would find other work centered around dancing, such as teaching or choreography. But as she examined her interests and values in a Crystal-Barkley course, Denise for the first time recognized her underlying life goals which included: "Helping myself and others experience the fullness of their talents and the exhilaration of top performance—whatever their work areas—aided by bodies in top condition." This goal, finally articulated, represented most of what had attracted Denise to dancing in the first place.

Today, after three grueling years of schooling secured by a patchwork of scholarships, Denise is a much-in-demand physical therapist at one of America's best-known hospitals. Long range, she wants to continue developing her "magic" through her own clinic. No doubt she will.

The pursuit of our goals is an ongoing, sometimes arduous task. This pursuit is infinitely preferable, however, to a quick, superficial, meaningless approach to life. *That* will dump a person out of the boat as soon as rocky seas are encountered.

As coaches we can help young people discover what is real for them—what they feel the energy for. Everyone encounters tough times; they're more easily surmounted when an individual has a driving enthusiasm propelling him.

WHERE GOALS COME FROM

People build goals from:
- How they spend their time.
- Things they love doing with their hands, head, or body (skills).
- Fantasies—the things they dream about.
- What they are doing when they have fun.
- How they want to be thought of by others.
- What they want for themselves and for others.
- What they do when no one is monitoring them.

The Family Business: A Help or a Hindrance to Goals?

Deanna's family owned a local chain of cafeterias, but her parents never pressured her to participate. Uncertain as to what field to pursue, she got a degree in business administration, figuring it would look good on her resume. Eventually Deanna opted to open another cafeteria under the aegis of the family franchise. "I wasn't able to figure out what I wanted to do," she explains. "I kept thinking, 'What's the best opportunity?' The family business seemed safest."

Deanna was successful in her venture but has regrets. "Looking back, I chose the family business because I couldn't come up with anything else. That isn't the best way to make a decision."

I agree with her assessment. Entering the family business by default undermines ego and self-confidence and leads to a narrow view of self and potential. The individual almost never thinks about his or her own goals. Even worse, young people may never believe that they can succeed without family help. They may also find that relatives and associates don't appreciate them as mature, competent individuals of achievement. Instead, as young adults, they often remind other family members of all their old childhood labels: "Joey always was unreliable"; "Suzy is poor at math"; "Ned is so shy"; "Kevin is so glib." And so on.

On the plus side, a family business can offer pride in heritage, opportunity, achievement, and fulfillment, as well as the great pleasure of knowing you're part of an enterprise built on the spirit and talents of your ancestors. Under the proper conditions, participating in family enterprise offers an opportunity to contribute and display talents in a uniquely satisfying relationship.

Following in a mother's or father's footsteps as a lawyer, doctor, teacher, or whatever invokes many of the same opportunities and hazards as does the family business. For the Kennedys, politics was the family business. Clearly, some family members were better suited to the venture than others, but all were expected to follow this route.

I believe that one of the keys to working successfully in a family business is to work somewhere else early in life. A few years of learning how other enterprises are run allows a young person to mature in neutral territory as well as gain credibility; he can experience making decisions and taking risks without fear of being prematurely shot down. He might also get new ideas for revitalizing an old family business. Should the "heir apparent" decide to enter the family business later, he or she will have confidence and a track record that commands respect. Even if your client has a thriving family business ready to step into, it's still essential for him to view himself as a totally unique individual with his own life and goals.

(**Note:** To look at the other side of the equation, whether you should go into business with your child in an effort to help him get started, see Chapter 11.)

Exercises and Activities

Things to Think on Alone

1. To what extent do you feel you have had the chance to pursue your own goals?

2. How do you feel that will affect your attitude toward your client?

3. Is it important to you that your son or daughter have status and wealth? Is this the same way you have felt about yourself? Can you answer "why?" to both of these questions?

Things to Think on Together

4. How would you—or do you—convey these thoughts on status and wealth to your client?

5. How do you feel about family members being in business together?

6. What do you think about parents' influence on their children's professions or work?

Things to Do Together

7. The Billboard Exercise: Tell your client, "A highly visible billboard is being given to you. You may put on it anything you like. You may never have another chance like this again. Create the message you want people to see. It can use words, images, or both. It can be personal or for the world. Obviously the message has to be to the point. It can support a favorite cause, be a business statement, or encourage or discourage behavior (like eating meat, smoking, or drinking).

Give your client 10 minutes—no more—to get something on paper. Do not discuss the results at this point.

8. What Needs Doing in My World, Part 1: The next time you can be quiet and alone, ask the following:

"Suppose you became an all-powerful ruler for a day. What in our society or in your own immediate environment would you change? What do you think needs doing? Don't feel constrained by the idea that you will have to fix it yourself; just think about what you would like *somebody* to do. Let your imagination run wild. You have the power to fix anything. It could be your car or the universe, your neighborhood recycling program or global pollutants. Write down exactly what you think needs doing in *your* world."

9. What Needs Doing in My World, Part 2: Ask, "Now that you have listed the changes you would make—which ones would you like to participate in yourself? How, and to what extent, would you help? For example, if you wanted to preserve the rain forest, would you: Develop new sources of food? Fund research? Organize a think tank of scientists who would then apply their efforts to the problem? Work with native populations? In your vision, what do you see yourself actually doing, and how deeply involved are you?"

10. Ask your client to review the exercises in Chapter 4. If he hasn't had a chance to do them, now's the time.

11. Next, put the results of the exercises in this section side by side with the exercises from Chapter 4. Study the patterns together. What predominant themes does your client notice? If he is slow to identify a theme, nudge him gently in the direction that you notice. (Please note, I said "nudge.") Say something like, "Look how often your love of animals is cropping up," or, "I never realized how important spending time outdoors is to you."

12. When your client finishes, ask, "What else is important in your life? What's missing? Personal health? Financial security? Time to improve your tennis game? Family?"

When the additions have been made, ask, "What comes first?" Make an attempt to rank these interests in order of priority.

13. Ask your client to weave all these loose phrases into one statement, placing some of the most powerful interests at the beginning and some at the end. The result will be your client's first rough statement of goals for life. This is a significant accomplishment.

For a sense of what a goal statement is, go back and take a look at Nancy's goals earlier in this chapter.

14. Which entry-level jobs do you think would most help your client pursue his particular goals? Think carefully about this (you need to fully understand your client's goals). Do some research among friends if you need to, be specific, and write down your ideas—always in relation to the goals your client has described. Ask your client to think about this, too. Talk about what you each came up with.

Chapter Seven

FINDING "THE" JOB

Driving on a Georgia back road I once ran across a sign that read, "Pick your rut carefully, you'll be in it for the next 20 miles." Our job is to help clients pick jobs carefully because they are likely to be in the tracks created by them for some time, good or bad.

The most common failing of job seekers is going after something before they know what kind of lives they want, which skills they wish to use, and what they have to offer to employers. Their approach is like turning to the newspaper's classified section and circling want ads blindly.

The second most common failing is going after a job without knowing anything about the job market. This chapter is about discovering which people, companies, or entrepreneurs need your client's unique abilities.

In pioneering his vision of the working world, John Crystal said every job is a need wanting to be met. In one way or another, when an employer offers a job, she is always buying a service she needs. This is true on every level: The dry cleaner needs a worker who won't mangle a silk blouse; the manufacturer of computer software needs a salesperson who can interpret its advantages to the public; the person in charge of the space shuttle needs engineers who are exceptionally attuned to the fallibilities of component parts.

As she has earlier in the Crystal-Barkley process, your client begins by looking within herself and then uses that

---

DESIGNING A SURVEY PLAN

1. What's the subject? Describe it broadly. (Example: commercial architecture, mechanical engineering, not-for-profit fund-raising.)

2. What exactly is it about this subject that intrigues your client? (Example: rehab of older buildings for shared office space and services.) Ask plenty of questions until your client zeros in on a tight topic.

3. Where will this survey take place (geographically)?

4. When will the survey be complete?

5. Who and where are sources of information?

    a. The people, places, data resources through which light is shed on the subject but are not themselves involved. (Example: librarians, associations, and consultants.)

    b. People who are buyers, clients, or users of the products and services closest to your client's refined subject.

    c. Those who produce or provide these services or products.

    d. The number of meetings with people in each category needed to ensure adequate information.

6. Questions to ask. (List the specific questions which might be asked of potential employers and contacts to reveal their needs.)

vision to guide her subsequent search for work. In this chapter we will revisit surveying, using it now to steer your client toward the right job.

Nancy, whose goal statement is highlighted in the previous chapter, won't be very successful in her job search if she simply looks into "producing exciting events." She must narrow her direction to what type of event, for what audience, for what purpose.

Because she loves the outdoors and would like to live away from big cities, Nancy decided to focus her inquiry on ski resorts in the Northeast. (Skiing was on her list of interests.) She had an idea that these resorts could use innovative special events to attract more customers, particularly in the off season, and possibly draw media attention. Nancy planned a survey to learn which resorts in New Hampshire and Vermont which might be most interested in promoting off-season special events. (It was important that Nancy not end up sidetracked by an ultraexclusive resort that wished to avoid publicity.)

The purpose of her survey at this point was to discover the needs of potential employers. Did anyone in the ski-resort business share her particular interest in using special events as a promotional and marketing tool?

This was a match-making survey—to discover if her skills and interests matched a potential employer's needs. When that match is struck, a job is the result.

Skills/Interests + Need = JOB

Once Nancy determined her survey objective, including the geographic area, she needed an overall time limit, names of people to see, questions to ask, and weekly objectives so she could monitor her progress.

Even though she had surveyed before, Nancy felt nervous about this new undertaking. A lot was at stake. She

NANCY'S SURVEY PLAN

Subject: Special Events at Ski Resorts.

Survey objective: To discover which ski resorts in Vermont and New Hampshire are most interested in promoting themselves, especially during the off season, through innovative special events which may attract media attention, by talking with at least 8 owners/managers, 15 people who have visited these resorts, and 10 people who write about or are familiar with the resorts, and to complete information gathering by August 1.

Survey sites: New York City, New Hampshire, and Vermont.

Possible sources of information: *The New York Times* travel section; travel agencies in NYC; ski associations and clubs; travel directories and books; Vermont and New Hampshire tourist and business bureaus; my friend Bill, who works at Killington; the resorts themselves; several friends who regularly go skiing; Uncle Alan who has a house at Stowe; travel writers.

Questions to ask:
Of resort managers/owners:

- What sort of events are planned annually? Monthly?
- What has been the response to these?
- How important do you feel these are in increasing numbers of customers?
- Tell me about your biggest problems in mounting these events.

- How have you recorded the data on the results?
- How have these events varied over the years?
- Could you describe what you feel was the most successful event?
- What has been your experience in securing media coverage?
- What difference has media coverage made?
- What event would you like to put on in the future?

Of travel writers:

- Which resorts do you feel put on the most noteworthy special events? Why?
- How do you find out about these?
- What do you feel makes these resorts exceptional?

Of skiers themselves:

- What sort of a job do you feel your favorite ski resort does in devising enticing special events?
- What influence does this have on your patronage?
- What would you like to see them do that they haven't?

Weekly and daily objectives: Working with her personal calendar, Nancy decided how much time to allow for off-site research, how much geographic territory she would cover in each week, and how many people she would see in that location each week. As the survey unfolded, she began to set daily objectives on her calendar. She circled a midpoint date when she would review whether she was on track for her August 1 deadline or whether she would need to accelerate her efforts.

warmed up by talking with people who might be indirectly knowledgeable about ski resorts in the Northeast. She also read as much current material about the resort industry as she could. As she acquired a working knowledge, her confidence grew.

She rehearsed how she would introduce herself by telephone and in person and then began setting up meetings with resort managers and others on her survey list.

Most people were interested and curious about her research. In the survey meetings she gathered information about the wants and needs of ski-resort managers and customers and about the story angles and deadlines of travel writers. Soon a picture of the problems resorts might have in producing special events began to emerge: time lag (generating plans far enough ahead for the press and promotional materials), estimating the number of people who would attend, last-minute snafus and cancellations, and handling the needs of different age groups.

After each meeting with a resort manager, she checked off what she liked and didn't like about the resort—ranging from management style to types of guests, physical setup, and environmental conditions.

Once, a resort manager preempted the survey and offered Nancy a job on the spot. Nancy responded with genuine appreciation and told the manager she would certainly keep the offer in mind if she felt the needs of this particular resort were a good match for her skills.

The point: Nancy would be the primary decision maker. Only if she felt conditions were right, after evaluating information produced by her survey, would she return to discuss a job.

You can help your client fine-tune his interests and begin to match them to an industry or field just as Nancy did hers. The first step is to help him build a focused survey, an approach that works regardless of the nature of the interest.

TIPS FOR SUCCESSFUL SURVEYERS

- Be absolutely clear about the reason for the survey.
- Show courtesy to the people who assist—friends, secretaries, receptionists.
- Gather information with eyes and feelings as well as ears.
- Engage everyone encountered in conversation.
- Listen more than talk.
- Dress as people in the places to be visited are dressed.
- Respect people's time constraints.
- Share information as well as ask for it.
- Stick to focused information gathering (no discussion of job).
- Note the special interests of people met, and follow them up.
- Ask if individuals could recommend anyone else knowledgeable about the subject.
- Thank people, both orally at the time of a visit and in writing within a week.

It demonstrates to the potential employer that this job candidate values himself enough to take a careful look before taking the plunge.

Take Matt, for example, who also used surveying to reveal a potential employer's need. In college, Matt and two friends opened a diner on campus, so he spent many, many hours working in a fast-food joint. He bacame fascinated by the problem of providing efficient, courteous service. During a school vacation he turned this interest into a survey. On his motorcycle he toured much of his region of the South observing how the big franchises operate. He viewed and timed service over and over again, watching traffic flow, assembly techniques, and all other aspects of quick-service restaurants whose kitchens are easily visible to customers. As Matt began to understand the problems, he also began to develop solutions. He used this research as the foundation of a proposal for speeding up service, then pitched it to the manager of a branch of a well-known franchise. (See Chapter 8 for Matt's proposal.) Now Matt works for one of the largest food operations in the world. His job? Consulting with franchise owners to help them increase efficiency and quality control. He worked his way up from a position with a local owner of several restaurants to one with the parent company.

Another client remembers watching her parents struggle to launch a small business during her childhood. Shirley's mom and dad were turned away from banks and had to find private funding for their ventures. Luckily the business survived, but it was a constant struggle. Fascinated by both investment finance and start-up businesses, in college Shirley majored in economics and after graduation surveyed to discover how small businesses could make themselves more attractive to lenders. Along the way she discovered that the dialogue between lending institutions and entrepreneurs was seriously jammed. Both bankers and small-business owners needed someone who could understand their unique perspectives and act as liaison between them.

This was Shirley's concept—which she eventually turned into a proposal for banks that exhibited an interest in working with entrepreneurs. She entered a training program in the bank that best fit her criteria, which included an interest in helping small businesses grow. Shirley worked her way up and carved out a niche in which she could use her dominant skills—strong communications, sensitivity toward people, financial savvy, and an eye for innovative marketing concepts. She became a lending officer with a growing regional bank and became known for her reliable lending decisions.

Developing a Concept

Your client's lists of likes and dislikes, interests, skills, and dreams all contribute to forming a concept of what he can offer a potential employer. His concept then turns into a survey tight topic, like Dan's idea that interior design in rehabilitated older buildings could contribute to worker productivity. Concepts continue to develop during surveying. They may be grand schemes or promise small improvements. They may fit an employer's existing job description, complement an existing project, or suggest that a new job be created. One concept is enough, but *the concept should be viable in more than one setting.* For example, Nancy could have put her special-events promotion concept to work for a manufacturer of golf clubs or a P.R. consulting firm just as easily as for a ski resort. The setting chosen, however, must reflect genuine interests.

Once your client has gathered enough information from her survey, she will turn it into written or spoken proposals. Her proposals will result in job offers if the potential employers' needs match what she offers. This match is what enables people to choose work that capitalizes on their most productive and creative selves.

Dan, whose survey you may remember from Chapter 5, emerged from college with a degree in commercial design, ready for the job market. His very specific concept was: "Creating glamorous office space in rehab buildings for allied professionals." Dan had visited and studied one such successful rehab in Santa Monica, California. The interior plan situated small, modestly furnished offices around a core of gorgeously appointed Art Deco common rooms. The tenants were 16 independent filmmakers and producers who shared the conference and screening rooms, a charming rooftop café, and a well-supplied central office fully staffed to meet their secretarial and administrative needs. Dan wanted

UNCOVERING AN EMPLOYER'S NEEDS

Background research and observation will reveal some of a potential employer's needs. Background research, for example, might show that the industry as a whole is suffering for lack of creativity, or from shrinking markets or labor-management problems. Observation might reveal a harried manager, or a badly organized office, or customers being kept waiting too long.

When your client feels comfortable in a survey meeting, he can discover much more through careful questions.

To Discover:	**Your Client Might Ask:**
Whether an employer knows that customers are being kept waiting.	What sort of wait do you think most of your customers experience? How long a wait do you feel is acceptable? How do you find the time to observe your employees at work?
Whether an employer has organization and scheduling needs.	It seems that you have a great many demands on your time here. How do you handle scheduling your appointments? How does your filing and retrieval system for documents work here?

	What have you found to be most frustrating in this regard?
Whether an organization's marketing is suffering.	Would you tell me a little bit about how you do market research here? Do you see any specific trends? Do you feel this trend is affecting your competition also?
What this person would most like to have done for him or her.	Have you thought about ways your work could be simplified or made easier? I wonder if you could describe these?
What the organization's needs will be in the future.	How do you see this organization's direction changing over time?
And, if this suggests urgency . . .	How fast do you think these changes will put pressure on you?

The object is for the surveyer to collect enough good information so he can measure it against his own criteria. In the discussion, the surveyer should be ready to describe the work he can do and enjoys doing most. These meetings are an opportunity to test whether a possible employer is interested in your client's talents without yet making the pitch.

to apply a similar concept to other renovations. His immediate problem was to discover who was in the throes of rehabilitating large buildings.

Dan knew he wanted to work directly for a developer who first acquired an old property and then modernized it for lease or sale. He wanted an opportunity to acquire equity in projects and was also interested in the sales aspect.

Dan knew of an old warehouse on the riverfront, which had just been sold. "It's a big unrenovated open space—very unusual," he said. "It would make a stunning professional space." He wondered who was developing it, and if it would be possible to get involved.

To develop a more specific concept for such a space, he asked himself some questions. Here are the questions—and the answers he came up with—that led to his concept:

Q: What kinds of professionals would like this kind of space?

A: Those wishing to present themselves to the public in a substantial and enticing way but who can't yet afford to secure their own lavish space.

Q: Who could these be?

A: Architects, media consortiums, insurance consultants, financial planners, artists, producers, designers, craftspeople.

Q: What would this space offer?

A: Luxurious common rooms and common services like food facilities, secretarial help, and other special features targeted to the needs of potential tenants.

Dan refined his concept for the space, profiting from what he had observed in Santa Monica. His idea was that costs for both developer and businesses could be kept down without sacrificing style. The first thing visitors would see on entering would be a glamorous, highly efficient common space. Dan's next step was to discover if developers might be interested in his ideas. How could he meet the developer who was rehabilitating the old warehouse?

On the outside of the property, a large sign listed addresses and phone numbers of the project's architect, general contractor, and the city planning board. Dan contacted each one, and in separate meetings he asked for thoughts concerning the site—advantages, obstacles overcome, any snags still existing. He also got the name of the developer and learned a little about his past projects. Based on this input, Dan further refined his concept:

> Using interior and exterior design, light, and furnishings to create efficient, unusual, lavish working environments ideal for shared space: In such surroundings, tenants will be more productive and will also present a winning face to their clients; the developer will be more likely to lease or sell his property at a top price to quality tenants.

His next move was to meet with the developer himself and learn his needs. Dan by now was an old hand at surveying and his opening gambit was smooth. He explained to the developer's secretary that he'd been doing research on the site and had several ideas that might be of interest—ideas he'd love to explore in person with the developer.

When Dan finally met the developer face to face, he briefly described his educational background and his current research on the warehouse project. He talked just enough to demonstrate the seriousness of his interest and the validity of his information. Having described his own interests

FIVE CRITICAL PIECES FOR SURVEYERS

Every surveyer should:
1. Know his strengths.
2. Know his desires.
3. Put information gathering first and decision making last.
4. Understand that his or her skills and interests are what employers need to fill jobs: Skills/Interests + Need = Job.
5. Be disciplined and persevering in information gathering.

briefly, Dan asked, "How do you feel about professionals sharing core support facilities?" The developer said he was already thinking of providing some shared space in the warehouse, but he had some interior layout problems.

Dan and the developer found they had many interests in common. Dan's ideas about creating a shared space fell on open ears, and he probably could have convinced the developer to hire him on the spot. However, Dan knew if one developer was interested, others might be, too. Because his concept was easily adapted to a variety of projects, he continued to meet with other developers doing similar work.

Dan targeted several other renovation projects within 60 miles of his town—the geographic area that best met his personal criteria for a living environment. In each case he checked to see how successful the developer had been at rehabs before, what was planned for the current project, and how far along he was with the job. He paid special attention to each developer's attitude toward preserving a building's architectural integrity. Two developers passed Dan's basic criteria. One was converting an empty school building into commercial offices; the other planned to restore a block of abandoned stores downtown. Dan set up meetings with both.

As it turned out, both developers had needs Dan was enthusiastic about filling. Surveying had led him to the point where he had some realistic jobs to propose. Ultimately, his first choice was the warehouse developer with whom he felt such a strong rapport, because he offered an excellent opportunity for future projects.

Surveying helped Dan learn enough about the real needs of potential employers to position himself as an appealing employee. It also gave him choices.

Job Seeking Is a Full-Time Job

Your client should be spending between eight and 10 hours a day on the process of surveying, developing a proposal, and presenting herself to prospective employers. Her task is to develop ideas about what she wants to accomplish, to research them, and determine their viability for people who may employ her or buy her services. She will work it out through the following:

• Knowing her foremost skills and talents.
• Knowing what she wants to accomplish.
• Knowing who needs what she wants to accomplish, and needs it enough to pay for it.
• Identifying the top people or organizations among them who correspond to her top criteria.
• Approaching them with proposals (see Chapter 8).

Tips for Getting Organized

1. Review your client's monetary situation and set a minimum budget. Can your client finance the job search? For how long? Does she need an interim part-time job? If so, the number of hours devoted to the job search will have to

MEASURING A POTENTIAL EMPLOYER'S INTEGRITY

Lots of heartbreaking stories could have been avoided if job seekers had taken a closer look before signing on with an organization. To measure a potential employer's standards, your client will have to know his own ethics. Once a person knows what he's willing to stand up for in life, there's a much better chance of recognizing it in others.

Suggest your client begin by looking at top management. What is expected or tolerated in the executive suite has an uncanny way of influencing behavior down the line. Do these people seem to be models to which your client would aspire?

There are a number of ways for your client to discover whether a potential employer's ethical background coincides with his own values. He can ask questions of current and former employees, contact the Better Business Bureau and ask whether any complaints have been registered against the company, and consult local and national newspapers.

be adjusted. Instead of eight hours a day, she may spend only four hours. Once the number of hours each day is established, set a time limit to complete the job search and block out that period.

2. Say she chose four months: Break down those months into measurable objectives. For example, by the end of the first month, she should have identified potential employers. At the end of the second month, she should know if they perceive the same needs she sees. At the end of the

Anyone considering a job with Dow Corning, for instance, would gain insight from reading up on the way that company responded to the recent silicone-implant controversy. Someone interviewing for a job at Time Warner would find abundant news about disputes among top executives, stories that outline how the company functions and in what direction it's headed. By the same token, the search for Lee Iacocca's replacement, played out in the national press, shed light on the values of Chrysler Corporation.

Other sources include a company's current and former clients, legal records of lawsuits or judgments, and vendors. If it's a small company, several years in business is usually an indicator of stability, and talking with vendors or customers will give an indication of ethical practice.

Your client can also glean information from his own observations while surveying. When your client asks a tough question, he should pay attention to both the answer and the delivery. Someone who looks you in the eye, doesn't hesitate or dissemble, and offers solid information probably doesn't have much to hide.

third month, she will have put together well-researched proposals. At the end of the fourth month, she will have made her proposals and is ready to make a decision.

No matter how urgent or extended the time frame is, the procedure remains the same. This scheme works like an accordion. Constrict or expand it to fit the time frame and plan activities day by day. Every day should have a plan and every week an objective. (Even with a long time frame, your client should plan to survey several potential employers on the same day or within a few days of each other to keep the momentum going.)

3. Advise your client to get out of bed early (and at the same time) in the morning. The biggest mistake job seekers make is to succumb to sloth—a morning spent in bed means critical time lost. Feelings of defeat will set in when your client is not on top of her schedule. She should decide the night before what to do the next day. Better still, she should use the weekend to plan her calendar for the coming week. Calls made in the afternoon to set up appointments help to start the next day right.

4. Anything you can do to help your client create "home-office space" will be a big help. It should be well stocked and inviolate, even if the office shares space with the kitchen or the bedroom. She will need good stationery—(see box, page 92), and she might want a business card too. Help her set up a filing system for correspondence and printed information. A computer notebook or a Rolodex with over-size cards can be used to track appointments and record the date of each phone contact, meeting, or letter.

5. Encourage your client to balance her life during this high-stress period, just as if she were employed. Make it easy for her to take care of herself physically, eat well-balanced meals, and take some extra vitamins. It is important to include leisure-time activities in her planning—playing rac-quetball, visiting a museum, having lunch with a friend.

Exercises and Activities

Things to Think on Alone

1. How have you made your own work-related decisions? How did you choose your present work or profession?

How much choice do you feel you have had? What changes (if any) have occurred to alter your feelings about your work?

2. Surveying is a way of life. Think of one aspect of your own work that might be interesting to investigate. Define it precisely. Who could tell you something about this? What would you say in approaching that person about your interest? What questions would you ask? How do you feel about doing this? Pondering such a prospect could give you some fascinating ideas and also reveal your own feelings about surveying.

3. What new skills have you developed over the years but neglected to integrate into your work? How might you consider doing this now? Would it help you and others? Who might offer insight on this subject?

Things to Think on Together

4. Discuss the benefits of surveying a work-related interest. Does anything about surveying worry you? Do either of you have any fears about it? If so, acknowledge them and talk it over. Since ignoring fears rarely makes them disappear, see if you can think of ways in which these concerns might be overcome. (Usually just giving surveying a try makes any fears about the process disappear.)

Things to Do Together

5. Likes and Dislikes in a Working Environment and the Community: Remember the Likes and Dislikes in People activity your client did in Chapter 3? Ask him to repeat the exercise now, this time concentrating on his likes and dislikes in a working environment and the community at large.

Ask your client to divide a notebook page down the middle. On the "Likes" side, he should list what he enjoys most in a *working environment*. On the "Dislikes" side goes absolutely everything that turns off your client. Suggestions include dress standards, ability to advance, deadlines and pressure, bureaucracy, supervisory styles, independent versus group work, meetings, variety of projects—everything of importance.

On a separate page, ask your client to do the same exercise for *community*. He should consider climate, flora and fauna, transportation, access to recreation and culture, proximity to schools and universities, and housing.

Encourage your client to build these lists to the ultimate. When *everything* is listed, ask him to go down each "Likes" column and place an asterisk by items that are absolute *needs* (versus items that would be nice but not essential). In the "Dislikes" column he should place an asterisk by items that are total *rejects* (versus items he would like to avoid but could tolerate under some circumstances).

These lists are invaluable tools for decision making. You will come back to them in Chapter 9. Doing this exercise also sensitizes your client to keeping his eyes open for the environment during surveying. These simple devices can make choosing a job a much less mysterious, and a tremendously more reliable, process.

To test the criteria, your client might ask himself, "What if they were fulfilled *exactly* as I wrote them?" This is like the story "The Monkey's Paw." Be careful what you wish for—you may get it.

6. Ask your client to return to the list of skills and aptitudes developed in Chapter 4. Now is the time to star those skills which he most enjoys and most wants to develop—in other words, the skills which are the most fun to use. A refined list of skills and aptitudes will be an essential tool for making a decision. (Keep this starred list to use in Chapters 8 and 9.) Does the job in question provide room to use and develop these skills?

7. Develop a list of questions for a specific employer that would elicit ideas about his needs. Questions should be based on your client's preliminary reading and surveying as well as on his own interests. For example, Dan might ask whether a developer is satisfied with the types of glass available for skylights; Nancy might ask about the ages of guests who had attended a previous New Year's Eve gala.

Chapter Eight

ESCAPING THE RESUME TRAP

N ow that your client knows so much about her skills and her direction, you want to be sure she doesn't spoil her creative approach by using an outmoded tactic such as the resume to introduce herself to possible employers.

"Resumes don't open doors, people do." So said John Crystal 40 years ago, and it is still his most quoted comment. I never ask to see resumes, and don't even know if my highly skilled and valued employees *have* resumes. Optimally, I wouldn't discuss resumes at all, but many job seekers still believe they are essential and most employers ask for them out of habit when conducting standard interviews.

For some, resumes appear to have the power and stature of the Ten Commandments, but, in fact, they're not that old or immutable. Resumes became standard around the time of World War II as a convenience for personnel departments overwhelmed by unprecedented numbers of job seekers.

The most dangerous assumption job seekers make is that resumes will get them jobs. Conservative statistics indicate that it takes an average of 1,127 resumes to produce a single job interview. That's *interview,* not job. Sending off a flurry of resumes is an unfocused approach to job hunting, and, as the numbers suggest, it has little chance of hitting the mark.

Worse yet, resumes can backfire. Your clients may inadvertently include the one thing that guarantees a rejection, and she has no way of knowing in advance. I can remember being turned down for an important board position because I mentioned my environmental-protection activities in a curriculum vitae. This outside interest was totally irrelevant to the company—just as irrelevant as someone's tap-dancing hobby is to a law firm selecting a new associate, or an artist's past bout with tuberculosis to a design firm. In my case, my environmental interests happened to rub an influential board member the wrong way because he assumed pro-environment meant anti-business.

Resumes may inadvertently highlight certain irrelevant past details, and they often do not focus on the needs and concerns of the potential employer. Inevitably, resumes force job seekers into defensive positions where education, employment histories, and lifestyles must be explained. That is, if your client ever actually makes it to an interview.

In large organizations, most resumes get no further than the human resources or personnel department, where the mandate is to screen out applicants. They are a quick read for the overwhelmed people in these departments who may have little experience with the positions for which they are charged to produce candidates. If a person has never been involved in manufacturing, assembling, delivering, or promoting a product or service, it's difficult to do a good job of selecting others for these functions. Nor do human resources personnel generally have the time and skill required to discover the unique qualities buried in each job seeker's credentials. Usually, the only propitious times to approach a human resources department are when a job seeker actually wants a human resources position, or after he has already landed the job with the line manager. Although human resources people eventually may be very helpful, your client should always place his first shot at the center of the target.

Even when sent to a specific manager within an organization, a resume can get lost. One executive who needed to fill a key position on her staff placed a newspaper ad. Sure enough, more than 600 resumes came in—and sat in a pile on her desk for months. Every week Eileen vowed to plow through the stack but never got around to it. One day a young man came to meet Eileen in the course of a survey, and by the end of their talk, she had offered him the job. So much for the unfortunate 600.

There's another hitch to resumes. Since they are credential-based, they tend to typecast people so that they have little chance to change or grow. Resumes tell what a candidate has done, not what he might accomplish in the future. Resumes ignore the candidate's passion and what he wants to achieve. They also ignore personality traits, values, goals, and interests. I often hear young people say, "I'm going out for this club [or I'm joining this association] because it'll look good on my resume." Adults frequently agree with them; but if we want to encourage productive development, we should urge them to choose activities that will feed their genuine interests.

If resumes don't work, what does? To land a job, applicants need to make a presentation that closely matches an organization's needs. The best method for doing so is in a personal meeting. Second best is a well-focused piece of writing. Meetings are usually easy to arrange with targeted employers identified during surveying if your client makes it clear that he has a concept to propose which answers an employer's need.

In a personal meeting, the candidate can demonstrate both brains and style. He shows off his communication skills and the way he makes intelligent decisions, and gives a clear picture of how he handles business—whatever that business is. The prospective employer gets to measure the candidate's energy and enthusiasm, personality and drive. Employers report their pleasure in receiving candidates whose focus is on the needs of the organization rather than on themselves.

A personal meeting is particularly crucial for young people with little work experience. If any quality distinguishes one candidate in a large field of aspirants, it is passion for doing what the employer needs to have done. Even if the candidate's work experience or education has gaps, even if he makes gaffes during the meeting, genuine enthusiasm is likely to sway an employer.

Greg, a young lawyer recently out of law school with a strong interest in holistic health, saw a blind ad, placed by an unidentified health organization, for a litigation attorney with malpractice experience to represent its 50,000 members nationwide. The ad requested a resume and letter to be sent to a post office box. Greg guessed that the company was a medical association looking for a lawyer to advise its doctors on malpractice suits. If he was right, the job didn't fully match his interests, nor did his experience fit the job specs. But the ad appealed to him because it mentioned it was seeking innovative ways of dealing with the escalating problems in the health services field. Rather than sending a resume, which he figured would be inadequate at best, he wanted to learn more about the company—whatever that company was!

Greg called his family doctor, a personal friend, and they came up with an educated guess that the organization was a well-known national medical association. Greg's doctor also suggested the name of someone in that company to call. Greg called, introduced himself, and, bringing a personal spin to the conversation, talked about his primary interest, which involved educating the public about the prevention of illness. Greg said that he understood the organization was interested in promoting holistic health and wellness. He never mentioned the ad, and when his contact asked if he were applying for a job, he answered, "No, I don't know enough about you to be doing that yet, but I am interested in learning about your efforts to make wellness promotion a paying proposition."

As a result, the contact arranged for Greg to meet with a few executives of the company. During the meeting Greg talked about his ideas to use various media, especially video (another keen interest, with which he had some part-time work experience) to help educate the public about various health issues.

The executives said their biggest problem was advising members on how to cope with malpractice law suits. They asked Greg if he had any ideas to help solve that problem. (Yes, it was the same organization which had run the ad—a fact that was never even mentioned.)

At first glance it hadn't seemed that the company's needs matched Greg's primary interests. But as Greg learned more, he realized it was a terrific opportunity to get the diversity he sought in his work. He came back with a long-range plan for developing educational tools (using video, naturally) to improve relationships between doctors and patients. If doctors had better print and film materials to inform their patients about health issues, he reasoned, the trust between doctors and patients would be improved, and ultimately this would have a beneficial effect on the malpractice picture. The proposal included practical suggestions with respect to settling as well as preventing malpractice suits. The executives were impressed with Greg and his ideas. They began to revise their concept of the job, realizing that hiring a single malpractice attorney could not make any appreciable difference in the overall scheme of things. Hiring Greg to implement his creative proposals, however, could contribute to changing the climate between doctor-members and their patients and Greg could work with outside counsel on litigation. The company redefined the job description in line with its preventive approach and Greg was offered the position. He never submitted a resume.

Eventually, particularly if seeking employment with a large corporation, the civil service, academic institutions, or in a highly technical organization, your client may have to submit a resume. But even in these situations, it doesn't have to be done at the start—it can be forwarded later. After the decision maker is "sold," he or she is much more likely to glean from the resume the valuable nuggets that suit the job in question.

If your client must submit a traditional resume up front—before a meeting—I recommend attaching it to an in-depth letter which closely resembles a proposal. He can ask that the letter be circulated with the resume and indicate on the resume itself that it's part of a package. If your client is asked to fax a resume, make sure he faxes a cover letter along with it and follows up by sending the original letter and resume by mail.

Types of Resumes

There are four types of resumes, plus portfolios for artists or designers. From least effective to most effective they are:

A chronological, or traditional, resume is a list of work experience and education, starting with the present and going backwards in time. Even hard-line resume believers consider this simplistic type of resume outmoded, and it is seldom used by savvy job seekers. Although I don't recom-

GOOD-LOOKING RESUMES

O nly your client—with your help—can develop the content of a resume or a proposal, so forget about resume services. As for typing it, a resume merely needs a sparkling clean look, not flashy graphics, so a PC or an electric typewriter will do the job.

- Use a typewriter or laser printer only (dot matrix printing is not clean enough).
- Use a standard typewriter font or close to it (rather than a "printed" typeface), so the resume looks tailor-made for the recipient.
- Use good quality 8½-×-11-inch stationery (only white, buff, or gray, with black or charcoal printing).
- Center name, address, and telephone number at the top.
- Maximum length: two pages (no foldouts).
- Any attempts at unusual or cute formats will not be appreciated, so don't even think about them.
- Spelling, grammar, and clean, clear format are important! Check and double-check, even if you use a typing service (they make mistakes, too).
- No videos or audiocassette resumes, unless specifically requested.
- Ask a trusted senior business or professional friend to review the resume once it is completed.

mend them, these resumes can still be shaped to respond to a specific employer's needs.

Under "work experience" include responsibilities and accomplishments directly related to the job being sought. If two or more similar jobs were held, focus on something different in each.

Under "education" list years of attendance and degrees earned, placing the most advanced degree first. If the candidate has a college degree, there's no need to include high school. A student still in college should list the number of credit hours earned so far and grade point average, if 3.0 or higher. Mention jobs held during school, special sports or academic affiliations, student government positions, and so on.

"Personal information" might include active pastimes that demonstrate ability for this particular job, information about professional memberships, military service, travel, languages, and hobbies.

A curriculum vitae is similar in organization to a chronological resume, but it offers a more complete list of accomplishments, including speeches and publications. It is most commonly used by academics, researchers, and some government specialists. It usually does not contain a description of the function carried on in each position.

A functional resume emphasizes how tasks were accomplished in the past. It is organized by function, i.e., administration, leadership, traffic management, planning, usually describing where and when these tasks took place.

Functional resumes are sometimes used when shifting to new fields in which the candidate has no direct experience. Because most skills are transferable, this kind of resume allows the candidate to demonstrate that she has the necessary abilities. People who have been out of the work force for several years and recent graduates with little work experience, whose skills may not be obvious, often lean toward functional resumes.

Although they offer greater opportunity for describing skills, I often find functional resumes difficult to read. Employers also tell me they are growing suspicious of them because they feel candidates often use them to mask inappropriate backgrounds. If your client chooses to develop a functional resume, she should write it in a very straightforward manner without embellishment, using lots of action verbs to illustrate what she was doing and clear identification of the setting in which the skills were performed.

A qualifications brief is an enhanced version of the functional resume. It is tailored directly for a specific potential employer. If you have to supply a resume, don't. Send a qualifications brief instead.

A qualifications brief begins by stating a specific, immediate work objective—a concise, interesting explanation of what the candidate wants to do. Everything else on the page flows from this objective, justifies it and supports it. The next section is "qualified by," which describes experience that directly promotes an ability to meet the objective. All information extraneous to the work objective is eliminated. If relevant, a summary of background or a biographical sketch may be included, but only if it closely relates to the objective.

When the candidate is very young, a qualifications brief offers an opportunity to highlight skills acquired in part-time work, extracurricular activities, academic pursuits, and family responsibilities, many of which may be highly transferable to the particular needs of this employer.

A biographical sketch is usually sent after rapport between potential employer and job seeker has been established. The sketch should describe your client's experience so employers understand why he is suited to their needs. A biographical sketch also lets a candidate include interesting side notes not normally covered in a resume. There's more room for creativity in this type of presentation, which may accompany or be used instead of a resume.

Before he begins such a sketch suggest that your client look back at the lists begun in Chapters 4, 5, and 6. The idea is to emphasize the skills, aptitudes, personal characteristics, and experiences which support your client's work objective, showing the employer that he is the "right" candidate. The sketch should begin and end with his strongest points.

NANCY'S QUALIFICATIONS BRIEF

Nancy K. Loomis
554 Newtown Parkway
Rye, New York 02112
914-287-0234

Objective: Position managing special events in a
Northeast ski resort with a reputation
for quality recreational facilities and
programs, which caters to families as
well as single people and which has a
desire to extend its year-round appeal
to a growing national market; where
superior logistical competency, creativity in developing and executing marketing concepts, team spirit, stamina,
determination, presentation skills, and
a sense of style are valued attributes.

Qualified by: • Experience in establishing a branch of
a nationwide membership association,
taking the lead in seeing this project
through from concept to fruition,
including convincing authorities to
grant headquarters' space, generating
initial membership, and planning first
year's programs—the organization is
thriving six years later.
   • Training by working as the assistant to
the manager of a popular gourmet
restaurant, which required me to greet
the public, plan special functions,

substitute for absent staff members in all positions, and work long hours.

- Assisting the banquet manager in a major hotel chain, where I was credited with devising an effective logistics control check system that is still in use.
- Helping a retail women's-apparel shop secure and present fashion shows, which increased their business by 10 percent.
- Introducing prospective students to my university campus, with a better than 70 percent acceptance and registration result.
- Volunteering at local camp for the handicapped, teaching swimming and team sports, and being asked to return to do my own team-sports program.
- Participating on the student council for three years in university.
- Acting in a little theater group, securing leads in four out of nine productions.
- Participating in Junior Achievement for three years, one of these as CEO.

Education: Florida International University, B.S. in Hotel/Restaurant Management, 1990.

Special Cooking Program offered by the Chaine des Rotisseurs, 1990.

Personal Information: Born April 8, 1968; in excellent health; active ski enthusiast; dedicated volunteer in children's and community causes.

Portfolios are most commonly used by artists, photographers, designers, engineers, and architects. They may include sample photographs; copies of project plans; charts; slides or photographs of artwork or installations; sample page layouts, diagrams; stories and articles by or about the candidate; and statistics or reports. Portfolios provide wonderful evidence of talent and potential. Each sample should be labeled with a brief comment about its important points. Always include a descriptive list of the portfolio contents and a biographical sketch or a curriculum vitae.

What Every Resume Should Contain

All resumes, regardless of type, profit by being targeted to the recipient, and modeled as much as possible to his or her exact needs.

All resumes have the candidate's name, address, and phone number centered at the top. Next, a work objective briefly states exactly what the candidate seeks to accomplish, with the focus squarely on the responsibilities, rather than a title. This pitches the resume to the organization's needs, not what the organization can do for the candidate.

In describing past achievements, make sure your client always uses action verbs in the *present tense*. Endless use of "was" and "did" suggests that skill is no longer up to date. Using *"ing"* words helps the reader visualize activities as if they were happening now: "Researching and presenting technical information; independently controlling work schedules."

Avoid pretentious creations like "liaised" and "interfaced."

Help your client emphasize the skills and experience he most wants to use, skills that are most important to this particular job. Every skill needn't be included. For instance, Marie types 100 words per minute, but she wants to move away from administrative assistant positions towards managerial roles. There's no need to mention her typing skills; that would suggest to an employer that she can do without support staff.

Avoid the word "I."

Pare descriptions to a minimum and quantify everything possible to *prove* skills (sales units, profits, time saved, grades).

Obviously, resumes need to be visually attractive but not cute—no posters, balloons, or kites, and definitely no videos or audiocassettes unless your client is a performer.

Keep descriptions truthful and accurate—your client may leave information out, but what he says must be true. Stick to the facts, no embellishments.

Keep resumes to one or two pages. (Proposals are another story.)

The Proposal

The best pitch is a proposal. On the face of it, proposals look like a lot more work than do resumes, but there's a distinction between effectiveness and ease. True, it takes time to craft a proposal, but the results are ample reward. Our experience at Crystal-Barkley shows that most clients get results with no more than three finely crafted proposals. Compare three with 1,127!

Proposals are effective for two reasons: Your client will have selected a few targets by careful surveying, and she will have honestly appraised her skills, demonstrating an obvious passion for the chosen occupation. The match between employer and employee will have been amply demonstrated before the proposal is presented. This is a far different scenario from an anonymous approach to random organizations with unknown needs.

After your client has selected three or four possible employers from all the people he's met with, it's an easy next step to call candidate number one, and say:

NANCY'S BIOGRAPHICAL SKETCH

Nancy K. Loomis
554 Newtown Parkway
Rye, New York 02112
914-287-0234

BIOGRAPHICAL SKETCH

From her earliest days Nancy Loomis has been involved in producing events and greeting the public in ways that have been highly entertaining for everyone concerned. Raised in Florida, the daughter of a scientist and an engineer, her creative turn of mind has been complemented by her disciplined upbringing and a B.S. in Hotel/Restaurant Management from Florida International University.

Foremost among Nancy's accomplishments while still in school was her spearheading the establishment of a new chapter of a national sorority on campus. She managed to enlist the support of students and the administration, form teams to carry out related logistics, attract an initial membership of 27, and simultaneously maintain a grade point average in the upper half of her class. In the course of promoting the sorority's aims, Nancy learned to enjoy making presentations and orchestrating events large and small.

Nancy held many paid and volunteer jobs during and before college. In fact her family dubbed her the "bionic kid" because of the energy level she displayed in pursuing her interests. From several lead roles with the little theater group to teaching at a local summer camp for the handicapped, she found she enjoyed the fruits of long hours of work.

There were many occasions for Nancy to demonstrate her project-management and events-planning talents: proposing and mounting fashion shows for a local women's apparel shop which increased the store's sales by 10% in the same month; assisting the manager of a popular gourmet restaurant; devising an effective logistics control system for a major hotel as Assistant Manager in her first job out of college; successfully introducing prospective students to her university (better than 70% acceptance and registration achieved); and team sports participation as well as teaching. Prior to college, Nancy participated in Junior Achievement and was CEO one year.

Nancy has always been interested in cooking. In 1990 she completed a Chaine des Rotisseurs special cooking program, and she is often host to her friends. She is a ski and swimming enthusiast, enjoying excellent health.

Presently Nancy is working with a talent agency and is researching the most productive ways to put to work her ideas on promoting business for ski resorts through special events.

PROBLEMS IN RESUMES
OR INTERVIEWS

What your client writes on a resume or says in an interview must be true. That doesn't mean your client has to tell everything about himself, especially certain information that might be disadvantageous. For example:

- Gaps in work experience or education can be downplayed.
- Periods of unemployment often can be legitimately termed "self-employed," "researching," or "consulting." An alliance with a friend's business or family enterprise may fill in the gap. "Providing marketing assistance to brother's printing business," for example, is legitimate, whether paid or volunteer.
- It helps to focus on what your client is moving toward rather than on a gap in past history.
- In recounting experience, refer to years, not months. This avoids awkward small gaps.
- If your client was ever hospitalized for extended

"You recall we were discussing your problems with giving timely service? I'd like to come back and discuss some solutions I've been thinking about."

Your client should make a similar call to each potential employer. This can be done simultaneously. No matter how attractive a particular job offer or an employer seems, it's dangerous to assume that it's the one and only. Having several alternatives is like having insurance.

A proposal places the focus on the present and the future. All good proposals contain:

medical treatment (this is increasingly common as so many people spend time in rehab and recovery programs), simply refer to this as time off for "personal development." (This situation is a good reason to avoid the traditional resume entirely.)

- If your client lacks the right degree, don't emphasize the *lack*; instead, mention what education or experience your client *does* have which may have been acquired in a nontraditional way. If he didn't go to college, for example, emphasize the work he did in those years, and what he learned.
- Don't put medical conditions on a resume.
- Don't use "fired" on a resume. In person, your client will always describe job severance in truthful, positive terms, emphasizing how long the work was productive and successful. (Because of the present economy, having been fired does not carry the stigma it once did, especially in certain professions, and having been "laid off" is not bad at all, because job performance is rarely a factor in layoffs.) On a resume, simply indicate the year in which your client stopped working with an employer.

1. A compelling statement of purpose (*why I am here presenting this proposal*).

2. A definition of the "needs" your client can address (*what I can do for you, the employer*).

Tip: What does the interviewer want to hear? Think of what you've discovered about his needs through surveying (in most cases you will have met this person before). What's lacking in the company? What's required to maintain—or increase—the organization's current level of activity or profit? How can efficiency or the look of a product be improved?

MATT'S PROPOSAL

Matt, the motorcycle-loving fast-food enthusiast we met in Chapter 7, first delivered his proposal orally to a regional fast-food manager, then followed up by presenting it in writing. His proposal includes every one of the steps discussed in this chapter.

[1. *Why I Am Here*]

For a long time I have been fascinated with the problems of efficiency in fast-food restaurants. This comes from having earned my way through school by working in cafeterias and concessions. I love good food and I recognize how important it is to people who have to get back to work fast. This summer, I toured the three-state region, eating at and closely observing numerous quick-service restaurants. I've come to some conclusions about what may work best with respect to filling customers' orders quickly and courteously.

[2. *What I Can Do for You*]

What I propose to do for your four restaurants is increase the speed with which customers are served. If your lines move faster than your competitors', your business is likely to increase. I also think I can improve the attitude of your counter help. (I remember you telling me how discouraged you were with the level of their enthusiasm.) They are very good in comparison to most of your competition, but I believe I can give them an extra spirit of enthusiasm.

[3. *How I Will Go About It*]

I suggest that I start with a single restaurant to show you what I can do. I could work as assistant to the manager, first tackling kitchen efficiency, then counter efficiency and attitude. First of all, I would assess why your kitchen and counter help are working here, if they enjoy their jobs, how much responsibility they want, and if they would like some variety of tasks. Then, based on what I learn, with the manager's approval, I would institute simple changes in procedure or sequence which they think would help. In this way, the people who have the greatest effect on the customer become part of planning improvements. I would need the support of your manager, which I don't think will be a problem, for, if I start on the South Beltway, Joe and I have already talked over these concerns several times. Later I can take my approach to your other locations.

[4. *What the Benefits Are for You*]

I estimate that you'll see measurable improvements in a month, and in six weeks your lunchtime wait should be cut in half. At the peak, it is running 20 minutes now, so this means 10 minutes or less. Your manager will be freed up to work on marketing and other matters. I imagine once we take my approach to other locations, you'll be able to deliver on an ad promising "The fastest and best lunch within 20 miles." I also predict you will have less turnover in help. We may be able to keep some of your school-age employees year-round on staggered schedules, cutting down on training costs.

I am sure I will have some interesting and cost-effective incentive raises to propose for your consideration after I have been on the inside for a while. These will enable you to retain help and keep spirits high. I know you would like to be spending your time scout-

Continued

ing out new opportunities rather than putting out
fires at your present locations.

[5. *Why I Am Qualified*]

By this time, you must be thinking, "How does
this guy know he can do all of this?" I suppose I'm so
sure because I have had lots of opportunity to work
with people the same age as your employees. In high
school I began working on the cafeteria serving line.
The manager pulled me out after three weeks to put
me in charge of interviewing and scheduling the
kitchen and serving help. We had a lot of fun that year,
and the cafeteria manager got me back the next two
years as his assistant. One summer, I was the dining
room manager for the YMCA camp at Lake Hiawatha.
The next year, I was asked back as assistant personnel
manager for all camp employees. In college, two friends
and I opened the first campus all-night diner. We ran
it for three years and then sold it to the college. Our
success sort of ran away with us. We had some heavy
scheduling problems to work out so that we could
each keep up our grades.

In summary, I'd simply like to say that I hope you
can see I'd be a better-than-average bet. Most important, I have come to you before any other fast-food
restaurant in the area because I like the quality approach you seem to be aiming for.

[6. *Next Step*]

Perhaps you would like to talk this over with Joe,
and then we can meet again. What would you say to
next Wednesday? This will give you time to think
about the timetable I suggest and the time I would
free up for Joe. I'm really very enthusiastic about what
we may be able to do together.

3. An outline of proposed steps for solving those needs (*how I will go about it*).

Tips: What can your client do alone? What can be done by other members of the team? What activities will take place over what time frame?

4. A paragraph outlining what the employer will gain. (*what the benefits are for you*).

Tip: What increases in revenue, goodwill, ease of working, or market position will result? You can offer improvements even at entry level: "I am good with people on the phone and can save you time there; I can organize the office and arrange your incoming correspondence in priority order."

5. Printed material, visual aids, evidence from your client's past achievements that prove he or she can do these things (*why I am qualified*).

Tips: If your client has done this type of job before, give examples which show the result achieved. Also use analogies which describe the success of a similar action taken in a different setting. Patterns or cycles that support your client's concept can also lend the kind of credibility executives need to sell the idea higher up. For example, one client drew an analogy between her concept for a nationwide wine-delivery network and the popular FTD flower-delivery service.

Printed statistics, diagrams, flow charts and tentative revenue projections are excellent support materials because they can be left behind with the proposal. Written material that can be passed around provides concise, accurate communication within the organization, so the proposer doesn't have to rely on one person's ability to restate the points.

6. An action step for the proposal recipient (*next step*).

Tip: Summarize the points covered in the proposal and suggest that the employer make the next move, i.e., consult a superior, meet with the unit's team, and so on. Try to establish a time frame in which this will take place.

Proposals make the case in an appropriate and compelling way. They are the tools the most sophisticated job seekers use to get what they want. Happily, their employers get what they want in the bargain. Proposals are the means for your client, like Matt, to seem virtually irresistible to someone who has needs which correspond to his skills.

Exercises and Activities

Things to Think on Alone

1. Do a mini survey for yourself. Ask 12 people—friends, co-workers, relatives—the same question: "How did you get your job?" You'll be surprised how few launched their careers by sending out a resume.

2. What assumptions do you have about resumes? How have you communicated these beliefs to your client?

3. If you were writing a proposal for your current job, what would you say? Is there a new responsibility you would like to tackle at your job? Perhaps you would like to consider writing a proposal for this task.

Things to Think on Together

4. Review your client's highlighted list of skills and aptitudes from Chapter 7. Together, imagine your client were investing her foremost skills on behalf of some "ideal" employer. What skills would she describe? Could these skills be a basis of a proposal?

5. Think about action words that will enliven the proposal: creating, inventing, monitoring for results, convincing—if these are appropriate for your client, they will win attention.

6. Gaps in education or experience can be turned into positives (see "Problems In Resumes or Interviews," page 150). Pick something perceived as a failing in your client's experience and see if it can be reframed in a positive light: Taking five years to earn an undergraduate degree might be repositioned to reflect "work on a double major" or "a change in major to gain additional insights into rapidly advancing fields."

Things To Do Together

7. Look at your client's highlighted skills and aptitudes list again. Narrow the top skills down to five and *rank them in priority.* These are the building blocks of future employment.

8. Working with this list of top five skills, explore with your client the settings in which she has made them work to the greatest effect. For example, if your client has good technical-writing skills, in what settings did she most enjoy using them? (Newspaper or magazine, corporation, independent research, academic environment.) Or, for what purpose did she most enjoy using them? (To educate the public, expand professionals' knowledge, explore environmental issues, help in scientific discovery.) The answers will give you a context which will be accurate for your client.

9. Review your client's five top skills and help her come up with proof that she can actually do these things. For instance, if she were excellent at writing clearly about technical matters, she might prove it by saying, "My essay on the effect of toxic substances in the water supply was selected for the school paper." Or "I earned the appreciation of my family for translating our VCR directions into understandable form."

The task here is to describe at least one set of *results* from each particular skill. Your client can use this as ammunition to back up her claims during written or verbal presentations. (The results of this exercise will be used in Chapter 9.)

10. Help your client describe her ideal job as if she were writing a screenplay: Exactly what does the workplace look like? What is she doing there? What product or service is involved? Who is her boss? Who are her co-workers, if any, and what are they doing? How much time does she spend in the workplace or away from the office? Make sure the environment of the envisioned office includes her top "Likes." (Refer to previous "Likes and Dislikes" lists for clues.)

She should also describe how the imagined job fits in with other important aspects of her life goals—family, friends, pets, access to cultural events, living and working environment.

Write down how this ideal job supports her intellectually, emotionally, spiritually, and physically.

11. Now, take this fantasy of an ideal job and together create a proposal to match it with the perfect employer. Include each of the steps for a proposal outlined in this chapter, and be very explicit.

Chapter Nine

PUTTING IT ALL TOGETHER

S teve came into my office waving a piece of paper. "Look," he said, "I've got a chance to take a trip to Albuquerque—all expenses paid—to negotiate for my uncle on a piece of property he wants to sell. This is just the part of the country where I want to live. Help me put together all the pieces of what I've learned about myself, so I can make the most of this opportunity."

Steve was excited about the prospect of finding a job in the Southwest, but he was also frantic with a lot of disjointed ideas swimming around in his head. This was the moment to fashion an "immediate specific work objective," the Crystal-Barkley name for the very-much-hoped-for next step in a person's work life.

Steve needed to get all of his information about himself wrapped up in a single statement that he could carry around emblazoned on his forehead.

The task is the same for you and your client.

First: Be sure your client's skill lists are in good order, with the five or six top skills—the ones he's best at and loves doing—precisely described.

Second: Revisit goals and decide on the most-feasible job to pursue that will lead in the right direction.

Third: Review all of your client's "Likes and Dislikes" lists, paying attention to the most critical items.

All of this information is important in making a decision. But it's too difficult for people to try to remember it all—all of the time. So only the most important items, those at the top of the lists, are used to define an "immediate specific work objective" (ISWO). Steve's ISWO turned out like this:

> A challenging supervisory position overseeing the maintenance, supplies, and logistics of a large academic or health-services institution in the Southwest United States, in which scrupulous honesty, superior attention to detail, facility with meeting crises, and ease in getting along with people under stress are highly valued.

How did he arrive at this detailed ISWO? He started by going through the above three steps. At the time we began to work with Steve, he was just getting out of the Navy, where, as a supply officer, he had learned to love logistical management. Crises which would have made many people nuts were actually fun for Steve.

By analyzing his life stories, Steve had identified nearly 200 individual skills. When you work with your client, you will also find several hundred individual skills. Many are either similar to or compatible with each other and can be grouped together and named as one skill area. Steve grouped his skills into 12 areas and ranked them according to the ones he liked best and the ones he was best at. Then he wrote down the five at the top of the list.

Steve's *top five skill areas* were:

1. Rising to the occasion with stamina and energy to quickly solve logistical problems.

2. With good humor, juggling multiple complex tasks.

3. Exceptionally organized in tracking complex physical inventory.

4. Dealing directly and fairly with suppliers and users of materials.

5. Effectively and amicably resolving disputes and mis-understandings.

When he came to write his ISWO, he made sure that he had included every one of these top five skills. This is exactly how your client will bring his own top skills to bear on his work objective.

Next, before he settled on where he wanted to put his skills to work, Steve reviewed his goals thoughtfully. Among the phrases in his goals statement were these words: "smoothing the way for people under stress in a stressful world" and "contributing to knowledge, learning, and self-discovery within an increasingly complex and demanding society."

Now, Steve was no academic. Nor was he of a scientific bent. Teaching or writing about science or other academic subjects plainly did not correspond to his skills.

We brainstormed together. What was this preoccupation with stress and relieving stress? People who are ill suffer stress. So do those working in large institutions, especially when they can't get what they need. Steve began to see himself as a master at troubleshooting for frustrated people trying to get the job done. Even as a little boy he was always the first to find exactly the right tool for the right job, or if he couldn't find it, he rigged up a substitute.

Since Steve was drawn to learning, what about a job at a school? Or a teaching hospital? Or a health-maintenance complex? Or a research lab? By analyzing his goals, Steve determined that his preferred job targets were academic or health-services institutions. In his ISWO he made sure to include "large" and "challenging," because the bigger and more complex the job, the more eagerly he rose to the challenge.

At this point, I had only one more question to ask. "What else matters to you so much that you must have it?"

In response Steve delivered the key words that would form the matrix of his ISWO: the Southwest, honesty, getting along, attention to detail.

Now he had all the information he needed to complete his ISWO. Steve was able to leave behind all of his notes and lists. His ISWO summed it all up. He knew exactly what he was seeking. All he needed now was a good survey plan to take advantage of his 10 days in Albuquerque. When he was in the Navy, Steve had developed an inventory-tracking system, and he now decided to use it as a basis for survey meetings with prospective employers. His survey would ask specific targets: How hard is it for you to keep enough inventory in the right place at the right time?

Steve identified 12 organizations in Albuquerque and eventually met with more than 30 people, sparing himself a lot of aggravation by confining the search to companies that could use his top skills. How irresistible he appeared to the potential employers he identified! Indeed, he was a dream come true to a harried university vice president and an overworked inventory-control manager at a teaching hospital. In fact, both offered him a job on the spot; he politely deflected the offers, redirecting attention to his survey topic. He promised to return when he had a better idea about where and how he could be most effective in their organizations. By the time he finished his survey, Steve had one other *preferred* target, for a total of three.

Steve now was ready to go back to his top three choices and offer them a proposal. His proposal, which he presented verbally, described exactly what he wanted to do, and was utterly compatible with his ISWO. He presented it first to his top choice, the teaching hospital, and it was immediately accepted. Steve now reports to the Senior Vice President for Administration and has just been promoted to assistant vice president. He works long, intense hours and plays hard in his off time, taking full advantage of the mountains and deserts which had first attracted him to the Southwest. On many weekends he and some of his friends from work participate in archaeological digs with the community amateur society in which he is active.

Sometimes, when he's back East for a visit with his parents, old friends remark at his terrific lifestyle. "I guess it just all came together," he replies modestly. He and I both know there was no "guess" about it. Steve put in the disciplined time to design the life/work scenario he's living.

When you get ready to coach your client through his next move, approach it just as Steve and I did. The process is the same whether your client is choosing a college, a summer internship, a place to live, or a job.

Ranking Criteria

A "criteria-ranking sheet" will help your client steer the course. All you need is a large sheet of paper and a ruler. Across the top of the paper list the target companies; down the left side, your client's specific criteria derived from her top skills, talents, aptitudes, interests, goals, likes and dislikes—literally everything that matters to her the most. (See exercise 7.)

How do you work goals into criteria? If one of your client's goals is, say, "maintaining optimum physical health by regular exercise," the location of the prospective job might be important. A rural area with lots of woodsy jogging and walking paths might afford an opportunity to exercise

STEVE'S CRITERIA-RANKING SHEET

Criteria	Perfect Score	Teaching Hospital	Doctors' Hospital	Lindsay HMO	Skyview Center	Syntech, Inc.	State U.
Located in the Southwest	20						
In need of logistical organization	20						
Reputation for fairness and honesty	20						
High value placed on facility/ environment	20						
Stable, straightforward, disciplined boss	20						
Autonomy in work	15						
Good-humored atmosphere	20						
Some place to go in the organization	20						
Willingness to provide ongoing training	15						
Salary and bonuses ($40K+)	15						
Health and dental plans	15						

CRITERIA	PERFECT SCORE	POSSIBLE EMPLOYERS					
		TEACHING HOSPITAL	DOCTORS' HOSPITAL	LINDSAY HMO	SKYVIEW CENTER	SYNTECH, INC.	STATE U.
Annual performance appraisal	20						
Minimum of travel	15						
Ability to impact whole organization	20						
Sabbatical program	15						
Permission to recruit team	15						
Private office	15						
Adequate secretarial support	20						
Contemporary office machines	20						
Openness to innovation	15						
Well-financed/ endowed	15						
Complex, growing organization	20						
Total Perfect Score	**390**						

STEVE'S COMPLETED CRITERIA-RANKING SHE[ET]
(After Surveying)

Criteria	Perfect Score	Teaching Hospital	Doctors' Hospital	Lindsay HMO	Skyview Center	Syntech, Inc.	State U.
Located in the Southwest	20	20		.	20		20
In need of logistical organization	20	20			20		20
Reputation for fairness and honesty	20	20			20		20
High value placed on facility/ environment	20	20			20		20
Stable, straightforward, disciplined boss	20	20			15		15
Autonomy in work	15	15			12		13
Good-humored atmosphere	20	15			10		8
Some place to go in the organization	20	15			15		15
Willingness to provide ongoing training	15	15			15		15
Salary and bonuses ($40K+)	15	15			15		12
Health and dental plans	15	15			15		15

CRITERIA	PERFECT SCORE	POSSIBLE EMPLOYERS					
		TEACHING HOSPITAL	DOCTORS' HOSPITAL	LINDSAY HMO	SKYVIEW CENTER	SYNTECH, INC.	STATE U.
Annual performance appraisal	20	20			20		20
Minimum of travel	15	15			15		15
Ability to impact whole organization	20	20			20		15
Sabbatical program	15	10			10		15
Permission to recruit team	15	15			15		10
Private office	15	15			15		15
Adequate secretarial support	20	20			20		15
Contemporary office machines	20	20			20		20
Openness to innovation	15	15			10		10
Well-financed/ endowed	15	15			15		15
Complex, growing organization	20	20			20		20
Total Perfect Score	**390**	**375**			**357**		**343**

every day, at lunch or after work, as would a corporation with an on-site gym. But a long commute every day would allow much less time for a regular exercise program. Each potential employer would get ranked according to its work-out opportunities, as well as according to other criteria.

All criteria that make it to the criteria ranking sheet are important, but even here some are more important than others. Each criterion gets a "perfect score," and these are set to clearly distinguish the most important. In Steve's case, the most important criterion's perfect was "20." Items slightly less important were given a lower number. Then all the numbers in the column are added for a "total perfect score." The idea is to see how close each target comes to a total perfect score. (See "Steve's Criteria-Ranking Sheet.")

A criteria list must be long enough to accommodate all desires and all possible targets. Steve's actual list was longer than this sample. We had to piece together two pieces of paper to accommodate all of his criteria and possible targets.

Having this model sharpened Steve's surveying. Following each meeting with a potential employer, he quickly recorded in pencil an estimate for each item on his list. If Company A offered a perfect geographic location, for instance, Steve gave it a "20."

If he wasn't sure exactly how a company measured up for one of his criteria, he gave it a best estimate. This way, the criteria-ranking sheet becomes a dynamic document that changes as your client gets more information. The sheet becomes enormously helpful in the final stages of decision making, it helps your client remember things he might otherwise forget or overlook.

When Steve began his survey, he had more than 12 possible targets on the list. Gradually, he narrowed them to eight and, finally, to three, all of which appeared to have needs he wanted to fill. These were the three which achieved the highest totals. Each had a score within 50 points of his "total perfect score." How the total score of each target compares with your client's perfect total gives him an objective answer for making a good decision.

We use this method in advanced consultation with clients who are considering a number of targets. But someone considering making a change within her present organization can use the same method. For example, should she stay where she is, doing what she's doing? Stay where she is, but reconfigure the job? Change the interior workings of the unit she is presently in? Switch departments? Become a consultant to the organization to do what she's currently doing, plus other things she wants to do?

In every decision-making process the criteria-ranking sheet is an invaluable guide.

Exercises and Activities

Things to Think on Alone

1. With your help, your client now has an excellent chance of getting a job which capitalizes on both her talents and aspirations. Do you genuinely believe that is possible?

2. Can you put aside any reservations you may have about the direction your client has chosen?

3. Do you feel you can openly encourage your client's pursuits? And often?

Things to Think on Together

4. Acknowledge that the hardest part of an effort is just before it comes to fruition. Share ways in which you can reinforce your client as she takes the last steps in the search for work.

Things to Do Together

5. Review your client's lists of "Likes and Dislikes" (people, working environment and community, Chapters 3 and 7) to help create a picture of his ideal working environment.

This is the time to formalize criteria for the "ultimate" job. Ask your client to rethink his top priority "Like" items in each category and formally write them down. These are among your client's *criteria* which will help him choose employers and also remain clear and focused for negotiations.

6. You and your client review all of his major skills and specific aspects of his goals that are especially important right now. You are getting ready to isolate criteria for making the best job choice. Refer to lists refined in Chapters 6, 7, and 8.

7. On a large sheet of paper, set up a criteria-rating sheet, similar to Steve's.

(a) Based on his top skills, list those that your client most wants to use in his next job. Referring to his likes and dislikes, list everything about the workplace that is most important to him, including the atmosphere, the physical layout, and the people he works with. And based on his goals, list those that could be advanced by or at least not be hindered by the targeted employers. The criteria list should be long and detailed, but also refined. Only the most important make it to the list.

(b) Even on this refined list, some things are more important than others. Which ones? Ask your client to determine which among the items on the list are absolute "musts." Assign them an arbitrary number. (Steve used "20.") This is your client's highest "perfect score." Other items on the list should be given slightly lower "perfect scores," depending on how important they are. They may be 18, 15, or even 10, for something that is relatively minor, but your client would like to get if he could. Add up the column for a total perfect score.

8. For each target surveyed, your client will record his ranking for each item. He should work in pencil so numerical ratings can be changed easily as he gets more information.

You can contribute by helping your client evaluate the information he gathers so he can make good estimates on his criteria sheet.

Chapter Ten

EFFECTIVE INTERVIEWING

O ften people say, "I don't know if I want the job, but I'll wait until they offer it to me to decide." In the same vein, career counselors often tell young people to go on as many interviews as possible— "for the experience." My view, however, is that pointless interviews are a tremendous waste of energy and time. It's much more valuable for your client to spend her energy focusing on what's inside—the skills she wants to use and the interests she wishes to explore.

When your client is unprepared, job interviews are potentially out-of-control, even esteem-ripping situations. Typically they pit an offensive interviewer against a defensive interviewee. Like resumes, traditional interviews almost always focus on the past, in the vague hope that it will predict the future.

Interviewers, who, particularly if they are in a personnel office, may know little about the actual job in question, may be trying to winnow a field of hundreds down to a handful of "qualified" applicants. Basically their job is to turn you down. Some interviewers are angry, tired, or bored. Others wouldn't know a good candidate if he came in wearing a banner, because the corporate goals are unclear or the job has never been clearly defined.

For example, Lydia interviewed for the associate health editor's position at a young-women's magazine but didn't get the job. Five months later, a manager from another division of the parent publisher contacted her, saying they were starting up a new magazine and hunting for an assistant editor. Was she interested?

"The manager sounded very harassed. We agreed it would be better to talk in person, so we made an appointment. She didn't give me much information about the publication, so I gathered samples of my editing and writing and figured we'd discuss her needs in depth at the interview.

"Well, she breezed into the meeting waving my resume— the one I had tailored for the health editor's slot—and immediately asked for my samples. I presented them to her, and she scanned my resume again, smiled brightly, and said, 'Tell me why you're the perfect candidate for this job.'

"'I'd love to,' I replied, 'but first you'll have to tell me what the job *is!*' Believe it or not, she couldn't answer me. If she had told me over the phone that they were in the midst of developing a concept for the new publication, I could have prepared some ideas rather than going through this totally useless 'interview.'" Unhappily, improbable as this situation seems, I find it not uncommon for employers to be interviewing to fill jobs for which they have not yet outlined the requirements.

When surveying has preceded the interview, it is much more likely that your client and the possible employer will have a balanced and valuable conversational exchange. Optimally, it is a meeting in which the job seeker and representatives of the organization make the first judgment on the mutual benefits of getting together.

What an Employer Needs

Employers hire candidates who demonstrate that their services are more valuable than what it costs to keep them on the job. This basic fact is usually overlooked by job applicants. Employers are extra sensitive to this equation now because current economic problems stem largely from high overhead. Therefore, during any interview, the focus must always be on the benefits your client offers. Interviews provide your client the chance to present herself compellingly. Every question is an opportunity to display personal assets.

It's easiest to do this if you know the employer's needs beforehand. Remember Nancy's story in Chapters 7 and 8? Before she proposed herself for a job, she had to figure out how the needs of ski resorts related to what she most wanted to accomplish in creating wonderful events.

You will want to help your client ensure there is compatibility before she suggests herself for the job. You want your client to ask herself: *"How does this employer's need relate to my objectives?"*

Deciding Where to Interview

Even if your client hasn't identified potential employers through surveying, she can still improve the traditional job application process by following these guidelines:

• Choosing only organizations which are of intense interest.
• Being sure skills and aptitudes are likely to match the needs of the employer.
• Locating potential employers from the local chamber of commerce and professional associations, rather than relying solely on want ads and job postings.
• Calling the specific department of interest and asking for the person in charge of the particular function for which

she is suited (accounting, research, sales, etc.); telling that person forthrightly why she's eager to work for this organization.

- When applying to personnel or human resources, asking if it is possible to speak with a manager in charge of the desired function.
- Even when time is short, finding out everything possible about this employer—before the interview.

Calling for Interviews

Even career salespeople admit cold-calling is tough work. Prospects are busy and often have trouble returning the calls they must, much less finding time to talk to strangers. It's critical that the job seeker make every second count. This means your client must write a script and practice it with you or a friend until it feels natural.

A script should include the caller's name and reason for calling (your client read about this individual, heard about her through word of mouth, etc.). It's nice to offer an appropriate compliment to the person or his organization such as, "You have a reputation for exceptional customer service." Describe the topic to be explored, mention that the visit will be brief, and suggest a time. For example, here's what Dan said to a prospective employer:

"Hello, Mr. Smith. This is Dan Sloan. You may remember we talked when I was completing my project on rehabs in graduate school. The practicality of your approach made a lasting impression on me.

"I am graduating soon and would like to speak with you about applying some of your ideas to other buildings in the downtown renewal district. Could I come by one afternoon this week?"

It's impossible to know the schedule of every business, but 9 A.M. Monday morning is bound to be hectic; Friday afternoons—especially in the summer months—may find people too wound down to be of any help. The hours between noon and 2 P.M. are traditionally devoted to lunch (catching people right before or after is good). Also, people tend to set appointments on the hour or half-hour, so calling at 10 minutes before or 20 minutes after the hour can be effective.

Setting up appointments may not happen as quickly as your client would like. Callers should expect to encounter receptionists and assistants, and they should be prepared to treat these screeners courteously, offering a clear, concise reason for the call. Encourage your client to keep trying; it usually takes several attempts to get through to most busy people.

The Interview Itself

Your client has three possible approaches to any interview:

1. Traditional: following the lead of the interviewer and responding to questions as they are asked.

2. Turning the interview into an information-gathering survey: gathering data to decide if this would be a good place to work.

3. Presenting a proposal: outlining exactly "what I can do for the organization."

Option one is not much of a choice. This happens when candidates are poorly prepared, answer random ads, or when they are taken by surprise with a sudden interview opportunity.

See that your client opts for number two or, even better, number three. The choice depends on how much she knows already about the organization and how probable the match is between the job and her skills and goals.

Your client should choose option two if she doesn't know much about the job but thinks the organization seems like a good match. Turning the interview into an information-gathering survey protects your client against snapping up a job offer in the wrong environment. (Read Chapters 5 and 6 carefully.)

Option three is ideal for job seekers who already know a lot about the field, the organizations in it, and this organization in particular. At the beginning of the meeting, the job seeker should continue to gather information to make sure her proposal is on track; later in the meeting she will orally present it. (See Chapter 8 for proposal format.)

Typical Interview Questions

For employers, interviews boil down to three basic questions:

1. Can the applicant do the job (are his or her skills, aptitudes, and experience appropriate)?

2. Will the candidate do the job (is she motivated; what are her goals for the future)?

3. Will she fit in (can this individual get along with our organization and work-style)?

Most interview questions are double-edged. For instance, when an employer asks, "Where do you want to be in five years," she really wants to know: Does this person know what he wants, or is he drifting?

Typical questions are aimed at:

• Goals
• Personal issues
• Education
• Current and previous jobs
• Compatibility with employer
• Compensation

Before going to any interview or making any kind of presentation, your client should think about questions an interviewer might ask and how he might answer.

CLASSIFIED ADS

Newspaper ads depict predefined jobs, which means there is little room for negotiation. Answering an ad usually locks the job seeker into a rigid sequence of resumes and personnel interviews—if his initial inquiry even gets a response. Worse yet, the job advertised may already be filled and may have been advertised only to meet fairness regulations. And sometimes "fake" ads are actually placed by employment agencies trying to find new clients.

Job seekers who choose to respond to want ads can still be winning candidates if they use the exercises in this handbook to develop a high level of self-awareness.

Before answering any ad, your client should reflect upon the specific element of the ad that attracts him. Next, he should zero in on which of his interests might add dimension to the job. Then he can clearly match these two vital elements in his own mind, so that he is sharp and well-focused in both his resume and cover letter as well as in the ensuing interview. That way he'll stand out from other candidates seeking the position.

Goal-related questions attempt to discover if the candidate's goals match the organization's.

What they say: "Where do you see yourself in five to ten years?" "Why did you choose this career?" "What do you want to do in life?"

What they mean: Do you have the commitment to stay with us?

TURNING AN INTERVIEW INTO A SURVEY MEETING

INTERVIEWER: Hello. Thanks for being on time. I'm sorry I had to keep you waiting.

CANDIDATE: I understand. Actually, I made good use of the time reading your annual report and learning something about the department from your assistant.

INTERVIEWER: I like your curiosity.

CANDIDATE: I'm very interested in the work you do here. My senior project was devoted to working on one aspect of it. [A teaser about qualifications.]

INTERVIEWER: I'd like to hear about that.

CANDIDATE: Gladly, but I wonder first if you could tell me about this position and exactly what you're looking for in the person who fills it?

INTERVIEWER: Here, you can read the job description for yourself.

How to respond: The best answer defines career goals in terms of values, interests, and skills the candidate wants to use. For example, instead of "I want to be a high school principal," it's better to say, "I see myself using my managerial skills helping teachers to be more effective."

A good general disclaimer is, "It's difficult to predict exactly what I'll be doing in ten years, but I'll be most effective. . . ."

CANDIDATE: [After reading.] I wonder—since two people never fill a position exactly the same way, could you tell me anything about what's not said here? What qualities you would value most for this job?

INTERVIEWER: That's an interesting question. Since the director of this department changed six months ago, I'm thinking we need to put a more action-oriented person in this position. Also someone who can handle customers as well as work with the team inside.

The interview has turned naturally into a meeting to explore the company's needs. As the candidate learns more about the company, he is also thinking about his own interests and criteria. This meeting can eventually develop into a mutual exploration of company needs and candidate's skills and interests. The candidate may conclude the meeting before the job is pinned down, leaving it open-ended: "I have some ideas about how I might fit into the job, but I'd like to think on our discussion and give you a call at the end of the week. Is that time frame all right with you?"

Personal questions are designed to uncover personality and attitude.

What they say: "What makes you angry?"

What they mean: Are you going to be able to get along with people here? Do you harbor resentments?

The best response: Your client should zero in on a single work-related issue, such as discrimination or white collar crime, and describe how he has coped with or eliminated such a problem in the past. Above all, the candidate should come off as one who is not easily annoyed or overwhelmed.

What they say: "Tell me about yourself?"

What they mean: How are you suited for the job?

The best response: This question tests the candidate's ability to organize thoughts and communicate ideas. He or she should describe how interests and abilities match the job. For example, Nancy might have answered, "I'm very energetic and love the excitement of putting an event together. I have tremendous stamina."

What they say: "What's your greatest strength?"

What they mean: Do you have the skills that are important to this job?

The best response: The candidate should always back this up with specific examples. Dan, our interior designer, might have said, "One of my particular talents is coming up with cost-effective designs. In fact, last year I was one of two students cited for fulfilling a reduced-budget assignment in the most creative way."

What they say: "What are your weaknesses?"

What they mean: Are you realistic about your capacities?

The best response: This question is not an invitation to true confessions. The candidate can describe an ability she already has that she's working to make even better. "I enjoy working with computers and I'm taking a class in desktop publishing to enhance my skills." Or, "One of the things I want to do is get lots of experience speaking before groups so I can polish my presentation skills."

What they say: "What's your biggest achievement?"

What they mean: How realistic are you about yourself?

The best response: The candidate should *always* choose an achievement that relates closely to the job.

What they say: "How do you handle pressure?"

What they mean: How will you perform on the job?

The best response: Help your client select work-related examples that describe how she meets deadlines, organizes priorities, and delivers the end product.

What they say: "How do you solve problems?"

What they mean: Do your values and style match ours?

The best response: Your client should answer based on his own style rather than what he thinks the company style is. Generally, a good answer describes how the candidate solved a problem in the past.

"First, I reviewed and clearly defined the problem [describe one specifically].

"Then, I thought about the pros and cons of various alternatives [describe these].

"I made a decision based on . . . [describe the specific decision made and why].

"As it turned out, it was the right move." [If the decision turned out wrong because of unforeseen circumstances, say how you corrected it.]

Your client can conclude the description by saying why solving a certain problem was interesting to him.

What they say: "What's your definition of success?"

What they mean: Are you as ambitious as we are?

The best response: A graceful approach is to offer examples from both working and personal life, stressing contributions to others. Always connect the answer to the work involved.

What they say: "Whom do you admire?"

What they mean: Are your views compatible with ours?

The best response: Suggest that your client name someone he genuinely admires, whose goals, values, and methods are also likely to be consistent with the organization's.

What they say: "How do you spend your leisure time?"

What they mean: Will your outside interests interfere with the job?

The best response: The answer should clearly show that your client has outside interests but they never loom larger than work. He should limit the response to two or three non-risky items.

One young singer entering business for the first time made the mistake of describing her extracurricular musical activities at length. Her eager description convinced the employer that she would never be fully dedicated to his job.

Education is another topic about which interviewers tend to ask young people a lot of questions.

What they say: "How important are good grades to you?"

What they mean: Are you motivated to produce your best effort?

The best response: "Grades are important to the extent that they reflect an aptitude for the subject. I am very motivated to develop proficiency in my subject."

If grades were high, your client can explain that he worked hard; if grades were low, he can mention extenuating circumstances like working full-time or raising a family, without leaning on the point too hard. (The less said about low grades the better.) Emphasize skills which may not be reflected in grades.

What they say: "What was your favorite subject?"

What they mean: Are the topics you like best similar to what's demanded by the job?

The best response: Your client should pick any job-related interest that demonstrates his top skills.

What they say: "How well did school prepare you for this kind of work?"

What they mean: Show me what you know about doing this job.

The best response: If your job seeker's major is inappropriate, he can concentrate on his job-related technical skills and any other talent that makes him especially suited for the job.

What they say: "Why did you pick the college you attended?"

What they mean: Does this person think things through and weigh alternatives?

The best response: Your client should describe factors like cost, location, and reputation. Above all, show how this choice was tied to goals at that time—or currently.

What they say: "Do you plan to continue your education?"

What they mean: Do you see your career as a long-term commitment or are you still casting around?

The best response: Career goals and possible ongoing education can be summarized and tied back to the job in question. The candidate should be specific about what he wants to learn and how he'll do it.

Current and previous jobs are topics interviewers always ask about, usually to back up the hiring decision. In other words, if your client can show she's done the job in some way before, the interviewer feels assured that she can do it again. Should she fail at some future date, the interviewer can't be blamed.

What they say: "What's your experience?"

What they mean: Are you prepared to do this work?

The best response: Again, the candidate should emphasize any skills related to the prospective job.

What they say: "What did you like most about your last job?"

What they mean: Are the responsibilities you liked best also demanded by the job in question?

The best response: Your client should pick her top skills, mentioning those she wants to use again and develop further.

What they say: "Why did you leave your last job?"
What they mean: Are you stable? Loyal?
The best response: Your job seeker should always answer that the previous job lacked some important challenge. Perhaps it was a static job without opportunity for growth. Perhaps the product and service were poor. Explain why the new job will be more permanent.

What they say: "Can you provide references?"
What they mean: Have you done good work in the past?
The best response: Your client should be specific and choose references who will indicate stability and commitment. If there were problems on past jobs, come clean—briefly. Share the responsibility for conflicts but always finish on a positive note, emphasizing those who will furnish good references.

Compatibility questions aim to discover whether the job seeker's goals complement the company's.

What they say: "Why are you interested in this company?"
What they mean: Do your goals match ours?
The best response: This is a place for your client to say that he shares the organization's commitment to certain values and welcomes an opportunity to use his top skills in this environment.

What they say: "What type of people do you have trouble getting along with?"
What they mean: How do you deal with people you dislike?
The best response: The key here is for your client to choose *traits* she has had trouble with—dishonesty, laziness,

explosive tantrums. She can talk about how she has worked effectively with difficult people in the past, even helped to resolve conflicts.

What they say: "Is there anything you dislike about the sound of this job?"

What they mean: How straightforward can you be?

The best response: This is tricky. Your client should shift the question from "dislike" to "concern," then pick an aspect which might concern anyone determined to succeed. For example, if your client is interviewing for a teaching position, he might be concerned that the classes are larger than the norm. He can take the edge off by saying that he welcomes the challenge. (If, in fact, he does.)

Compensation questions often come up early in the meeting. It's important for you to counsel your client to deflect them until the end. Discussion of specific numbers should be avoided until a position is offered, and, even then, ideally the employer will speak first. If pressed, your client should mention a salary range typical to that kind of work (which he will know by having surveyed in advance), and express confidence that an agreement will be reached.

What they say: "What's your current salary?"

What they mean: I want to get you for as little as I can.

The best response: Many employers feel they can offer people the same or somewhat more than the salary they're currently earning. Suggest your client duck the question, particularly if it comes early in the interview. She can explain that when they have determined the job is a good match, she'll be glad to discuss salary requirements. When quoting a previous salary, she should avoid lies or exaggerations. (Employers have their sources, too.) It's often possible for your client to show that her current or past salary is an inadequate measure for the new job (the responsibilities may be greater in the new job, or perhaps there are more people to supervise, or the hours are longer or more erratic).

Is This the Right Job?

For every serious decision, your client must ask:

- What do I want to accomplish?
- What will this move do for me? (Think of status, professional development, increased-earnings potential, and the fit with goals and preferences.)
- Will I need to develop additional skills for this job?
- What is the compensation package? (Include special savings or pension plans, vacations and holidays in the calculations.)

Help your client think out the specifics of the situation, such as:

- What's the commuting time?
- What will the transportation costs be?
- Will I need a new business wardrobe?
- How much time do I have to make a decision?

You and she should review her specific criteria and discuss how well each might be met and if the employer seems to have the same criteria. She could also ask family or friends what they think about the opportunity.

Negotiating Compensation

Negotiating salary is the last step in any job-seeking process, to be taken only when both sides have agreed on the job seeker's value to the organization. It may take several meetings for your client to get to this point. Negotiations don't have to be competitive—the best deal actually does work for both sides.

By the time the offer comes, your client will have a clear sense of what to look for in terms of compensation. Through surveying, he will have learned what similar jobs pay. If he is uncertain, he can get some quick information from college placement offices, the Bureau of Labor Statistics, other professionals in the field, professional associations, trade magazines, newspaper ads, the *Occupational Outlook Handbook,* and the *National Business Employment Weekly.*

The employer measures the job in relation to the organization's overall needs, how much revenue your client might generate, your client's previous offers, salary history, education, and experience, perhaps even his appeal to the competition.

Items are negotiated in this order:

1. Compensation (salary and commissions).

2. How work is evaluated (timing of performance appraisals and standards used to determine bonuses).

3. Fringe benefits (medical, pension, stock).

4. Perks (expense account, clubs, moving costs).

5. Working conditions (support staff, office, orientation/training, vacation, and resources such as consultants, computer software, membership in professional associations).

6. Continuing education and training (tuition allowances, conferences).

7. Career path (advancement, promotion).

You can help your client visualize an ideal (but realistic) negotiation. Ask her to outline, in writing, both sides of the conversation, including all of the above points and describing everything, even facial expressions. The ideal scenario includes: Opening (social talk); agenda (meeting objective); discussion (address concerns, resolve differences); conclusion (agree and/or identify issues still to be resolved); close (finalized deal); leave (friendly good-bye).

Following an outline is crucial, because after a job starts,

TURNING AN INTERVIEW INTO
A PROPOSAL PRESENTATION

INTERVIEWER: Come in. Refresh my memory. How did we find out about you?

CANDIDATE: I answered your ad in the *County Register.* Also, one of your researchers here may have recommended me. Al Jameson? He and I were volunteers together on the Alpha community project.

INTERVIEWER: Oh, yes. In fact, Al spoke to me about you just yesterday. He said you were very skilled at analysis of mathematical data.

CANDIDATE: That's one of my skills. I'd like to hear more about how you view the responsibilities of this job.

INTERVIEWER: Aside from what you already know, I can tell you that this is going to require long hours and a good bit of solitary work. We need someone who knows when to get help, because no one will be at your side.

it's usually too late to negotiate additional benefits. Making an outline is simple if your client has thought out her needs in advance.

Take Nancy, for example, who ended up negotiating the position as Special Events Manager for a ski resort.

After her survey meeting with the manager, Nancy made

CANDIDATE: I understand what you mean. I had a summer project last year working for an author researching the statistical basis for her theories. I had some of the data ahead of time because I was able to tap into some complementary research a classmate of mind had done.

INTERVIEWER: That's the idea. You've got to know not only when to get help, but how to get it. Is there anything you're not good at?

CANDIDATE: I guess I'm not too good at working with a team whose technical proficiency is weak. I'd like to concentrate on describing exactly what I can do for you. If I understand your needs correctly, you're seeking. . . ."

Who's in charge of this conversation? Answer: Both of them. The candidate is about to restate the company's needs and then launch into his presentation, describing how he will be able to fill those needs.

a proposal designed to stimulate business during the off season. She suggested a series of events tied to the history of the nearby town and a second program capitalizing on a nearby summer arts festival. In her proposal she proved her organizational skills and energetic follow-through by citing examples of her significant school and voluntary experiences.

Based on her proposal, Nancy was offered a newly created year-round position, and the manager was now ready
to settle the question of compensation with Nancy. At the
beginning of this, their third, meeting, Nancy and the manager joked a bit about how taking care of skiers on holiday
had completely worn him to a frazzle, and now *he* needed
a vacation, preferably somewhere where it never snowed.
After the friendly small talk, the manager asked Nancy what
she had in mind as a salary.

Through her conversations with people in the industry
Nancy had learned that beginning salaries in similar resorts
ranged from $25,000 to $30,000. But she didn't want to be
the first to name a figure. The ensuing discussion went
something like this:

NANCY: I have an idea of what may be appropriate, but
              I'd like to hear what you think is possible under
              the circumstances.

MANAGER: It's difficult to say. This is a new position, and
              the owners don't want to go out on a limb for it
              moneywise.

NANCY: I'm sure you must have some sort of range in
              mind.

MANAGER: Yes, but I'd like to hear what your needs are.
              After all, you have never held a position like this
              before and I've gone to some lengths to justify
              your suitability to the owners.

NANCY: I hope I made that easy for you by showing you
              the results I achieved elsewhere.

MANAGER: Yes, indeed. That's why we're at this point. What
              do you feel would be a fair salary?

(Forced to declare first, Nancy wisely named a range

slightly above the minimum figure she had in mind, but not so much as to scare the manager.)

NANCY: Surveying comparable resorts tells me that somewhere between $27,000 and $32,000 would be in order.

MANAGER: That's a little on the high side for us. We were thinking of $23,000 to $28,000. I'd rather start somewhat lower and raise you later, after we've been able to show some results. I'm sure you know few people at ski resorts earn more than $30,000.

NANCY: I do know that. I appreciate your high overhead and short-season problems. The results of my work should help increase visitors both during and out of the season. But this is a twelve-month job for me, which means I won't have an opportunity to earn elsewhere during the summer months.

MANAGER: What would you say to $25,000?

NANCY: I'd say you're making an effort to meet my needs. I would be more comfortable with $27,000. I've taken a look at housing costs here and they seem astronomical to me.

MANAGER: We may be able to help you with housing. Let's settle on $26,000. That's as far as I'm willing to go at the moment.

NANCY: Okay. I understand where you're coming from. What's the bonus or raise possibility if I do a really good job?

MANAGER: I'd say it's very good. I like bonuses, because if you bring in money, it's there to pay you.

NANCY: Could we agree on a performance standard that would determine the bonus?

MANAGER: Normally we would sit down a year from now, take a look at how you've done, and offer you a raise and/or a bonus.

NANCY: How about doing that in October? I will have been here six months by then. I should certainly have had an effect on your summer volume and generated some good P.R. to boost winter activity.

MANAGER: Fine. I'd be more than willing to do that.

NANCY: I assume you have standard medical and health benefits?

MANAGER: We can put you on our Blue Cross/Blue Shield plan. We pay half and you pay half. I'll give you a folder on the coverage.

NANCY: Are there any other fringe benefits?

MANAGER: In the strict sense, no, except for disability insurance. But there are some nice side benefits of being a management-level employee: ski pass, shuttle-bus pass, and breakfast and lunch at the lodge Monday through Friday.

NANCY: That's great. Especially because I know I will need to entertain some reporters and travel writers on-site.

MANAGER: I'll probably help you do that. If you need to take someone to dinner, we'll cover it, of course. As standard procedure, I want to be notified in advance of any P.R. visitors.

NANCY: What if I need to travel to see them?

MANAGER: What do you foresee?

NANCY: Oh, just to Boston or New York.

MANAGER: We would expect you to drive and would cover your mileage at the standard rate. We would cover modest hotel expenses. One of your first tasks here will be to make a detailed budget, which I will approve.

NANCY: I can also see it as being advantageous for me to visit other resorts occasionally for comparison purposes and to pick up ideas.

MANAGER: Not too much too fast. Once you're showing some results, we can build things like that into the budget.

NANCY: It sounds as though I won't have any trouble talking with you about these things as time goes on. I'm anxious to get started. By the way, where, exactly, will I be working?

MANAGER: We're going to have to carve out space for you— and space is at a premium here. You should be near my office in the lodge. Why don't we take a walk around?

(The office situation seemed impossibly cramped to Nancy, but she didn't want to give up the strategic location in the lodge proper. After studying the space a bit, she suggested an L-shaped sound panel be installed at the quiet end of the manager's outer room, where a window let in natural light and offered a beautiful view of the mountains.)

NANCY: I think this will work fine. I anticipate doing most of my own secretarial work, but if there's an extensive proposal, is there someone who can help me?

MANAGER: We share a secretary here and I think we can work out something. When can you start?

NANCY: Virtually as soon as you can set me up in here. How about two weeks?

MANAGER: Perfect.

NANCY: You mentioned an idea about housing?

MANAGER: There are some nice apartments near the shuttle route downtown. Our assistant reservations person is vacating one. We can call him before you leave today.

NANCY: When would you prefer me to take vacation?

MANAGER: You have two weeks, not to be taken for six months. Then, as long as you can work around your special events, you can take your vacation anytime. I'll need a written request at least two weeks in advance. We don't give standard holidays here because they are our busiest times. Instead, everyone has ten discretionary days and we simply juggle so not too many of the office staff are off at once.

NANCY: What days would I have off during the week?

MANAGER: For you, Sunday and Monday would be good, but, again, we juggle a bit.

NANCY: I realize in a situation like this we all have to help each other. I hope to develop into an important member of your team.

MANAGER: I'm counting on it.

NANCY: Would it be helpful if I drafted a letter summarizing our understanding?

MANAGER: Absolutely. If you get it to me by tomorrow, I'll formalize it by week's end.

NANCY: No problem. So my start date would be the fifteenth?

MANAGER: Yes, indeed. Welcome aboard.

The entire negotiation was achieved in an easy give-and-take manner. Nancy managed to have most of her criteria met. She didn't press for items beyond the ski resort's capacity, such as continued education or tuition allowances.

The secrets of this negotiation are common to all good negotiations:

• A relaxed, friendly tone.
• An excellent understanding of the two realities—the candidate's and the employer's.
• The order of negotiable items—observed without deviation.
• Securing the offer in writing—preferably drafted by the candidate so all bases are covered.

There's no sleight of hand here, no magic or mirrors, just two people wanting to get the job done. And, as we've seen, that makes the best magic of all.

Exercises and Activities

Things to Think on Alone

1. Do you still believe it's a good idea for your client to go on as many interviews as possible just to gain experience? Why? What do you think of alternate ways to learn how to become a practiced interviewee, such as role playing or Q & A sessions?

Things to Think on Together

2. Before any interview, ask your client to think back on his criteria-ranking sheet (see Chapter 9) and keep his top priority "Like" items in the front of his mind.

Things to Do Together

3. Help your client create a telephone script to set up an interview and practice it.

4. Role play an interview with you as interviewer and your client as job candidate. Discuss both of your impressions afterward. (See tips on role playing in Chapter 11.)

5. Create a negotiation scenario, and practice it.

Chapter Eleven

HELPING YOUR CLIENT: DO'S AND DON'TS

T here are five fundamental things coaches can do to help their job seekers. You can use these strategies from the very beginning of surveying all the way through interviewing and making decisions. They are:

- Diffusing fears of rejection.
- Rehearsing or role-playing upcoming meetings.
- Debriefing following meetings.
- Helping to plan and schedule surveys and interviews.
- Evaluating progress.

Diffusing Fears

Suppose you've supplied your client with a list of contacts, but he is not following up. Something is wrong. Maybe you're pushing contacts your client doesn't want or offering the names of people in organizations that don't meet his criteria. Some youngsters accept a list of names because they think they "should," but deep down they're not interested. Or they are terrified.

Fear is not uncommon when people are looking for jobs. It's in making contacts that your client is most apt to display his fears. I have dealt with many sophisticated men and women who had to be virtually led by the hand to make contact with an unknown person. The way to diffuse the fear is to ensure that your client is:

- Approaching people on the basis of genuine enthusiasm.
- Aware of the skills and talents which make him an attractive, engaging person equipped to discuss his enthusiasms.
- Calling people only after doing background research on the field and company.
- Clear about the purpose of the requested conversation.
- Practiced in carrying on a conversation which will be interesting to the contact. (See "Role Playing," below.)
- Starting with the least potentially important contacts first.

Practice and self-knowledge automatically diminish fear and build confidence.

Role Playing

Role playing is an especially effective way to help your client prepare for meetings, interviews, presentations, and negotiations. Before you start to role-play, though, make sure your client:

- Has a clear-cut objective.
- Has a good list of questions, if he's doing a survey.
- Is well informed about the organization and field, if he's presenting a proposal.
- Has a good idea of what he'd like to do for this organization—the concrete advantages his proposal offers the employer and how he'll go about achieving them.

How to Role-Play

1. Role playing at its best involves three people—your client, yourself, and a third party. Your client plays himself, the third party plays the prospective employer, and you play the role of an observer who watches to see what works and what doesn't. You are more concerned with presentation than with actual content.

The third person needn't know anything about your client's field of interest ahead of time. Your client simply tells him or her the title and the level of responsibility of the person he or she is playing, and the kind of meeting it is (survey, interview, or proposal presentation). Then, like any actor, the third party has an idea of how to respond in a manner consistent with his part.

2. Set aside 10 to 15 minutes of uninterrupted time in a comfortable place. Equip everyone with pads and writing implements. Try to set up the room and seating arrangement to parallel the actual meeting place. As the observer, sit off to the side as if you are behind an invisible screen.

3. Begin the meeting. No one should break role, but if someone does, don't react. The players can talk only to each other. If they're having trouble concluding the role play you might enter as the "secretarial assistant" to warn of the next appointment, but that's the only time you should interfere.

Things to Watch For

How comfortable is your client? Are her questions smooth and direct? What is her body language? Is she observing the rules of surveying or presenting proposals? How effectively is she using restatement to test agreement and understanding?

Concentrate on the interaction. Is your client appropriately mirroring the behavior of the person she's meeting with? If that person is laid-back, your client will want to appear to be equally relaxed, not poised impatiently on the edge of her seat. Conversely, if the interviewer is excited and high-strung, your client needs to be energetic without going to extremes.

Look for defensiveness in your client. Notice if she summarizes well and articulates an action step to follow; she will not want to conclude without an agreement to take a concrete step within a given time frame. Pinpoint a date when one party is expected to get back to the other.

4. When the role play is over, everybody usually takes a deep breath, because the game is always harder than the real thing. Be quick to offer positive reinforcement. Say, "Congratulations. You did a great job." Immediately compliment your client on the part of the "meeting" she handled best.

During debriefing, *first,* ask your client how she felt during the meeting—a lot of information comes out of this seemingly innocuous question. You can give encouragement along the way, but primarily you want to give your client every opportunity to vent her feelings. Ask questions like, "How did you feel about this?" "How do you feel the "prospective employer" was reacting?" "Did you feel well informed?" (Be sure to ask about some content issues, even though the process, rather than the content, is your main concern now.) Don't rush the answers.

5. Next, turn to the "prospective employer" and ask, "What were your reactions to the role play—beginning with the pluses." He may have negative comments of varying degrees, but your job is to help your client maintain her morale, so she can learn from the experience. If the third party launches into a litany of errors—"She talked too fast, she waved her arms, she rambled too much"—do not interfere unless it goes on at length. You can temper these comments later when you begin your own comments with a positive statement.

6. After your client and the third party have aired their comments, it's your turn. Chances are they have already mentioned many of your own observations. Unless these were especially important, offer only new observations from your list. Concentrate on big issues—particularly positive ones. In any case, always start with what you liked best in the role play.

7. With input from all three parties, there may be a second round of observations. However, don't beat the subject to death. Allow no longer than 15 minutes for both rounds.

8. End the role play by asking if your client wants to do it again before going to the actual meeting. If she wants to repeat the role play, it's a good idea to wait a day or so to give her time to digest everything she's heard and possibly do additional research. A different "prospective employer" may be invited to participate.

Remember, your client can—and should—role-play every new type of meeting situation. It's more fun than you might think, and the benefits are tangible.

Debriefing

Debriefing after meetings is enormously important for clients and a perfect occasion for you, the coach, to act as a sounding board. When your client returns from a meeting, always ask upbeat, open-ended questions. Reserve most commentary until the very end of the conversation; you don't want to introduce the "parental voice" and interfere with your client's reactions.

Some good debriefing questions:
"How did it go?"
"Did he make you feel welcome?"
"What sort of day did this person seem to be having?"
"Did you feel you were dressed appropriately?"
"What would you think about going to work dressed that way every day?"
"How did you feel about the look and feel of the place?"

"How comfortable were you in that environment?"

"How do you think you read the person's needs?"

"How does that compare with what you thought his needs would be?"

"How many other people may be part of the decision?"

"How do you think you might meet them?"

"How much time did he give you?"

"When is your follow-up date with this person?"

Encourage your client to talk about what he learned in the meeting and underscore the action steps to take next. Favor neutral questions ("How do you think you did?") over leading questions ("You look concerned—what went on?").

Instead of asking, "What could you have done better?" ask "What might you have done differently?"

Self-criticism will come out naturally in the debriefing—and, inevitably, your client will find more faults than really exist. Your task is to encourage him to look at what went well and turn the discussion toward what he can do in the next meeting. Always encourage by emphasizing the positive and leave the negative alone—your client already knows the negatives.

Planning and Scheduling

This can be a tough issue, full of pitfalls for parents, because it can resurrect all the old relationship patterns and the urge to say, "Do it this way." "Why haven't you done this yet?" The best thing you can do is give your client an example of your own planning and scheduling system. Show how you keep your calendar, cope with high-pressure times, and set up your files.

This issue is very personal. Perhaps you favor an electronic datebook, a home-computer tracking system, tickler files (file folders tagged chronologically to be dealt with at the appropriate time), or a big desk calendar with large squares for writing in appointments and deadlines. Remind your client that it's hazardous to keep separate desk and pocket calendars, since it's easy to forget to transfer the information from one to the other, and therefore to miss a date. I like using a Rolodex with big cards to record names and addresses as well as the date of my most recent contact, a note on what kind of contact it was (phone call, fax, letter, meeting), and the names of people who support this contact (secretary, assistant, deputy).

If you're a poor organizer, say so, and help your client locate someone more talented in this regard for advice. On the other hand, if you're organized to within an inch of your life and your client isn't, don't rush in and set up a system for him. Should your client ask you to set up a system, however, make sure that he participates in the process. Ask questions like "What do you think you can commit to?" "How much activity do you think is feasible?" "About how long does it take you to do X and Y?"

The best system is the one your client will follow. Even if you help design a system, your client should always set the due dates. You can help your client lay out monthly activities, but he's the one who must be at the meeting, write the report, make the proposal. So remind him not to set an inhuman schedule. We can all accomplish just so much.

Occasionally I run across someone who has developed a sophisticated system, then spends all her time writing lists and filling in calendar squares. Pure procrastination. How can you move this type along? You might say, "I can't help but notice how wonderful you are at organizing and how much you enjoy it. Have you ever thought of incorporating scheduling and planning into your job description?" Don't laugh. People do make careers from scheduling: freight expediters, construction-project managers, congressional assistants are just a few.

On the other hand, if your client's calendar remains empty, he is suffering from inertia. He needs to learn to work harder on his own behalf, just as he would at work for an employer. You might say, "I wonder if you're feeling a lack of energy because you're just not as interested in this topic as you initially thought you'd be?" Or, "I know you have a law degree, but could the problem be that law just doesn't fascinate you?"

Evaluating

Evaluating—running a reality check—is done through all of the steps of the job-search process. You can help your client discover weak spots in his plan and monitor his progress; and when he has concluded his search and is ready to make a work decision, you can help him evaluate everything he has learned.

Does your client:

* Know enough to make a proposal?
* Have a good overview of the industry?
* Understand the different functions within this industry?
* Feel positive about the field on the basis of what he has learned so far?
* Make realistic connections between the job and his skills?
* Understand how long it will take to gain status in this particular field?
* Seem to have a compatible style with the organization under consideration?

You want to be sure your client doesn't come to premature conclusions. Listen carefully. Observe your client's attitude. Do her eyes light up when she talks about an organization's services or products? When does she become energetic? Notice that behavior and reflect it back to her.

When the time comes for your client to consider a job offer, as with any important decision, it's a good idea for her to have a change of scene first. Getting away for a few days relieves the sense of imminent pressure. People under pressure tend to make decisions based on a few isolated facts rather than on the whole canon of information gathered. A fresh, and refreshing, setting reduces background noise, calms the mind, and helps thoughts flow more clearly.

Special Do's and Don'ts

Anyone involved in a job search may be experiencing some serious tensions. The pressure of finding a job when out of work or being in a miserable work situation can make good decisions seem impossible. When your client is under a lot of pressure, how can you best help?

When to Help

Most obviously, be sure to help if your client *asks* for help. Even if you cannot take active steps, you can always provide psychological support. Also be sure to help if:

- A client is in the throes of a crisis that may have warped his good judgment (i.e., has just been fired, is going through a divorce, or is recovering from a death in the family).
- You perceive impending disaster—for instance, your client is about to hire on with the same kind of employer (or do the same kind of job) that he's hated and failed at in the past.
- An illness or family tragedy is interfering with the job search.
- You notice a marked change in behavior which may indicate depression, other illness, or an addiction.
- The financial situation is so severe it threatens your child's

WHEN YOUR CLIENT IS ABOUT TO MAKE A MISTAKE

Our job is to emphasize the positive. We don't want our clients to become absorbed by what they're *not* good at, rather with what they *can* do well.

Still, there are times when our obligation to people we love means trying to keep them from going down disastrous paths. When you observe negative behavior that threatens your client's well-being, you can say, "I must tell you how I see this and its potential consequences." For example, "Your consistent impatience with your future partner is certain to lead to a serious rift."

Try to discuss your observations. Your client may be so determined that nothing penetrates, but you owe it to him to explain your reservations.

You might write down your concerns, which will allow him to contemplate your remarks in privacy without having to defend himself on the spot. Be careful about putting your opinions and feelings in writing, however—the written word is permanent, and it carries a much greater sting than oral criticism. If you do put your thoughts on paper, try to be encouraging and positive even in the face of your fears. Wait a few days before giving your written comments to your client—sometimes in just writing down the issues, you change your mind.

However you choose to express your thoughts, cushion them with kindness and support. Say, "I don't own all the truth, but this is how I see things."

Pose some questions for him to consider:

If it weren't for the availability of this job [partner], would you have chosen such an opportunity?

How would you rate the values of this organization against your own?

What in your experience to date gives you some evidence that you will enjoy this work?

If you feel as if you're banging your head against the wall, try this:

- Look at exercise 1 in this chapter and ask yourself again the first five questions. Are you sure you're being objective? Could past parental patterns be controlling your opinion?
- If you are certain this decision spells disaster for your client, don't stand back and let the drama unfold. If you can't talk to your client, find an intermediary. If your client is single, there may be a close friend, lover, or roommate who could intercede. (Never approach anyone in your client's business environment because you may undermine his credibility.)

  If your client is married, you might talk to his or her spouse confidentially. (Be sure the situation is very critical before taking this step.) Explain your concerns and ask him or her to consider using his or her influence. Your client's spouse can then tell you whether he or she sees the issue in the same way.
- Offer your client a relevant article, or book to read, or a consultation with a professional. Suggest that he consult these before making his decision.
- Repeat, "I've offered my opinion, but regardless of your decision, I'm here for you. It doesn't alter our relationship."

actual existence, or his family's welfare (you may be unable to offer money, but psychological support and help exploring options is critical at this juncture).

• Your client is unjustly (or justly) accused, ranging from a behavior or performance issue on the job, right up to a misdemeanor or felony.

Whatever the situation, be careful about projecting your own perceptions onto it. Is your opinion tainted by your client's past? Though familiarity with your client's history is beneficial, you may need to update your perspective—to see what's happening today, not what happened in teenage or childhood years. It is important not to lock people—least of all our children—into past expectations.

When Not to Help

Don't help if your client specifically requests that you stay out of his affairs. This can be tricky, because the request may directly conflict with a real need for assistance. In this case, try to suggest other sources of help: friends, a spouse, a respected teacher or coach, printed and data resources.

Don't interfere if your client is certain he's doing fine in the job search. You may be impatient for results, but your client has to move at his own pace. A good coach will watch and applaud.

Don't speak to contacts in your client's behalf.

Never help when your client is talking with a contact. I've heard many stories about a parent answering the telephone and becoming involved by chatting with an important contact or a potential employer, only to leave exactly the wrong impression for the circumstance. Even a well-meaning conversation may paint your client in a disadvantageous light. Your discourse with your client's contacts should be minimal, even if that person is your close friend or business associate. You may have forged the connection, but that's as far as your role goes. Never ask the contact, "How did my daughter do?" "Were you impressed with her credentials?"

Similarly, discourage your client from referring the contact back to you. George and Maria ran a thriving small mail-order business. Although they had no plans to hire an office assistant, when friends begged them to take on their grown daughter, Gwen, they agreed it might be a good fit.

They met with Gwen, explained the business, and outlined her duties. When it was time to talk salary, Gwen said, "I'll have Dad call you about that. He's a good negotiator."

George and Maria were flabbergasted. "But we're not hiring your father," Maria said. Somewhere along the line, Gwen's father had convinced her that only he could make a deal for her. If your child has relied on you to make decisions in the past, now's the time to change. Say, "If you've got any questions on how to handle this, we can discuss it in private, but do the deal yourself."

A few other caveats:

• Don't put words in your client's mouth by speaking before he has a chance to tell you what he thinks.
• Don't refer to your client in childlike terms.
• Don't talk to other people about your client's situation without his permission.

Going Into Business With Your Child

Frequently, parents become business partners with their children in an effort to help them. Occasionally a child actually hires a parent in a subordinate role, and we have seen some interesting cases of this recently.

Should you get involved in a new family business for the sake of your child? If so, how deeply? Should you invest money? Time and skills? Co-sign loans? Would your involvement be temporary or permanent? All these issues need to be discussed and resolved from the onset. Settle as much as possible up front, in writing.

Questions to ask yourself:

If you are becoming involved in a child's business, you should be able to answer "yes" to at least two of these questions. Even if you study the issues and decide all indications point to a "no" verdict, you may choose to become involved anyway. After all, you're still a parent. I understand the propensities, having been in this spot myself. At least, you will be forewarned.

- Does the business make sound economic sense?
- Do you like the product or service?
- Is it in a new field you want to learn about, or in a field you already love?
- If you are going to actually work in the business, will you be using a skill you enjoy using?
- Do you have the time to do what will be expected of you?

The issue of your compensation should be resolved from the start. Many of us are reluctant to take a salary from a child. While you may be tempted to "just help out" without pay, you will actually be doing your client a disservice. He'll never get a chance to demonstrate whether the business can hold its own. And he'll be in a worse situation if you should stop working, because then he'll have to pay someone to do your work and the money might not be there. If you like, agree to a short period of time when you'll work for free. After that, you should get a competitive salary.

If you're an investor, establish ground rules for financial reports or feedback. What information do you want and how often? Determine when you'll get reports and whether you'll be consulted on business decisions. These are assurances your client would have to provide an outside investor. If your client fails to comply, insist that he follow through.

Recognize whose territory is whose. No matter what, even if you're the 51 percent investor, in this case, it's still your client's business. If you want out later—as an investor and/or worker—treat your client with the same courtesy and professional respect you would any other associate or employer. Give notice. Leave bridges intact. If there's a problem with the investment, talk it over, then follow up by putting it in writing, gently but clearly.

Some parents have a highly developed expertise, exceptional negotiating or organizational skills, or an electronics or other technical ability. Putting these at your client's disposal as he establishes a new venture is perhaps even more valuable than taking an equity position. Since you could easily take these skills elsewhere for compensation, your client should appreciate your contribution as he would appreciate the services of any other qualified consultant.

Parents may not need or want equity participation. If you have other children you might work out an agreement whereby any monies you actually give to one child to begin a business are deducted from that child's portion of your estate (unless they are returned). If you do opt for an equity share, write out an agreement concerning the mutually agreeable terms whereby you can sell that equity.

Exercises and Activities

Things to Think on Alone

1. If you feel your client is about to make a bad decision, ask yourself:

How well do I understand the dynamics of this situation?

How much do I think my client's behavior patterns have changed since childhood?

What evidence do I have that the old habits that formed my opinion are still present?

Have others observed the same habits or behavior patterns?

How happy does my client look when discussing this opportunity?

How open is he to talking over this decision with me or others?

Might my client feel guilty about taking my help/money/assistance (if that is part of making this decision)?

How do my dollars affect the decision?

Things to Do Together

2. On the verge of any decision—whether to accept a job offer, whether to go into business or go back to school, even whether to make a pitch for a promotion—create a simple pros and cons list. You and your client make separate lists of all the things *in favor of* and *against* the decision. Read your lists aloud to each other, comparing and contrasting them.

PART II

SPECIAL SITUATIONS

Chapter Twelve

IS COLLEGE ALWAYS THE RIGHT CHOICE?

There's no question that a college degree has dollar value today. In 1991, college grads under the age of 30 earned four times more than their non-degreed counterparts. (In 1973, they earned only twice as much.) In 1988, 59 percent of all high school graduates enrolled in college immediately after high school, compared with 49 percent 10 years earlier. In very affluent communities, that figure rose to nearly 90 percent.

Yet a degree does not guarantee safety in times of economic distress. One has only to recall the Black Monday that rocked the financial community on October 19, 1987 and put thousands of well-educated adults out of work, or, more recently, to read about the massive layoffs at the country's biggest corporations to have this fact driven home.

It is true, however, that many extremely successful people never finish college, or enroll later in life. For example,

Steven Jobs and Stephen Wozniak, founders of the extremely successful Apple Computer, Inc., both dropped out of college to pursue their goal of creating an affordable, accessible personal computer.

So if a college degree doesn't predict success or guarantee a more secure income, what is the college decision all about? College can be a wonderful time of discovery, a place where possibilities unfold and passions are explored under the tutelage of dedicated professionals. On the other hand, it can also be a four-year tour of duty undertaken on autopilot.

At the critical juncture, between the ages of 18 and 24, young adults are trying to discover meaningful roles for themselves in the larger world. The most important task for them is to build their self-esteem and measure themselves against a larger life canvas instead of the family portraits. College offers a protected environment for fledglings to gain self-assurance. But confidence building isn't confined to classrooms. Anything that gets your client out of his or her childhood milieu, that sets the brain in motion by exposing him to the new and untried, is a learning device.

The best way to increase self-confidence is for young people to expand on areas in which they already have had some experience and success. Success in small steps breeds confidence.

For example, Terry told me, "I was always fascinated with the idea of being a television host, but I was afraid to speak in front of a camera. After high school I got a gofer job at a local TV station. Then I was promoted to assisting the producer of a local talk show. I hung around with the technical crew, soaking up their expertise. I got a lot of good feedback about what a quick learner I was, and my confidence just shot up. Within six months I had learned how the pros create a broadcast from concept to finished video. If I go to college, I will probably study communications, and I might even get my courage up and try on-camera work."

Phil also fine-tuned his direction in life when he bypassed college. "In high school I loved my music courses. Every year, I won first chair in the band's and the orchestra's clarinet sections. I expected to go on to college but couldn't decide what to concentrate on." Phil's high school guidance counselor advised him to get a teaching degree, but teaching "didn't sound right" to Phil. Confused, he opted to spend a year studying music privately, supporting himself by working as an administrative assistant for an artists' management company. Twice a week he gave music lessons to kids in the neighborhood to see what teaching felt like. Phil's private teacher played in the orchestra of a popular Broadway musical, and invited him along to sight-read the score with the pit musicians.

"As soon as that thundering applause engulfed me, I was hooked," Phil says. "I knew I'd never be satisfied going directly into teaching without giving myself the chance to play publicly—in an orchestra, in a chamber group, or even in a small jazz combo. I'm glad I gave myself breathing room. What kind of teacher would I be if I was bitter about lost opportunities?"

Why Go to College *Now*?

While college is usually a vital step in a young adult's educational and emotional development, it is not necessarily the *next* step after high school. An automatic leap into college reassures parents that children are progressing, but we needn't stick to such narrow criteria. Regardless of what choice your client makes, the four to six years after high school should be spent exploring interests.

If your client goes off to college halfheartedly, nobody wins. Technically, she's living up to your expectations, but there's no fire, no focus. Maybe she will party too much or take no-brainer courses just to pass the time. The point now is to be certain that your client is 100 percent engaged—meaning that she *wants* to do what she's doing.

Sylvia says, "I never once thought I had a choice of doing anything but going straight to college after high school. I chose a double major in medieval history and English. In my junior year I studied in England and traveled on the Continent. Suddenly the world opened up to me and I began questioning my goals. I began to see new directions to explore—like arts administration or teaching English as a second language—but I was trussed up by my major requirements, and there wasn't time to take electives.

"When I came home, I told my parents I wanted to leave college for a while—I wanted a chance to explore these other possibilities. My parents turned up the heat. 'Just finish your last year and you'll have a degree, then you can do what you want.' I felt guilty, so I returned to school in the fall.

"It was an awful year. Everything seemed to fall apart. I could hardly drag myself to classes; my grade point average fell. What made it harder, my roommate, a committed architecture student, was totally wrapped up in positioning herself for graduate school; and I didn't have any idea why I was working for my degree.

"Since graduating I've been floundering, and my roommate is loving graduate school. I'm wondering what to be. I sincerely wish I hadn't been pressured to tie things up neatly in four years. I feel worse off than when I began."

A Look at the Options

What, if not college? Identifying both skills and interests (see Chapter 4) will suggest alternatives your client may wish to elect: an interim job or apprenticeship, travel, the military, alternative school programs (see the resource section), or volunteer activities. These opportunities also can be appropriate after college if your client is unsure of direction.

Remember, the choice your client makes is a choice *for now*. If your client puts off school, the college fund can earn another year's interest. And, in some cases, a parental subsidy is appropriate and worthwhile for this interim learning experience. It could be a lot cheaper than paying for the wrong degree.

Frank's family, for example, sought alternatives when he couldn't seem to settle on an area of concentration nor make a commitment to school. Through friends, his family heard about a South American archaeological camp whose leader had a reputation for inspiring his young helpers. They introduced the idea to Frank, who loved outdoor adventure, and he took to it readily. His parents knew the terrain was rugged and the work would sometimes be dangerous, but the chance to fire Frank's motivations seemed worth it. And it was. Frank loved the experience. He was stimulated by the adventure, and his confidence grew, along with his skills in surveying, forestry, and building temporary camps for special expeditions. This previously lackluster student became a resourceful and innovative wilderness team leader, easing the way for the more academically oriented members of the archaeological teams who visited the campsite. After this "year off" Frank decided to join the army, where he was chosen for Green Beret service. Following a highly praised tour of duty, he returned to civilian life and found work building unique modular houses in Montana. He is putting himself through college there at the same time. He fully expects to become part of top management in his creative construction firm.

Travel/Work

A 1991 Time/CNN poll of Americans in their early twenties found that 60 percent of those questioned wanted to travel extensively while young, reflecting one of America's most popular obsessions, the lure of the open road. Today, however, adventurers often forgo the classic great-cities-of-Europe tour and visit distant ports of call instead. More and more young people with wanderlust take working trips, where they join crews helping to build dams, chart rivers, clean up after oil spills, or join in archaeological digs. For example, Eastern Europe is eager for English teachers right now, and anyone interested in the changing world could choose to go there. (See the resource section for sources of information on opportunities abroad.)

Social Contributions and Volunteer Work

Twentysomethings often want to enrich society, but our most pressing problems are too large and complex to fix easily. Many young people feel cowed by the ghost of the 1960s. Money was looser then, tuition costs were more manageable, jobs more secure, and it was an easier choice for kids to drop out temporarily.

Today's students are often afraid to take time off. They worry that the good life may disappear before they are launched in their careers. Pressure to get going may accelerate until it forces poor decisions. That is a recipe for frustration and defeat. So, if your client feels he'd like to volunteer, but is afraid of wasting time, ask him to think about what he really needs to be accomplishing now—i.e., enhancing skills and developing new ones. It is also a time for practicing discipline and developing a lifestyle in keeping with his values. Volunteer work should be chosen with these objectives in mind.

For example, Gloria says, "Since he was a teenager my son worked as a volunteer at a hospital for handicapped children. He loved working there, and had all the patience in the world with the kids. His love for children trying to overcome problems became the central passion of his life. He is now a special-education teacher and feels he has found his role in life."

Our evidence shows that when people choose work they deem "valuable," they are able to sustain their commitment during periods when money and/or recognition are scarce. The psychic reward compensates. The lesson here is to urge your client to hold to a direction consistent with what she thinks matters in life. In the end, this makes for a highly committed and highly desirable employee.

Work-Study Programs/Internships

Another option is a work-study program or internship, offered through some colleges and universities, in which students can work in their field of interest and receive both monetary compensation and college credit. Northeastern University, in Boston, Massachusetts, pioneered this concept by offering a full four-year work-study curriculum. Today, many colleges and universities across the country offer these programs and coordinate internships with local businesses and not-for-profits.

If your client needs to work to help pay for college, it should at least be in the direction of possible interest. For example, working in the cafeteria offers insights into restaurant and institutional dining, catering and nutrition; tutoring can provide a feel for teaching; home-care helpers may learn more about geriatric care or child development.

Good sources of information on work-study programs include *Peterson's Guide to Four-Year Colleges* and *Where to Start Career Planning*, by Carolyn Lloyd Linquist and Pamela L. Feodoroff, also from Peterson's Guides.

Educational consultants—people who help students plan their education—also can help students identify and select relevant adjunct programs. In this book's resource section you will find profiles of several educational consultants, as well as information on a nonprofit organization called Independent Educational Consultants Association, which lists members around the country who are dedicated to helping students identify the best educational opportunities. They are found under "Career Counselors and Educational Consultants."

Short-Term and Part-Time Jobs

Summer and part-time jobs are a great source of inspiration, especially when they allow your client to explore new areas of interest. Unless she shows an overwhelming enthusiasm for one kind of work, encourage her to pursue a variety of

FULL- OR PART-TIME STUDENT?

At some point your client may have to decide whether to juggle school and part-time work or to devote herself fully to her studies. Her sense of direction for her life and her ability to handle multiple tasks simultaneously, as well as financial considerations, will play into this decision. Here are some of the pros and cons for each scenario.

Full-Time Student

Pros	Cons
Perhaps an easier and less-stressful way to work toward a degree.	Removed from the real world. Can induce ivory-tower thinking.
Full enjoyment of campus life.	Less opportunity to test interests and assumptions in real world.
Earlier receipt of a degree.	
Could be less expensive.	Can force premature closure on career path.

interests—it will open more doors. Trying different jobs is also a good way for kids to measure their values and worth in numerous settings while discovering what they enjoy.

Many kids approach their first employers with a "What can you do for me?" attitude, instead of one that emphasizes "What I can bring to you." They fail to realize that they have plenty of skills to offer and make the mistake of focusing on what they hope to gain from a job, rather than what they hope to give it. There's usually something a client does

Part-Time Student

Pros	Cons
Fewer courses, forcing more academic focus.	Less time for studying and academic learning.
Can more fully explore how academic interests relate to work interests.	Can be stressful.
	May not feel a part of campus life.
Better view of real-life conditions and the whole work/life picture.	Takes longer to finish degree.
Less dependence on parents financially.	Could be more expensive overall.
Opportunity for reinforcement of interests or timely warning of weak interest if work is related.	Takes longer to incorporate electives into study at most institutions.

recreationally, academically, or as a hobby that translates directly into an employment skill.

Can your client type or use a computer? Does she have a green thumb? Maybe she tends the neighbors' pets during vacation periods and nurses wounded birds. A nearby zoo may have summer volunteer or paid programs that use just those skills. Does she have athletic abilities? If so, how about coaching or leading camp activities? Is your client a good driver? Maybe delivery or chauffeuring will be appropriate. Once you start thinking in this vein, the list grows and grows. Jobs slinging burgers or delivering messages can be learning experiences too, particularly if these jobs are varied.

Sandra worked in the shoe department of a department store for one summer. After listening to women complain endlessly of discomfort, she decided to study shoe design, and now designs beautiful shoes that are easy on the feet.

Jeff spent a summer as a delivery boy for an elevator company. He became interested in the construction of office towers when he'd deliver materials to job sites. After high school he worked part time for an architect and learned even more about building. "Construction—how buildings stand up—fascinates me," he said. Jeff went on to college and studied engineering. "Now I'm learning more about what I want to do with my education. I thought I wanted to build skyscrapers, but now I'm more interested in constructing good low-cost housing. It somehow seems more important to me."

Sandra and Jeff are representative of hundreds of seemingly too-good-to-be-true outcomes of exploring through well-chosen "kids' jobs." The common theme for both was they chose work that appealed to them.

Working in the Family Business

Instead of college, perhaps your client wants to spend a year working in an uncle's factory or an aunt's real-estate office.

This can be a wonderful way to gain experience, but, generally, I think it's better for a young person to test himself in unfamiliar territory and gain the confidence that comes from surviving outside the family's protective wings.

Perhaps your client has already spent a summer working in the family business and liked it so much he wants to go back. Even if he loved it, encourage him to pursue a similar line of work for somebody else. That way, he will gain a measure of self-confidence and will invite more respect from family members if he later joins the business.

Vocational Schools and Apprenticeships

An academic education isn't a mandate for everyone. A vocational school may be an appropriate alternative, particularly if your client is genuinely interested in the field he's learning. Nor are the two types of education mutually exclusive. Your client may opt for vocational school and switch to college later, or vice versa.

Apprenticeships are another good, albeit sometimes hard to find, alternative. For Beth's brother, an apprenticeship opened up new worlds. She says, "Chris is brilliant at anything to do with electronics or computers but only squeaked by in high school. My folks sent him to a computer school and he quit, saying, 'They're not telling me anything I don't already know.' Then he went to an electronics school with a job-placement program, but he was bored and didn't take classes seriously. This kid can take a VCR apart and reassemble it in under an hour! My parents couldn't figure out what would help. He just wanted to be left alone to tinker."

In the old days Chris could have been apprenticed to an electronics company, but apprenticeships are not nearly as common these days. Chris's mother thought she might rediscover such an option if she could find the right person. She talked to the man who came to repair the computer in her office; she eavesdropped on conversations on the bus when someone talked about jobs in the electronics industry. She tried to be open to people whom she might otherwise pass by. One evening at a party she fell into conversation with a young scientist who worked in a robotics laboratory. "How did you ever come to do that?" asked Chris's mother. "It was an accident," the man replied. "I started out to be an engineer and just sort of stumbled into this field. Now I'm totally involved in it."

Would he be willing to talk to Chris about robotics—what it was and what training it required? Certainly. The result: Chris got a job cleaning up the robotics lab, and

APPRENTICE PROGRAMS

Has the apprentice system disappeared in the modern world? Traditionally, artisans and craftspeople spent years studying under—even living with—a master, painstakingly acquiring the knowledge and skills vital to their professions. At the end of this period, the apprentice might join the master as a junior partner or strike out in his or her own business. Times have changed but whether yo1pur client wants to become a potter, tattoo artist, plumber, silversmith, photographer, chef, machine-tool manufacturer, or financial analyst, it's still possible to find an apprentice program. Some of the ways you and your client can do so: Look into college "mentor" programs; consult career counselors and educational consultants; check out videos, audio cassettes, newsletters, and journals about the field your client is interested in; and query the associations related to the field.

quickly became a valuable right-hand man to the staff. In an environment where innovative ideas are welcome and exploration is in the air, Chris feels completely at home. He is surrounded by intensely involved people—just like himself —who take time to listen and talk about science and new technologies.

In the absence of formal apprentice programs, it takes the sorts of innovative inquiry carried on by Chris's mother to produce avenues of work and learning. You and your client can do it, too. (See Apprentice Programs box.)

In college mentor programs, many of which are open to the public for a small fee, professionals make themselves available to provide information about different careers. Some offer internships or apprenticeships, or entry-level positions, which sometimes lead to an offer of a permanent job. Contact your local university for more information about mentor programs.

A good resource for apprentice opportunities is Al Sakarov's *Off-Beat Corners: State Directory of Unusual Work*, which lists more than 10,000 alternative groups and organizations.

Many career counselors and educational consultants are also good sources of information. David Denman, an educational consultant in Mill Valley, California, for example, specializes in designing developmentally enriching opportunities for his clients. His program, which he calls "Time Out," places students in internships, apprenticeships, and study abroad. David has even placed two teenagers with the real Crocodile Dundee in Australia.

Exercises and Activities

Things to Think on Alone

1. Think back on your own life—when you were 18 years old. Did you go to college? If so, why? (Because you "had" to, because everybody did, or because you wanted to?) Why do you want your child to go to college?

2. What did you major in? How has your degree helped you in your work/life? How has your college experience shaped your work/life?

3. Can you stand the idea of your child not going to college? How would you deal with a decision like that?

Things to Think on Together

4. Ask your client what benefits he expects to derive from college.

5. Explore what he hopes to learn in college.

6. Discuss what she envisions doing in daily life six years from now. How do these visions fit with going to college or not?

Things to Do Together

7. Reverse Lottery: Tell your client, "We're terribly sorry, but we have no money. You can still go to college, but you can't count on the family's financial support." Then ask your client to write out a scenario for the next few years. Remind him that any choice is fine as long as he is willing to support it.

Options might include (but are not limited to): a work-study program, applying for a scholarship, taking out student loans, forgoing college and entering the work force full-time; working part time and studying part time, leaving home and going on welfare (wild as that may seem), working full time and saving for college in the future.

This hypothetical exercise reveals the level of your client's commitment and readiness for college. What's most important at this stage of his life is expanding knowledge and experience. How would your client choose to do this?

(You might want to make this a long-term exercise. Give your client a day or so to respond. If he is determined to go to college, suggest he do further research to find financial aid. He may well discover new sources of funding and a wealth of innovative work-study programs.)

8. A Year Off Before College: Tell your client, "You've just been given a year with total financial support. You can spend any amount of money, but you can't go to college. The only restriction is that you must write down what you will do with yourself—where, *exactly*, will your activities take place and what will you learn from them?"

The responses may be hedonistic pleasure seeking or full of meaning. Often, what seems to be simply thrill chasing turns out to suggest a variety of perfectly possible work directions. (There are people who lead adventure-travel expeditions!)

These activities will inevitably suggest whether your client is ready for college, now or later. The advantage of approaching decision making in this manner is that you both will see the picture simultaneously.

Chapter Thirteen

COACHING YOUR CLIENT THROUGH COLLEGE

I t used to be that the college years were primarily a time of self-discovery—young adults benefited from four years of college, *particularly* if they didn't know what to do with their lives. Today, because most interesting work requires a high level of knowledge which can be acquired only over time, students may be cajoled into naming their majors early—sometimes while still in high school —and applying directly to a specific department or college within a university. They're asked to make a career choice early and get on track.

But, for many students it is simply too early to commit to a narrow profession or field of work while still in college. And premature decisions made under pressure can have devastating emotional and financial costs. While no education is ever completely wasted, if a graduate discovers that his major has no bearing on his work interests, this can be a traumatic outcome for both him and his family. Yet it's a worse scenario if the graduate pursues a career because he feels trapped by his degree.

The truth is, majors seem rarely to be an indicator of subsequent work any longer. Many CEOs tell me, "Give me an English or History major any day, because these people have judgment based on understanding of how people and societies have reacted to each other over the years, and they usually can communicate well with others. I can always send them to business school later or train them to work according to my corporate style." The judgment which one gains from sound liberal arts training makes for good business and often good ethics.

Entire books and a growing cadre of professional counselors are devoted to the process of helping students select colleges and majors (see the resource section), so we'll just touch on a few issues here.

Choosing a College

I'm always amazed how people enroll in colleges they've never visited or thoroughly investigated. In addition to reading brochures and bulletins, your client should subject potential colleges to the same scrutiny that their admissions offices apply to applicants. He should make every effort to see the school before committing and if that's impossible, he should talk to people who have been there, especially those who share his interests. Find out when the next alumni group will meet in your area (or in the closest metropolis) and whether your client can attend. Often you can arrange for someone in the group to meet him and introduce him around to others at the meeting. Are there local undergraduates available to talk on the phone or to meet with when next in town on vacation? Are there men and women at your job who attended the school your client's curious about?

Some colleges offer overnight orientations for prospective students, with group tours and opportunities to meet department heads. Your client would be well advised to take advantage of these and to arrange one-on-one meetings with students and professors, or at least visit classes. She should go to classes in the company of *one current student,* if possible, rather than in a group of prospects. Topics to ask about include required courses, what majors are offered, interdisciplinary studies, extracurricular activities, and the campus atmosphere. This information is every applicant's due, and any school that values his or her participation should willingly provide answers. If officials aren't cooperative, your client should tap into the unofficial network of informed people (students, retailers who sell to the students, townspeople) who have daily experience with the college and are there for the talking to. Your client can sit at a coffee-shop counter and get into a conversation with someone on a neighboring stool, browse in a bookstore and engage salespeople in answering questions, or stop by the campus pub, where talk will be free. Occasions to pick up information informally can be easily generated.

Max came to see me when he was a junior in high school, contemplating college applications. "I haven't a clue how to begin *thinking* about schools," he admitted.

We talked about his interests and Max said, "I love cars." "Well, what about cars?" I prodded.

"I love the intricacies of car engines," he answered. "I'm especially intrigued by engines that don't run on gas."

This led us to a discussion of alternate energy sources, which held great fascination for him. Armed with a deeper awareness about his interests, Max started a survey of schools. He wanted to know where people were studying alternative-energy sources. Who was building cars that run on electricity, solar power, methane? What institutions were they affiliated with? Had they won any awards or grants, pioneered new studies? Who had gone the furthest in making a new car? In model building? In electronics and engineering?

Soon Max had a list of colleges where men and women were working on the cutting edge of alternative-energy sources. He had identified places that could feed his curiosity and provide a stimulating milieu. Now he was prepared to begin the application/screening process.

There are more than just academic criteria for your client to take into account. It's important for her to decide whether she wants to live at home or away. If the latter, does she want to be within driving distance, or further from home? Now's the time to ask her: "What do you envision yourself doing with your leisure time? Is climate important? Do you want to be near a big city or in the country? How big do you want your classes to be?" These questions are designed to help your client focus on the larger picture of how she will live her life at college. (See exercise 4.)

Remember, no amount of studying offers life experience. Your client can get a great education at a mediocre institution, if it is combined with opportunities to learn and absorb from the surrounding culture and environment. Conversely, even an Ivy League education, bereft of extracurricular activities, may fail to stimulate genuine learning.

Choosing a Major

I groan when I hear of advisers telling freshmen they must pick a specialty. When my own children were faced with this ultimatum, I urged, "Tell them you don't want to commit now. You're there to explore. No one has to choose a major so soon." It was an uphill battle.

Students out of tune with their courses may end up with good grades, but the work holds no meaning for them. Often they have simply learned to regurgitate what the professor expects. For example, Bonnie majored in French because she had an aptitude for languages, and she had no overwhelming interest in other topics. She was not an avid conversationalist and had little emotional love of France or commitment to the related subjects she studied. Some of her course work was enjoyable—for example, she learned a lot about French architecture and made a trip to France with her family, which she loved—but she never read a French book that wasn't required for school. When she graduated from college, she still could not identify where her interests lay. Recently she said, "I haven't even thought about French since I graduated. I'm all burned out from having to practice it so much. Do you think this is unusual?" From someone whose major was French, I thought it was a very sad comment.

The best advice is to hold off the "major" decision for as long as possible. It's always smart to pursue a general course of study for at least two years. Every future specialist profits from a solid liberal arts foundation. The chef-in-the-making attending culinary school may at some point want to write a brochure offering his services, or perhaps a cookbook. A musician may one day find inspiration in historical themes (consider Tchaikovsky, Wagner or Verdi). Scientists who write lucid prose may wind up alongside Diane Ackerman and Stephen Hawking on best-seller lists of the future. Students should steer clear of specialization until they have a good idea of their aptitudes and interests. Sometimes this means starting in one college and then transferring to another that offers a better course of study in the chosen field.

By their junior year, however, students have to make a choice. If your client still doesn't know what to study, together review his interests and skills, brainstorming all the possible work to which this could lead. Identifying an interest like hiking in the woods can help a person decide on a college major. Dive to the heart of the matter: As your client recalls this pleasure, ask him to describe its specific appeal.

Is being outdoors the best part? Getting exercise? Observing birds and animals or plants? Navigating trail maps along well-traveled paths or blazing through the brush? Perhaps he uses the walk to spin extended fantasies about the past, imagining himself a pioneer, or ponders the lives of those who inhabited the area a thousand years before. What seems like a simple walk can be a source of many related paths to follow.

Use Surveying to Choose a Major

Your client can use some of the same techniques to choose a major as she will later use in choosing work. Sheila entered college with a genuine love of art. "I can't draw, can't sculpt, can't paint," she admitted, "but I adore art in all its forms. If only I could have a career that's linked to art in some way."

Sheila made inquiries and learned that in addition to galleries and museums, many corporations maintain art collections, private collectors employ curators, and countless foundations exist devoted exclusively to the arts. What she didn't know was which major—business, fine arts, or art history—would best fuse her passions and aptitudes with a realistic vision of the future.

During her first two years at university, in addition to completing her standard college requirements, Sheila took art history classes and signed up for art courses for fun. She learned that some schools offered a master's degree in arts administration but remained uncertain whether this was appropriate. Would such a degree be too narrow and self-limiting? Sheila envisioned business majors as stuffy number crunchers, and art history majors as moles who sat in dark rooms all day staring at slides. At a crossroads, Sheila decided to investigate the alternatives by conducting a survey at her own university. (See Chapter 5 for a full description of the art of surveying. This research tool is ideally suited to choosing both a school and a major.)

Her objective, she said, was to discover what major would provide the best background for pursuing work in either arts administration, promotion, or curating. She gave herself a deadline for a completed survey of the end of the second grading period of her sophomore year.

She began by trying to think of the publications and people who could lead her to those personally involved in the art world. She concluded that these included the college librarian, national art magazines, as well as biographies of legendary collectors such as Peggy Guggenheim and Bernard Berenson. At Crystal-Barkley we call these "off-site" sources of information.

TAKE IT EASY

B efore your client has to choose a major suggest that he read some college catalogs cover to cover—even descriptions of courses he'd never envision taking. He may find he's drawn to new ideas, new disciplines. Then he could do a little surveying on what's of interest. This may offer an even wider scope than auditing a class, and it's not as time consuming.

Auditing classes, however, can be a good way to take in information without the stress of additional work and premature commitments. A student may wind up being fascinated by previously unexplored topics and want to take some courses for credit. Auditing is a good way to feel free to look around without being committed.

Sheila's "on-site" sources—the people who actually were in the field—included professors and students in the art history, arts administration, and business departments, the owner of an art gallery in her hometown, the editor of an art magazine, the director of the college art museum, the director of alumni fund-raising, and a curator at a large city museum.

Sheila had many questions. Of the professors and students she asked what courses were required for each major? What percentage of students from the three departments went directly into the art world, what percent to graduate schools? Were students happy with the professors and their course work? What did they plan for the future? What specific work were the graduates actually doing? Sheila also thought about whether she liked the students she was meeting. After all, they would be her classmates and future colleagues. She asked department heads whether course work could be tailored to suit a particular interest or specialty. Did they know anything about M.B.A.'s in arts administration and have any advice about their value? She asked the campus fund raiser what his daily responsibilities entailed, because she recognized that raising money is an important job at nonprofit arts organizations. She also asked what his background had been.

Sheila asked the magazine editor and the owner of the art gallery how they had come to be in their professions, what they studied in school, and solicited their advice about art-related careers. In particular, with the gallery owner, she explored how to raise capital for art investment. She asked everyone whether there were things they wished they had done or studied.

When she completed her personal conversations with these people, Sheila spent several weeks evaluating what she had learned. "After my survey I decided it was probably the financial and marketing side of art which would most intrigue me," she said. As a result, she chose to major in business, with arts-related electives. "Art is my great love," she explains. "I am already pretty knowledgeable about the history of art and the contemporary art scene. A business major offers a strong grounding in topics I can't pick up independently, like accounting and marketing. I feel I'm opening another door, multiplying my possibilities after graduation. If I hadn't done

ADVANCED DEGREES

S adly, even as a college degree often seems to be a prerequisite to upwardly mobile employment, a bachelor's degree itself is being devalued in a few sectors. Marjorie, who runs a successful semiconductor business in Silicon Valley, complains that to ensure the quality performance she used to get from college graduates she now has to hire Ph.D.'s. Thus, even with a B.A. our kids may be only halfway through their educational trek toward professionalism, depending on the field.

Although advanced degrees are clearly necessary for certain professions—law, medicine, social work, for example—graduate school may also be a convenient way to put off entering the real world. Your client may be daunted, thinking "undergraduate degree" equals "not very valuable." If your client is contemplating additional education, this is a good time for you both to ask: Is graduate school really necessary? Could it be an avoidance tactic? Does he or she really love learning that much? Can that passion be put to use in another way?

a survey, I would have automatically gravitated toward art history; it was the path of least resistance."

Sheila has yet to determine exactly what aspect of the art/business world she will go into, but she's confident that she's developing the skills and experience to give herself good options.

Activities and Exercises

Things to Think On Alone

1. Have I (tacitly or overtly) encouraged my child to pick a college or major because of family tradition?

2. Do I expect my child to excel in the same subjects I did?

3. Do I see college as primarily an academic experience (learning for the sake of learning), an academic/vocational experience (learning for the sake of a career), or an educational experience (a time of social, intellectual, and experiential growth)? What have I communicated to my child?

Things to Think on Together

4. Ask your client to describe what activities would fill an ideal day on campus. What would he like most to be doing? With whom? Under what circumstances? What would he dislike most? This is a good time to start thinking in these whole-life terms.

5. Ask your client: What home-centered tasks have you enjoyed doing? What do you feel you do best? For instance, did your client get pleasure from painting the house, planning meals, working out a budget on the computer, helping to redecorate the living room or to design an extension to the house? All his answers will point to the intersection of interest and expertise.

When this is done, also ask, What in school have you enjoyed, and why?

6. This is a particularly good time for your client to read biographies of people whose life work matches his own interests.

Things to Do Together

7. Adult Survey: Have your client ask at least six adults (relatives, friends, neighbors, or perhaps your business associates), "What did you major in?" "Why?" "How did your major ultimately relate to your 'real' life?"

This exercise is an easy introduction to surveying and opens your client's mind to the possibilities colleges offer. It will also make it clear that majors don't automatically predict career paths. Aunt Agatha majored in biology but went on to become a medical illustrator, not a doctor. William Carlos Williams went to medical school and worked as a doctor but joined the ranks of history as a poet. Preston Sturges took over his mother's cosmetics business and even invented a kiss-proof lipstick before finding his true vocation writing and directing brilliant film comedies like *The Lady Eve* and *Sullivan's Travels*.

8. Newspaper Headline: Twenty years from now, a newspaper runs a feature story about your client. Ask her to visualize the headline. It should represent what your client most wants to see—any accomplishment or inner aspect of her life (Jones Cures Cancer; Jones Adopts 12 Children of Different Races; Jones Gets Hole in One; Jones Fluent in Five Languages).

Then ask your client to describe her life to the thousands of curious readers. What would she say? What would she want to be true about herself? She should include all of her dreams, accomplishments—not just career goals, but all aspects of her life, including the kind of person she's become, the experiences she's lived through, the kind of life she's living and where she's living it, what kind of friends she has, and her family relationships.

9. Real Life Course: What if you could take a class at your university that uses the world around you as a laboratory? You can do *any* job in the whole world for one semester and receive credit for it. This is an imaginary exercise, but I know one woman who did it in real life. She chose to edit a local newspaper in a small California town. She learned the finer points of meeting deadlines and writing concisely. She learned about circulation, advertising sales, production, distribution, and more. This is your chance to create an ideal job for one term only. What would it be? What would you expect to contribute? What would you expect to learn? Be specific.

10. Your client has been given a year's free tuition to study anything he wants from any university's curriculum— no strings attached! Your client must choose the college and the curriculum. Will he try many different things? Or concentrate on one field? What does this choice reveal about your client's current course of study?

Chapter Fourteen

OUT OF WORK
AND DESPERATE

W hen a job ends—voluntarily or not—most people engage in a flurry of activity, usually followed by a kind of paralysis. Many young people make rounds of phone calls, send out lots of resumes, and then sit at home waiting for the phone to ring. As the days go by they feel increasingly helpless, while on the sidelines their parents grow increasingly agitated.

Having an out-of-work child can create pressures that may put you both to the severest test yet. Just when you thought you were in the homestretch, you may find yourself with a dependent child again. It's natural that parents' eagerness to get the problem solved and get on with their own lives sometimes produces counterproductive words and actions.

Helping an adult child in this situation is something like walking through a mine field 20 years after the war. It's easy to trigger unresolved emotional explosions left over from when your son or daughter was young. That's why so many kids dread telling their folks when something's gone wrong.

Jack, a 24-year-old graphic designer, remembered calling his dad to say he'd been fired. "I could hear him tensing up right through the phone wires. I knew he thought it was all my fault!"

Broke, Jack moved in with his dad, Charlie, a retired civil servant who had been recently widowed. He had sold the family home and moved into a small city apartment. Now, at a time when father and son each needed privacy to reshape independent lives, they were cramped together in a small apartment, both living on Charlie's limited income.

Charlie wanted to help but secretly resented his lost privacy and the drain on his income. In turn, Jack's guilt over his dependence on his father made him surly and disagreeable. "Dad doesn't understand what it feels like to sell yourself in today's market. He thinks I should get a night job while I'm looking for a new position. How can I get psyched up for big job interviews if I'm exhausted from waiting tables or driving a cab at night?" he said.

Jack thought his best bet would be another job like his previous one because "that's where my experience lies." Charlie thought Jack wasn't trying hard enough. "He needs a job *now*. Nobody ever asked me what *I* wanted out of life!"

Actually, this was a perfect time for Jack to broaden his base and explore his interests, skills, and values. If graphic design was still the main skill he wished to use, how would it fit with his primary interests and values? Jack could use a period of unemployment as an opportunity to explore this and shape his future. And his father could help.

Charlie's most important role was to bolster his son's self-esteem when things were looking bleak. Regardless of the circumstances, people tend to blame themselves for being out of work, wondering "What did I do wrong?" "Will I ever be able to get another job?"

Only people who feel good about themselves can go out and meet people and make effective proposals. This takes disciplined work and lots of encouragement under the best of circumstances; when a person feels desperate, it's an extra-tough assignment. But you can help your client get through it by keeping him focused on the positive. Now is the time to reinforce what your client has going for him and help him implement a realistic strategy.

Obviously, it doesn't help your client to blame others exclusively. We all can learn from our mistakes. But in trying to find a balance between "It's all my fault; I hate myself" and "It's all my boss's fault—that rotten s.o.b.," you can help your client deal with his feelings and gain a positive outlook.

What Happened?

Step one is discovering why your client is out of work. He may have been laid off in a general company purge, in which case there should be no shame involved. He may have been fired for poor performance or for cause. Being fired for cause implies a serious violation of rules or even legal transgressions. If this is the case, you may never learn what really happened.

It's also possible your client became so fed up with the job that he quit before finding another job. Perhaps he has a history of bouncing from one job to the next, never finding a happy situation.

How Do You Feel About It?

Every situation is different and arouses different emotions. Both parent and child are likely to be very worried, and your child may well be frightened. Some parents also feel a renewed burden; a few see a chance to reestablish the dependent parent-child relationship. That may feel good to the parent but doesn't usually help the adult child. Test your own emotions by asking yourself: "How do I feel about my own child

COPING WITH JOB LOSS

1. The best thing for your client to do is get away for a long weekend to a quiet place he loves (forget glitzy weekends that cost a fortune). The idea is to help him regain his equilibrium, reduce noise level, and get in touch with his values and feelings. He can go alone or with his spouse or a close friend.

Parents can help here, either by paying for the trip, taking care of home responsibilities (pet-sit or baby-sit)—whatever you feel comfortable with that will help. Suggest that your client take along a journal and record his feelings, such as what he'd like to do next, wished he'd done, learned from this experience.

2. Next, help make a financial plan. This may include eliminating credit cards, taking out a loan, moving back in with the family, relocating, or earmarking money for further education.

3. Based on this financial plan, your client should select an appropriate time period to engage in the job search—from two weeks to a year.

being in this jam?" List the aspects of your life that might be affected if your adult child becomes dependent again.

When parents help an adult child in trouble, there is an obvious potential for conflict. Parents sometimes:

• Want to dictate the child's next step.
• Give the help they choose, which may not be what the child wants or needs.
• Make life so easy for the youngster that she fails to do anything for herself.

4. Help him make a plan to balance daily activities: eight hours of working on the job search five days a week and the rest on sports, family time, leisure time, or whatever your client enjoys.

5. Be sure your client surrounds himself with upbeat people. This means avoiding "friends" who have a negative attitude. It also means taking a breather from others who may be so discouraged about their own situations that they impose their bleak outlook on your client.

6. Make a list of everyone your client knows who is or might be knowledgeable about or involved in his preferred area of work.

7. Help him make plans to talk with these people about their view of the trends affecting the field, what the field needs, and their own professional objectives.

8. Be cautious about job-search clubs. Your client will not want to be presented as one of 1,000 people—all out of work. Perhaps it's safe to use a club's office and telephone, but he must do his own thing. You want potential employers to see him as a resource rather than someone desperate for a job.

- Permit the situation to trigger old immature parent-child relationships that are no longer appropriate.
- Through their own accomplishments unknowingly weaken a child's confidence.
- Disrupt their lives to the extent that they resent their child.

It's very easy to fall into some of these traps. Acknowledge the hazards to yourself and attempt to build a strategy to help your client deal with the situation but at the same time, don't put pressure on her. And don't make up her bed!

Do implement a division of household duties, plan alternate nights out to preserve independence, and so forth.

How to Help

The last thing you want to do is to increase your child's anxiety by nagging, with questions like "How many interviews have you had this week?" "Did you answer any ads today?" "Do you have enough money?" Let your client offer this kind of information of his own volition. But throughout the process, you *can* ask, "How can I support you in the job search? Tell me what's going on? Perhaps there are some practical things I can do to help?" Try to listen quietly before offering counsel. Because you are walking in a mine field, you might want to get some outside help.

For example, let's say you believe your child is repeating old problem behavior, and you're afraid it will happen again on the next job. Instead of going over the same territory with your client again (and risking an explosion), recommend a wise outside person to explain how he or she resolved a similar situation. For example, Joan knew her daughter Tiffany had a lifelong problem getting along with authority figures. Joan suspected Tiffany had been fired for not being deferential to her boss, a strong, capable, demanding advertising executive. Instead of accusing her daughter, she said, "I know that when you're feeling exasperated, you tend to blow off steam. You might want to talk to Edith; she dealt with a similar situation at her office. She might have ideas about alternate strategies that may come in handy in the future."

Joan spoke friend to friend, coach to client, not as a finger-pointing parent. Instead of holding herself up as the owner of all wisdom, she wisely guided Tiffany to a source outside the family.

Whenever you see the red flags of old parent-child behavior patterns flying again, relieve the tension and give yourselves perspective by inviting the advice of a knowledgeable, kind person whom you both respect.

Should I Help Financially?

When it comes to money, there is no one "best" choice on how to handle it. How you help—and how much—depends on your own and your client's personal resources and your client's frame of mind. Sometimes offering money makes the client feel more like a failure. A handout from Mom or Dad may translate as a loss of respect and a lack of faith.

Your feelings are also important. If you take money from a cherished fund earmarked for something else, you're likely to resent it. Resentment risks damaging the parent-child relationship, and you wind up losing more than capital.

Still, your client's financial panic must be addressed so that he is free to move on to the more important issue of finding a right new job. And it must be addressed from the perspective of his unique circumstance.

Max was doing fairly well running two downtown boutiques, but business hit a slump a few months before a balloon payment on one of his loans was due. He turned to his parents, who were reasonably well off, for help.

Part of Max's overhead was the high rent he paid on his uptown apartment. His parents offered him a rundown bungalow they owned in the suburbs. They would give him title to the house outright if Max would live in it. From Max's perspective, the house was too far—about an hour and a half on the train—from his stores and his friends. His entire social life would disappear, and it would affect his being on hand at the stores. Also, to make it livable, the house needed a lot of work, which meant taking time and capital away

FIRED!

People have a way of doing exactly the wrong thing when a crisis strikes. The automatic reaction most people have when they are fired is to broadcast it to every friend, family member, and colleague who will listen. It's natural to feel rejected and want sympathy and vindication, but it is rarely a good idea for everyone to know the story. It paints the new job seeker into an unattractive corner. Who wants to hire—or recommend—a loser? (Unfortunately, that's often the image the complaining individual unknowingly projects.)

Instead, the person who was fired must immediately regroup—and I mean in the first hour after absorbing the shock. He needs to begin looking at the positive aspects of the situation. The sooner he starts talking positively, the easier it will be to genuinely *feel* positive. Do not let the cement set.

Regardless of how much he hurts inside, the message to repeat to himself, and to others, is: "It's time

from his boutiques, just when they needed it most. Max declined the offer—but he still needed help.

His parents were annoyed. They saw only the advantages of their offer—Max would be relieved of monthly rent—and refused to see the disadvantages. When his parents declined to offer other help, Max struggled alone against the rising financial tide. He lost one of the stores but managed to retain the other, although he remains saddled with debt. To this day, both Max and his parents remain resentful.

The parents weren't realistic about their solution, and

for me to move on, so I am now seeking an opportunity to. . . ." Or, "I want a chance to work under different circumstances so that my skills in _____ can develop."

The less said about the circumstances of the departure, the better. Keep the emphasis on what went right, not what went wrong. There are always good lessons to be salvaged about what to seek or avoid in future working conditions.

Additionally, anyone who has been fired should negotiate as favorable a recommendation as possible. Often recommendations can be secured in writing as part of the departure package.

This is no time for your client to speak his mind and go off in a huff. He needs to make every effort to maintain cordial relations with the past employer, because none of us needs enemies to haunt our histories.

Urge your client to leave the past where it is and move his emphasis to future plans, professional development, and the desire to use his best skills and seek accomplishments.

Max, extremely anxious in the midst of this crisis, was unable to give a clear picture of the demands on him. Since both parties could view the dilemma only from their own prejudiced point of view, a wise third party could have helped a lot.

If your client can't talk freely to you, castigating him for losing his job or having financial troubles will only make matters worse. Everyone has money trouble some time in life. Try to create an environment in which you can sit and talk about money without laying blame.

A creative approach is to start with a monthly survival budget. Literally, sit down with your client and figure out all the unavoidable expenses. This will accomplish several objectives: determine whether you might be able to supply the amount required, provide a realistic basis for deciding whether a move back home is essential, and suggest whether a sale of the client's assets or a loan might provide enough help. Depending on your own finances, you may decide to underwrite your child's expenses, either with a loan or an outright gift.

Loaning or giving your child money is an obvious and logical choice if you can afford to do it. If you are worried that he will take advantage of your generosity, you can also set a time limit on financial help. For instance, without withdrawing himself emotionally, Charlie might have told Jack, "I think it would be great if you moved in with me for three months while you're looking for a new job." Or, "I'll pay half your rent for eight months."

Parents can also provide access to money from other sources, including other family members, trust funds, or bank loans. For instance, you might refinance your mortgage to cover your child's large expenses or pay off a loan for him, or you may consider co-signing a loan with your child.

Another way to help financially is to invest in additional training for your child, particularly if she wants to learn a skill that will help secure a new job, such as a course in public speaking or planning or management. Don't encourage your child to retreat into academia as an antidote to the real world, but specific skill enhancement can be enormously useful, especially if it turns your child in the direction of genuine enthusiasm.

No matter how much money you decide to offer, it never precludes your personal support. Believe it or not, some people write a check, but forget the child's other needs—a parent's open mind and caring heart.

Interim Jobs

Parents can help in ways other than giving financial support. You can also contribute innovative ideas for earning interim money. The point is to figure out how your client can earn the most money for the effort, while preserving time and energy for the job search.

Interim jobs boost self-image and help alleviate anxiety, but they need to be chosen with care. Your client should take a job that suits his personality. For one person, tending bar might be fun, another might feel embarrassed.

Ideally, even an interim job should be in the arena of your client's ultimate interest, particularly if your client *thinks* he wants to change fields but isn't certain. An interim job related to the field of interest may provide tremendous amounts of information, and it may turn out to be exactly the stepping-stone needed to progress in this new direction.

Another good interim solution is arranging to be an outside supplier or consultant to a past employer, assuming cordial relations have been maintained. Increasingly, this is an attractive option to both employee and employer. Frequently, too, this arrangement turns out to be the source of a permanent new business.

An interim job will automatically reduce the time your client has to spend surveying, so unless the job is directly in the field of interest, your client will have to extend the time frame of the job search. But in all likelihood, the boost that the interim work will give your client's psyche will more than compensate for the extra time.

Volunteer work is also a good bet. Although it doesn't produce income, volunteer work keeps your client in the swim of activity, teaches skills, and helps maintain a sense of self-worth. (However, the work shouldn't be so time consuming that it diverts your client from job hunting.)

Perhaps your client has a hobby that translates into a product or service that could generate income. I know one family who runs a mail-order food-canning operation out of the garage. They pickle unique food—from watermelon to green tomatoes—and ship them throughout the country. The business started as their son's weekend hobby.

Another woman I know painted ceramic tiles as a hobby. Her neighbors fell in love with the patterns and commissioned tiles for their homes. Ultimately, her mother set her up in business. Now she's painting bathroom and kitchen tiles for contractors and interior designers throughout the city. Her business currently employs 12 people and is growing rapidly.

Moving Back Home

If you both agree this is a good option, treat your adult child as you would any other friend on a long-term visit. You would expect him to cook some meals, clean his room and pitch in on the common spaces. Keep it light. Say, "I'd love to have you back—it will share the load—but this is what I need you to contribute."

Regardless of your particular family dynamic, establish a date when you will sit down together and talk about how the living arrangement is working out and how the job search is progressing. For example, Charlie and Jack could have gotten off to a better start if they had set a date when they would sit down and reevaluate their arrangement. This would have kept the return visit from being entirely open-ended, and it also would have avoided the setting of a premature date by which the job search had to be concluded. Knowing that you're supposed to talk when a particular date rolls around also means that when the time comes, feelings can be expressed without any blame or guilt attached.

If your adult child is moving back home with a spouse and children of his own, you can expect to have a lot of fun and a very special time together—or you can find yourself living in a tension-filled house of horrors. It helps to set ground rules in advance. For instance, how often are you and your spouse willing to baby-sit? Try to set up private time and private space for each family. With good humor, anything can work, but it does take an extra measure of flexibility on your part.

In whatever "at home" arrangement you make with your child, bear in mind that the underlying purpose is to help him be productively and happily employed again. Don't let the logistics of living together be a drag on that. If the home duties you require interfere with the time your child/client needs to be out surveying, interviewing, proposing, or studying, your hospitality will be more of a hindrance than a help.

Revisiting Skills

You can turn your client's most devastating job loss into a positive experience by asking:

- What did you learn doing this job?
- What did you accomplish?
- Which skills did you use most on this job?
- Which were your best skills?
- Which new skills were developed during the job?
- What might have made this job a better experience?
- Can you look for those circumstances now in a new job?

Ask your client to revisit her skills by telling stories about the job. What may start out as a litany of complaints will inevitably reveal at least a few positives. She will recall what she learned from the experience and will begin to remember the good things that occurred. No job is all bad. The skills she liked to use most will help point the way to the next potential employer. She will also be able to evaluate the aspects of the job, the people, and the environment that she most enjoyed. This kind of evaluation will sharpen her judgment for the time when she is ready to choose her next employer. (See exercise 5.)

TOUGH QUESTIONS, SMART ANSWERS

Whether your client is at a party or on a job interview, he is likely to encounter friends and total strangers who ask uncomfortable questions. Here are some of the most typical questions and positive ways to redirect the conversation.

Q: "How long have you been out of work?"

A: "Let me tell you what I've been doing. I'm involved in the most interesting investigation. . . ." Your client should launch into a description of his latest survey. If he keeps his response quick and upbeat, he need never answer the original question.

Q: "What are you doing now?"

A: "I'm researching an idea I developed about how to do X." The idea is to always relate the answer to new work. In a job interview, your client can describe some ideas he has about solving a particular issue and explain that he's given himself a time frame to explore them. He *is* working on something important—researching for himself.

Q: "Why did you leave your last position?"

A: If your client was fired in a general layoff, he should say so. Usually he will have an opportunity to mention something proactive he did, like electing to take advantage of a severance package. If the firing was not part of a layoff, the answer should be truthful, but without ever using the word "fired." What *can* he say? Something like:

"I had completed my project, and there really wasn't additional work in the areas for which I am most suited. It was time for me to go." Or:

"A new manager was brought in who wanted her own people." Or, if worried about an unfavorable reference:

"My boss and I didn't see eye to eye on what I viewed as a serious business matter."

Nothing should be said to denigrate previous employers. Canny interviewers respect the professionalism of job candidates who do not bad-mouth former employers or co-workers. Whatever your client does, he must not talk about this event at any great length. He should be brief and positive.

If fired for cause, suggest that your client avoid mentioning the previous employer at all. He should say simply that it was time to go because his interests lay in another direction. Firing for cause is usually stealing or otherwise breaking the law. Try to make sure that whatever got him in trouble will not occur again. He could approach smaller companies, which may not run the extensive background checks a large corporation does. He can start to rebuild his reputation from there.

This positive review will also help your client see the old job in a happier light. She might even be able to ask:

• What could I have done a little differently?
• Was there someone else in the department who fared better?
• Why did that person get along better?
• What did he or she do?

Pondering these questions may reveal something about the company's culture or her own behavior that she wants to avoid in the next job. The key to helping your client get a better perspective is to keep asking questions that help her reflect positively on the past.

I had a client who was desperate to quit her job. To the outside world she was a successful, high-profile political adviser. Yet she hated this job so much that she was unable to write a single life-story vignette about her work. Finally, I prodded her to choose one isolated event and describe it. She wrote about a report she had prepared for a congressional candidate, but she belittled herself and dismissed the report by saying, "No one paid attention to it, anyway."

I kept after her. "How did you develop your idea? How did you decide to make certain recommendations?" I bombarded her with "how" questions that required responses. Eventually she was able to salvage the positive and recall some subtle triumphs.

Revisit Goals

A job loss is also a good time to revisit goals. Was the last job really leading in the direction your client wanted? Perhaps he was crunching numbers while dreaming about financial planning for middle-income investors.

Help your client develop a little survey around a new concept of something he would like to accomplish next. It may seem remote to your client that he actually *can* afford to think about what he'd most like to do at a time when he feels so desperate, but explain that his future welfare depends on it. Once he gets into surveying (as described in Chapters 5 and 6), momentum will begin carrying him, and you will both feel better. Being out among people inevitably leads to serendipity—that fortunate coincidence of luck and the ability to recognize it.

Activities and Exercises

Things to Think on Alone

1. When your child is out of work, be open about your own feelings. To sort these out, consider:

• Do you and your client disagree about his next move?
• Does his being out of work bring back memories of similar situations of your own? How did you feel about these? (For example, "When I lost my job, no one ever helped me.")
• Do you feel your client is out of work because of "the same old thing" he's been doing since childhood? (It may be true, but if you voice it, you will help create a self-fulfilling prophecy.)
• How do you feel about helping your client financially?
• Does his being out of work make *you* feel inadequate?
• In the past, would you have liked to quit a job, but stayed on for financial security? If your client quit his job, do you resent his decision?
• Are you afraid that your client won't be able to fend for himself without you?

2. Do you and your spouse agree on how much help to give, whether emotional or financial? If not, how will this difference of opinion affect your child?

Things to Think on Together

3. What are the benefits of your child/client moving back home? The disadvantages? How could the terms of the "move in" be adjusted so that benefits are maximized?

4. How can you ensure that any financial help you give doesn't demoralize your client or make her feel dependent?

Things to Do Together

5. Look back at this last job, and think about its positive aspects. Draw a line down the center of a page in your notebook and put "Positives" on one side, "Negatives" on the other. List what was good, if anything. What was accomplished? Think beyond skills. Maybe the location was fantastic, or the sense of balance between home and work was excellent.

On the negative side, list all the aspects of the job your client disliked, even hated: What working conditions were unpleasant, what the people were lacking, what support he didn't get that he needed—all the things that really ticked him off.

Use these two lists to help determine criteria for the next working situation.

6. Help your client structure a survey plan on paper (see Chapter 6). Make a special effort to think of appropriate contacts for your client to visit or consult with. Optimistic assistance is the order of the day. It has never been more important for your client to present himself in a focused, confident manner. Your attitude will give him a model to follow.

7. During the ensuing job hunt, role-play typical interview questions so your client will feel comfortable answering toughies like, "Why did you leave your last job?" "How long have you been out of work?" "Were you fired?" "Why?" "Did you and your former employer have any disagreements?" "What salary were you making?" (See box "Tough Questions, Smart Answers," page 258. Also read through the interview questions in Chapter 10.)

Chapter Fifteen

"*I Hate My Job!*"

P at's first job after college was as an administrative assistant in a public relations firm; over the course of two years she worked her way up to assistant account executive. For a while Pat found the work stimulating, but eventually she tired of the long hours, demanding clients, and tremendous amount of detail work. Ironically, it was her compulsive attention to minutiae that won her kudos from her boss. "Nothing slips through the cracks with Pat on board," he often said.

She didn't fare as well when it came to writing press releases. "That's one skill that really gets you promoted in this business," she said, "and I don't have it. I'd rather have my teeth pulled than write another press release."

Though she wanted to try something new, Pat felt typecast. "My resume is all public relations," she said. "Where else can I go?"

Another of my clients was a professor of economics named Michael. His outgoing personality was a hit with students, but he was a little too unorthodox to play the politics necessary to ensure tenure at his university. Through various connections he was offered an analyst's job on Wall Street. Michael's friends and family thought this move was too good to be true. Not only had he, according to his parents, found a berth in the "real" world as opposed to the "ivory-tower" world, but the pay was phenomenal.

When this gregarious fellow reported to work, the firm relegated him to a quiet back office, well off the beaten track. He was expected to spend each day generating analyses by pouring over vast numbers of computer printouts and publications. Michael liked the analytical part of his job but felt totally isolated. Everyone else seemed too busy to talk to him. Before long, he hated his work. He began to suffer severe stomach pains, sleepless nights, and a host of other psychosomatic symptoms.

Pat and Michael reacted quite differently to their unhappy work situations. Pat hadn't a clue about what she wanted to do nor what she was qualified for. Looking for a way out, she entered law school. Three years later, degree in hand, she still didn't know what she wanted to do.

By contrast, Michael took a good look at himself and set about revolutionizing his life. First he examined his skills, his likes and dislikes, and married them to his goals. He knew he wanted to get back to using his presentation skills, and he wanted to interact with people.

Michael came up with an idea for an annual publication telling businesses how to get the least expensive, most efficient long-distance telephone services for their needs. Then he set about surveying to find out if anyone was interested in his concept. When he got a favorable response, Michael put up his own money to publish the first issue. Product in hand, he got himself booked on the seminar circuit, teaching business representatives how to make the most of his information. That was 10 years ago. His enterprise is thriving, with innovations in each new edition of the book.

Pinpointing What's Wrong

Quitting is not always the best or only answer to "I hate my job." In fact, an unhappy job situation can be an ideal laboratory for exploring the future. By examining the dynamic of the unhappy job, your client may discover what he really wants to do. Sometimes careful analysis will reveal changes your client can make—in himself or in the job—to drastically improve the situation. Some people, after analyzing their skills, interests, and goals, decide to remain with the company but switch divisions. Others choose to move on.

No decision should be made in haste. (If your client quits his job suddenly, he is likely to precipitously choose another job that also makes him miserable. What we don't resolve, we tend to repeat.) If your client can analyze his problems, he may feel less trapped and more calm. You can help him do this by engaging him in an in-depth exploration of what is wrong and what is right about the present job. These conversations will be highly productive. For one thing, they will make him feel that he's begun to take action and will drain the sense of urgency from the situation. This is important because your client needs to buy time. Even if he does decide to quit, the conventional wisdom is that it's easier to get a job if you already have one. (In reality, that's not the case, but as long as our psyches make us think so, it seems to work that way.) If your client decides it would be wiser for him to hang onto the job for a while, relations must be stabilized.

When a client is in trouble on the job, the most important thing you, the coach, can do is remain open-minded. Instead of offering a quick fix or a criticism, keep listening. "Tell me about it" is still the best comment any friend can make.

As your client talks, what seems like global job misery begins to break down into specifics. Unhappiness on the job generally involves one or more of eight serious problems.

Now is the perfect opportunity to delve into these conditions and pinpoint your client's real concerns. Your client may think she faces only one of these issues, but it's worthwhile to review them *all.*

IDENTIFYING THE PROBLEM

To pinpoint job problems, try these questions:

- How did you feel when you first took the job?
- How long have you felt unhappy?
- Can you remember a particular event that triggered your unhappiness?
- What aspects of the job have you enjoyed the most?
- How often do you get to perform them?
- Do you think your boss values your skills?
- How important do your skills seem to be to the organization?
- What do you hate most about what you do?
- Has this dislike gotten worse lately—or did you always feel it?
- What do you find yourself dreaming of doing instead?
- If you could change one thing about your job, what would it be?

Encourage your client to write down responses as well as tell them to you. Probe his answers by asking, "Why is that?" "Tell me more about that."

PROBLEM
1

"I HATE MY BOSS"

This is number one on the hit parade of job problems. The boss may demand work your client doesn't enjoy. Maybe their communication is faulty. Perhaps their goals and values clash. Any time there is a conflict between employee and boss, it's wise for them to sit down and discuss the issue (unless there have been previous, unproductive conversations).

Communication is often the problem. Perhaps this boss likes receiving information orally, and your client showers her with memos. Or vice versa. Perhaps this boss doesn't like sweating the small stuff, and your client runs every detail past her. If faulty communication is part of the toxic mix, suggest that your client observe how his boss likes to receive information from others. Does she ask to be kept constantly up to date via memos? Or does she prefer to get a big picture of staff activities at weekly meetings. A simple change in approach may ease tension. Once communication improves, your client may find the boss isn't so bad after all.

All that said, sometimes employee-boss relations are unsolvable. To avoid repeating the same problem in the future, your client should analyze "boss" qualities that he likes and dislikes. Then when surveying to scope out his next move, he should measure a prospective boss against this list of criteria. If a boss doesn't measure up, chances are history will repeat itself.

PROBLEM
2

SKILLS

Inadequate skills are another common problem. Your client may not possess the right skills for the job, or perhaps he has the skills but doesn't enjoy using them.

Refer to your client's life stories to see how he has performed various skills in the past. What are his best skills? Do

TACTICS FOR CONVERSATIONS WITH AN IMPOSSIBLE BOSS

Advise your client to proceed along these lines:

• Begin with something honestly flattering.

> ("Your presentation to the management group today really piqued their interest." Or, "Your approach to convincing Al to buy from us was a good lesson for all of us.")

• Ask if it is a convenient time to talk for a few minutes.

> ("I wonder if you could give me a few minutes now? Or would later in the week be more convenient?" Or, "I would appreciate spending a few minutes with you to explore some issues on my mind. When this week do you think you might spare some time?")

• Decide ahead of time what you would like to result from the conversation—write it down and begin gently.

> ("For some time I have been thinking I might be more productive for you in _____." Or, "It would be a great help to me if you could give me some honest feedback on how you like _____.")

• Suggest ways this boss might get more of what he or she wants.

("Would it be possible for me to be assigned to understudy Grace for a week? How do you think that might work?" Or, "How would you like it if I were to do some research on Al's emerging market in South America?")

- Propose an action step to capitalize on your boss's reactions.

    ("This is very helpful. Suppose I draw up a tentative schedule and have it on your desk day after tomorrow?" Or, simply, "I appreciate what you have said to me. I'd like to think about it and get back to you with some constructive suggestions by next week.")

- Confirm your appreciation of the attention given to you, whatever the outcome, and restate the essence of what you have heard.

    ("Thank you for what has been an important few minutes for me. I didn't realize before that you perceived my sales approach as too soft for this company." Or, "You were really good to give me your attention when I know you have a lot of other things on your mind. And now I understand your feelings about the problems I have been having meeting my deadlines.")

- End on an upbeat note.

    ("I'll see if I can make this talk worthwhile for both of us.")

they come naturally? Usually our best skills do come easily, almost without training.

Remember Pat, the public relations account executive? Her mother couldn't understand why she had trouble writing press releases. She remembered Pat's straight-A record in English and countless well-written research papers. She thought her daughter's academic writing skill automatically translated into public relations. She made the common mistake of generalizing skills. Pat later said, "In P.R. you have to write 'hot' copy. You need a style that punches across the story in an exciting way, and you either have it or you don't. That just wasn't my talent."

On the other hand, your client's skills may be perfectly good, but he may not enjoy the context in which he's required to use them. He may like public speaking, for example, but not what he's talking about. A skill enjoyed under some circumstances may be intolerable under others.

Now is the time for your client to reexamine his skills and identify them at another level. Pay attention to how the skill was best used and the environment in which it was most enjoyed.

For example, if your client is a "good writer," what kind of things does she enjoy writing most?

• Novels or poetry?
• On-the-scene journalism or in-depth analyses?
• Advertising jingles or lyrics to a Broadway musical?

Under what circumstances does she most enjoy this skill?

• Completely alone or in collaboration?
• In a staff setting or freelance?
• On assignment or with the parameters up to her?

Break down each skill in the same manner. Is your client "detail oriented"? How does she keep track of things?

- How many issues she can successfully monitor at once?
- Does she write everything down or keep it in her head?
- Does she group similar tasks together or work through each one methodically?

Is your client an "effective communicator"?

- Orally or on paper?
- In a discussion or when giving a speech?
- With groups of similar professionals or the general public?

If your client discovers that her aptitude for the skills needed for the current job is weak or nonexistent, it's unlikely that additional training will fix things up. Good skills usually come easily. Chances are if she hasn't already begun to pick up the skill on the job, it will probably be an uphill battle.

One glaring exception to this rule is public speaking, which always improves dramatically with training and experience. This important business skill intimidates most people, and nearly everybody needs improvement, which comes with lots of training and practice.

There are two other exceptions: number crunching and computer literacy. Many people are terrified of numbers—but most can benefit from learning more about accounting, budgets, investments, and many other business accounting procedures. Basic computer literacy can also be learned by most people. If public speaking, numbers, or computer literacy is the skill problem, training can definitely help your client improve his performance on the job.

If it turns out that weak skills are the root of the problem and training will not ameliorate it, a job may still be preserved if your client wants to try hard enough. Is there someone else in his department who enjoys doing the task your client doesn't? Is it possible to work out a trade? This may mean switching jobs within the unit or simply redefining the job description.

It's possible that your client has an important skill that he never gets to use on the job. Perhaps this is the root of his job dissatisfaction. He might propose to restructure his job to incorporate this skill. Or another department in the same organization might value the skill.

PROBLEM
3

TROUBLE WITH MY CO-WORKERS

Sometimes co-workers just don't click. There are any number of possible reasons: conflict in values, differences in abilities, gender issues, political gamesmanship, attitude problems—all these can cause a basic rift among co-workers that may be virtually uncorrectable. It's true that co-workers don't have to like each other to function together effectively, but they do need to have similar approaches to work.

Tanya came to me because she felt out of place in her job as a production coordinator for a large printer. Tanya, who is task oriented by nature, had previously worked compatibly with a mentor-boss on a few projects, but, for the most part, she preferred to work alone. Doing the job well was her chief concern. She'd rather be right about the job than be on the right side of her boss or her co-workers. While pleasant, she didn't hesitate to say what she thought, even if it was not what people wanted to hear.

Unfortunately, her office then was extremely political (a go-along-to-get-along sort of place), and Tanya made few friends among her co-workers. She felt shunned by her colleagues, causing her to retreat into herself even further. Ultimately her boss eliminated Tanya's job as a way of firing her. Half of her co-workers were sorry to see her leave because her work was excellent; the other half were delighted because they felt Tanya just "didn't fit in."

Once Tanya stopped feeling rejected, she was able to glean some valuable information from this experience. In choosing her next job, she made sure that she had a boss who had a reputation for high work standards and who valued his staff's end product.

Personality mismatches are common problems, and workers in a politically-charged office often don't play fair. Perhaps a co-worker is climbing over your client or taking credit for his work. It's important that your client let the boss know about his contribution. He might say, "Joe did a wonderful job putting this report together and I wanted you to know how I helped—I provided data for sections three, four, and five, and the charts. I'd like to have another opportunity to do this kind of work in the future."

The next time, your client should put his name on his work, back up his contributions with documentation, and make sure, in little ways, that his efforts come to the attention of others. The object is to protect himself without ever criticizing his co-workers. Another strategy is to ask to enlarge his work team, thereby widening the circle of compatible people.

Conflicts with co-workers can also be gender issues. In some professions men outnumber the women (and vice versa). Women may believe the men in their units are moving faster than they are, and resent this.

If your client feels she is being overlooked in her company, she should ask herself why others in her unit are getting more attention. Has she asked for more responsibility, a promotion or new projects? Team spirit is a fine concept, but more often it's every woman (or man) for herself (or himself), so your client should not expect the corporation to nurture her.

If your client has been teamed with a co-worker he hates, he might try coping with the situation before quitting. The problem may or may not be resolvable, but there are ways of trying. Perhaps the team can be reshuffled and your client reassigned. He can say to the boss, "We're just two people who don't think the same way. I'd like to explore a

SEXUAL HARASSMENT
AND DISCRIMINATION

I f your client is being either sexually harassed or discriminated against, that's a more than adequate reason for being unhappy on the job. Federal laws, executive orders, and selected federal-grant programs bar discrimination in employment based on race, color, religion, sex, national origin, and handicap. It would be a good idea for your client to discuss the offense on a confidential basis with one or two knowledgeable friends outside the workplace before taking any action internally.

Legal action should be carefully weighed: It is difficult to build an airtight case, a great deal of time and negative energy will be consumed by the process, and, win or lose, your client will carry the action like a brand. It makes sense to proceed only if the odds of winning are high, if your client is not counting on working in the same industry again, or if she (or he) is determined to make the way easier for others with similar complaints.

This doesn't mean that your client should give up

different assignment where I think I could be more productive." Better yet, your client can try to figure out in advance what the boss might need and shift the focus from personality conflict to an opportunity for the organization. Once again, find the need and create the job.

There are lots of reasons for mismatches. Perhaps neither the product he's working on nor his co-workers have anything in common with your client. I heard a former without a fight. It's just that every battle has a price, and she should be aware of all the consequences. Every case and every individual are different.

There are other choices for effective action: confronting the offender clearly, firmly, and calmly; presenting the case to the human resources or personnel department, with evidence plainly in hand; or deftly diffusing inappropriate references or implied discrimination with humor. Humor can be a powerful weapon, if your client has the skills to pull it off.

By and large, if your client is in an organization or is working under a boss who condones sexual harassment or discrimination either tacitly or by behavior, urge him or her to make plans to leave.

For information from the Equal Employment Opportunity Commission write or call: EEOC, 2401 E Street NW, Washington, DC 20507 (202-634-6922).

In the "Advocacy Groups" section of the resource section you will find organizations for specific groups, such as the handicapped, minorities, and women. (Martha Merrill Doss's book *Women's Organizations: A National Directory* lists more than 2,000 women's organizations, local and nationwide.)

professor, speaking at a college career-planning center, share her "success story" with other professors who had been denied tenure. With the center's help, she had orchestrated a switch from academia to a major chemical manufacturer. She had never dreamed she would work with chemicals, but the job paid handsomely and used her research savvy.

She had to relocate, however, leaving a town with cultural resources she valued and many close friends. When questioned, she commented, "I miss having someone to talk to—all my co-workers like to talk about is who won the basketball game last night. I wonder if they even know who Mozart was. It wouldn't be so bad, but between the long hours and my long commute, I can't seem to find the time to get into the life of the community, such as it is."

The saddest part of this tale is that neither she nor the center which had "helped" her suspected she had unnecessarily traded away her quality of life. Trouble was surely down the road, for money can't compensate for unfilled personal needs.

PROBLEM 4 — MISMATCHED CORPORATE AND PERSONAL VALUES

Corporations have personalities, too. They may be highly competitive or laid-back, rigid or unconventional, staid or risk-taking, ruthless or consumer-sensitive.

If your client's personality and her employer's don't match, there can be trouble. For example, if your client is highly entrepreneurial, but her corporation is restrictive and conservative, tending to squash creativity, she probably will not thrive there. Likewise, if your client is a casual person who despises the navy suit routine, she should avoid formal companies with their spoken or unspoken dress codes.

Terry was a speech writer who landed a job working for a major auto manufacturer. The first day on the job he rearranged his office so the desk faced the window, to take advantage of the beautiful view. And he shut his door to cut down on noise and concentrate on his first assignment.

That afternoon he was called on the carpet by his superior. "Offices are expected to have a standard arrangement, with desks facing the door. Doors are to be open at all times," he said, spouting company policy. Luckily, they were able to reach a compromise. Terry conformed to policy three days a week and worked at home two days.

More disturbing is if your client is at odds with the employer's values and ethics. What if the organization is not too precise about honesty and your client is? Or the company is fanatical about schedules and your client isn't? Or suppose your client doesn't value his employer's product or service? These are fundamental and inescapable problems. Your client will never be happy if he compromises on ethics or values. (See box "Measuring a Potential Employer's Integrity," page 128.) He should ask not only, "How important is this job to what I want to accomplish with my life?" but "Is the way they go about doing it in tune with my standards?" If the answer to the latter question is "No," then he should start thinking about ways of achieving his goals that are.

One of my clients was a broker who loved the financial world, but she was tired of helping the rich get richer. As enthusiasm for her job waned, she wondered what to do. Eventually she developed her own firm specializing in asset management for foundations and wealthy individuals whose priority was investing in innovative educational programs, which happened to be at the center of her own goal structure.

PROBLEM	**"I'M SO BORED!"**
5	If your client is not performing challenging tasks or moving forward on the job, she's bound to get bored. Boredom is an indication that she's

practicing her skills at too low a level. The thrill is gone.

As boredom takes over, we become less disciplined and less creative. But ultimately it's the person who's bored who is responsible for enhancing the job. Suggest that your client carry out a small survey within her unit or the organization overall. Perhaps she can uncover a need and make a proposal to do something that will be a real challenge.

Susan, for example, took a part-time job doing mindless office work for a national cooking magazine. For the most part, she typed recipes into a computer. After the first month, she was utterly bored but held onto the job for the paycheck. By the second month, Susan realized she was being asked to input many of the same recipes over and over again as special editions of the magazine and cookbooks were prepared for publication. In the present computer system, recipes were stored just long enough to transmit to the type house for use in a single issue. In other words, the magazine was using its sophisticated computer like a typewriter.

A computer buff herself, Susan set to work devising a program that stored recipes for easy retrieval. It allowed every recipe to be accessed by title, main ingredient, or any other important characteristic, such as whether it was a dessert, soup, appetizer, bread, entrée, and so forth. The program cut the workload dramatically, and the magazine paid handsomely for her contribution. She got her challenge and was justifiably proud of her accomplishment.

Your client should also be on the lookout for opportunities within the company. Perhaps he can volunteer for an intercompany task force—from organizing the company picnic to brainstorming a new product line to starting a volunteer group. Surveying within the very organization your client already works for can pay big dividends.

PROBLEM 6	**"I'M STRESSED OUT!"**

Entry-level jobs are reactive in nature—someone tells you to do something and you do it. Perhaps your client feels pressure to perform at top speed, forfeiting careful planning to get the job done. Often he doesn't have a full understanding of how what he's doing fits into the company's purpose, and is left to simply react to the next demand. This can lead to high stress. A young person new on the job may feel he has to do everything alone to prove he's worthy of having been hired, which just makes it all feel worse. If your client is feeling stressed out, here are some remedies that may help.

Identify the source of the stress. Ask your client to list the sources of pressure she feels on the job. A highly demanding boss? A period of high demand in the organization? No control over decisions? Incompetent co-workers? Fear of poor performance? Anxiety about skills? Time pressures? Outside pressures? Uncertain business climate? Just knowing where the stress is coming from helps put things in perspective and gives your client a shot at remedying the situation.

See the big picture. Your client can reduce anxiety by learning why a particular task is important. He can ask, "How does it fit in with the department's work? What other results are we looking for?" Equipped with a glimpse of the future for the company, he will feel less stress.

Ask for help. It is important for your client to ask for help before becoming completely overstressed. Often there are resources in place to help him out. Colleagues may be able to devise ways to meet the unit's load in a fair manner. Some chores may be divided. Perhaps another employee can be called on for help or a temp could be hired to handle minor paperwork.

Slow down. New technology, everybody's helper, causes stress all its own. As the intervals between communications become shorter—with the advent of faxes, electronic mail, overnight mail—decisions must be made much faster. On a low level, faster may be better; but at a high level of decision making, faster often leads to poor judgment. Sometimes the way to reduce stress is simply to slow down—not respond quickly, even if technology permits rapid turnaround.

Stress busters. Every job has periods of intense pressure. Periodic stress can be reduced by taking a 15-minute nap at lunchtime, going for a walk, exercising, or playing a game. Anything that gets your client away from his desk—especially if it gets fresh oxygen into his system—is a boon. Encourage your client to be good to himself. If he has to work late at night, he can send out for a nice dinner instead of grabbing a hamburger at his desk. When someone is under pressure, it's important to eat right and get enough sleep. Especially, get enough sleep!

Most young people believe they're immortal. They figure they can work out at six in the morning, be at their desks by eight, go for drinks after work, eat dinner at ten, disco at midnight, and be ready to go again at six the next day. Actually, they *can* do this—but not forever, and not without repercussions.

PROBLEM
7

LOUSY ENVIRONMENT

A tiny windowless office . . . an impersonal cubicle in an open-plan office . . . piped-in Muzak . . . a sealed building with stale air . . . a long commute via public transportation or on congested roads . . . insufficient light . . . poor equipment . . . proximity to smokers . . . too much noise . . . too much quiet. The list of unpleasant working conditions is long and usually quite personal—what bothers one person doesn't faze another. Even if your client carefully considered the working environment before deciding on the job, environments can change. Offices move, bosses change, workers get reassigned, and cutbacks limit refurbishing.

In some cases it is easy enough to deal with the issue directly. For instance, if your client is unhappy with her chair, she could search the office for a replacement or go out and purchase one that suits her. The company may or may not be willing to reimburse her, but either way, the issue has been speedily resolved.

When Kay was hired by the promotion department of a trade-publishing house in the early 1980s (before a computer on every desk became de rigueur), she was appalled to discover she had access to only two ancient manual typewriters.

"I was a fresh kid, and I complained within two weeks. My job consisted of writing and revising copy for three catalogs a year, plus brochures, a status report, and countless memos. I told my boss I simply could not turn out the quality work she expected with what amounted to antiquated tools. She laughed, and ordered up a slick electric memory typewriter. My co-worker was amazed—she had accepted the old typewriters as one of the givens of her employment. It never occurred to me *not* to complain! Working to deadline was hard enough. Good tools were needed to do the job."

If your client loves his job but hates the working conditions, encourage him to take matters into his own hands. Perhaps he can negotiate to work at home some of the time. He could use performance as a bargaining chip; for example, when he turns in the next project, he might try negotiating for a better office, a door that closes, access to voice mail, his own telephone, or whatever means the most to him.

If nothing works, and if the environmental issue is severe, it's definitely worth seeking a change in employment or a transfer within the organization. It will be imperative in this case for your client to survey well before proposing the change.

| PROBLEM **8** | **"NOBODY APPRECIATES ME"** |

Frequently, I find this is more the fault of the person feeling unappreciated than anyone else. Some bosses give praise, plus a dash of criticism—but the employee hears only the negative (which may not even be negative, rather merely a suggestion for even better performance). Sometimes a boss is lavish with affirmations, but is unable to give generous raises and the employee feels slighted.

Your client should observe whether others in her department are getting kudos. Perhaps the whole department is neglected. This suggests that either the unit is undervalued by the organization or the unit's boss is ineffective. If it's just your client who feels unhappy, perhaps she can find some clues in the work or behavior of others in the unit. What kind of assignments do they have? Perhaps hers aren't as valuable. Are others getting plum assignments because of good relationships with superiors? Seniority? Accomplishment? Good bosses give employees feedback—pro and con—close to the event. If response to her work is not forthcoming, your client should not be afraid to ask for it. In other words, both being and feeling appreciated is sometimes a matter of managing a boss skillfully.

Your client can initiate conversations to let the boss know how hard she is working to achieve the desired result, what steps she is taking to ensure timely delivery, and how she is training herself to a higher level of proficiency. If time is too short for oral updates, suggest she regularly write memos: "Just to Keep You Up to Date," or "In Preparation for . . . ," or "Conclusions on Project Completion."

Performance Appraisals. Many people are so task oriented they worry about getting the job done but fail to position work so others will notice. It's possible for your client to take an active stance without being obnoxious, and the performance appraisal is the standard opportunity. Whether the annual performance appraisal is informal or quite strict, with a lot of paperwork, your client should prepare a list of what he's accomplished in the preceding year and be prepared to back it up in a factual, but not boastful, way ("I'd like to demonstrate the kinds of contributions I have made"). These accomplishments should relate to the expectations laid out at the last appraisal or at the time your client moved into the position.

Your client and his boss should discuss setting up mutually acceptable measurements for performance. That way he will have realistic objectives and feel proud of himself when he achieves them. It's important to learn how to give ourselves some pats on the back, since we can't always depend on others for praise. Ultimately, if your client still feels that his boss doesn't appreciate his work or by nature is incapable of giving appropriate praise and guidance, he should make this a very high item on his criteria list for choosing his next boss.

If any of these issues continues to seem intractable after attempts to better them, your client should definitely make plans to find other work. The status quo is unacceptable. Not addressing these issues invites discomfort far greater than mere job unhappiness, including settling into apathy, getting fired, becoming ill, or taking out frustration on personal relationships. Your client can begin surveying while adopting coping strategies to make his remaining time on the current job more bearable.

Occasionally psychological counseling is indicated. Are other things going on in your client's life that contribute to a negative frame of mind? Is your client ending a personal relationship, having money problems, coping with an addiction, ill health? Problems in any one arena—work, health, or relationships—affect performance in all three. If your client can improve one area, he'll begin feeling better. Then, it will feel more possible to work on changing the others.

Activities and Exercises

Things to Think on Alone

1. Are you adding to your client's stress? Ask yourself:

- Am I heaping more demands on him?
- When my client spends time with me, do I increase pressure by asking, "What did you accomplish today?" "Have you gotten that report out yet?" "Closed that deal yet?"
- When I ask questions, do I remember to offer help?

Things to Think on Together

2. Some people are very sensitive to their work environment. The wrong conditions can literally destroy their performance. How sensitive is your client to her environment?

• Is she affected by the amount of light?
• How important is comfort, and what's her idea of comfort?
• How much interest does your client take in how his bedroom or apartment looks?
• How action oriented is your client, compared to what is demanded by his job?
• How much quiet or noise does your client naturally surround himself with? Are her working conditions similar?
• Does your client seem to be surrounded at work by the kind of people she enjoys and respects?

Things to Do Together

3. Taking Measure of the Boss: Ask your client to reread and rethink his "Likes and Dislikes" and "Admirations" lists. Ask him to reflect on how his boss compares.

4. Taking Measure of Me: Does your client have the right skills for the job?

Part 1: Ask your client about the times in which he remembers performing his top skills well. In what setting was he performing these? Who else was there? List each event in its context and look for the common denominators. Are there similarities to these in his present job?

Part 2: Ask, "What was special about the skills listed in Part 1? Help him choose adverbs or phrases—such as "diligently," "vividly," "with extraordinary detail," "carefully," "humorously," "with little preparation," "rising to the occasion"—which characterize the way he applied each one. These qualifiers shed light on *how* your client works. With this awareness, he is more likely to seek and find a working environment in which his kind of behavior is appreciated and rewarded.

5. What I Need in People: If your client feels like a stranger in a strange land at the office, ask him to recall the circumstances in which he felt most comfortable in the past. Who was there? How was he interacting with them? What were they wearing? How did they respond to your client? What did he care about that they cared about also?

With this information, ask your client to return to his "Likes and Dislikes in People" list (from Chapter 3) and amplify it. The next time your client chooses a job, he will have a better handle on the people part of the equation.

6. The Values Match: Are your client's values mismatched with those of the company?

Part 1: Look back at "What Needs Doing in My World" in Chapter 6. Since completing this exercise, has your client changed his ideas? If so, he might revise the exercise. Is the organization your client works for doing any of the things he lists?

Part 2: What about goals? What does this employer have to do with your client's chosen direction? Reread Chapter 6.

7. Bored?:

Part 1: Ask your client: "Who are the most interesting people in your life? And where are they—in your company, in the family, in a club or an association?" Your client may want to make plans now to spend more time with these people, either socially or professionally.

Part 2: Ask your client to analyze every aspect of the previous two weeks. What did he do that was not particularly enjoyable—that he did not absolutely have to do? How could he change his patterns to make life more interesting?

Part 3: Sometimes people bored on the job are also bored outside the job. Suggest that your client revisit her interests list and add to it. If she were to carry a notepad everywhere, even keeping one by her bed, whenever she had an idea about an interest, she could jot it down. Could this new interest become part of her current job?

8. Reducing Stress: Ask your client when he last had a good laugh on the job? Off the job? Create an interest list (see exercises, Chapter 4). Activities that produce laughter or involve your client in genuine interests will make him relax and could reduce stress on the job (a company baseball team, a reading club, a special-education conference). Come up with a second activity that could be introduced off the job (running at lunch, joining a health club, starting a music group).

9. Analyze Likes and Dislikes in the Working Environment: This is a very individual issue. What you might find trivial may drive your client up the wall. Toby loves working on projects requiring tremendous concentration in a bare room. Lydia gets twitchy if she doesn't have pictures on the walls. Sam likes clutter and gadgets.

Help your client list the ways in which he's worked most productively in life. For example, did he do his homework at a desk in his bedroom or at the kitchen table with the TV blaring? (Refer to exercise 5 in Chapter 7.)

10. Unappreciated? Ask your client, "What do you think your foremost achievements have been in the past year, on or off the job?"

If your client says the entire year was a waste, keep probing. Even a bad year can be turned into something good. Say, "Hey, I'm proud of the way you've stuck it out this year. How do you think you did that?" This should reveal some of your client's skills, and also build pride and self-esteem.

Ask your client to write down his achievements as if he were going to present them to an appraiser. Then ask him to actually do so by telling his boss. Even if it's not time for the annual review, his boss may be open to this discussion if your client presents it as an opportunity for both of them to get more out of the situation. He shouldn't couple this with asking for a raise.

He can open with: "This is where I think I've been and where I am going. Do you think I'm on track?" And he should ask for feedback.

FINISHING TOUCHES

There is one quotation I carry with me in my appointment book. It comes from Helen Keller, the famous deaf and blind speaker and author:

"Life is a great adventure, or it is nothing at all."

You want your child's life to amount to *something*, preferably to encompass more joys than sorrows, to be satisfying, reasonably secure, and, I urge you to add, *to be lived in a spirit of considered adventure.*

No amount of money, prestigious title, or comfortable surroundings can compensate for boredom. Once boredom and apathy take over, it's hard to fan the spark which puts the luster on life. Contemporary parents and children are so concerned about the difficulties of surviving in an uncertain economy that there is real danger of taking all the fun out of the quest for work—which usually takes all the fun out of working, too.

Disciplined pursuit and fun and adventure are not mutually exclusive. The *discipline* part of it, which you as a parent and coach have been instrumental in providing, will ensure that your child/client's adventures are in tune with his goals and will free him to have fun along the way.

In the course of this book, you and your client have acquired new decision-making tools and possibly a new way of working together. With your help, your client has taken or is on his way to taking a significant next step in life: getting a satisfying, appropriate job. This is no mean feat.

Even so, I have the audacity to now ask, "But what about the rest of your client's life? Surely this remarkable individual in whom you have invested such care and energy adds up to more than 'a person with a job'!"

What about the job after this one? What about the other aspects of his life (his interest in exploring primitive cultures, film noir, or outer space; playing the piano; protecting the environment; maintaining his health; nurturing loved ones; or any one of a host of issues which flavor goals and create well-integrated, satisfying lives)?

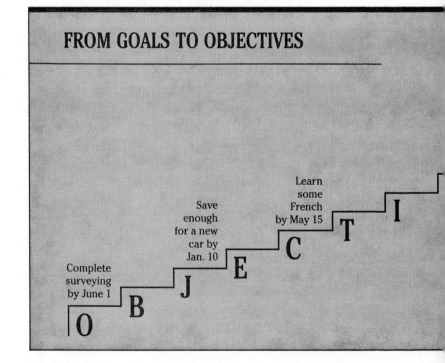

FROM GOALS TO OBJECTIVES

Learn some French by May 15

Save enough for a new car by Jan. 10

Complete surveying by June 1

O B J E C T I

The final step in the Crystal-Barkley process addresses this question. It involves outlining a plan of action for life by literally illustrating your client's goals—what he wants to be learning, working at, helping others to do, changing in the world, or doing for fun—and creating some tangible steps toward achieving them. Having a clear view of goals makes it easier to continue when the going gets rough.

After your client is over the excitement of landing the right job, suggest he review his notes and put together his own picture of his goals and objectives. And I do mean that he should literally draw a picture. Actually drawing the picture is an important part of being able to make it come true. We have learned at Crystal-Barkley that the more clearly our clients actually envision themselves in their ideal scenarios, the closer they come to getting them.

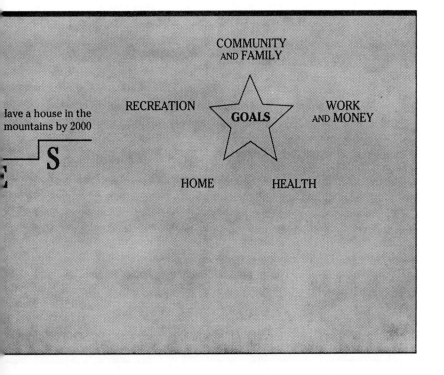

In his picture your client will first illustrate his goals, the centerpiece of this distinctly personal work of art. One person's goals may look like a star, another's more like an octopus with many arms waving in different directions. Someone else's may look like a castle on a hill. It doesn't matter, as long as the image conveys your client's vision of his goals.

Next, your client will find a way to draw in his objectives, the practical steps he plans to complete by certain stated times. Write in the dates. Objectives are subject to additions

A POSTSCRIPT—COMING TO TERMS WITH UNORTHODOX CHOICES

What to mention to your bridge or poker buddies, your boss or your running partners, when you have a child who is pursuing life as a clown, a whale tracker, a surfing instructor, a cartoonist, a sheepherder, a rap singer, an evangelist, an extraterrestrial life researcher, a doll maker—or any one of a host of other occupations which seem beyond the pale of normal existence? Especially if you are worried this son or daughter may never survive economically.

First, don't say anything, until you feel positive about your client's choice.

• Think about how this occupation seems to match your son's or daughter's goals, abilities, determination, stamina, and lifestyle preferences.
• Do some research to learn how the top people in that particular occupation achieved their success— their trials, rewards, and the economic or physical

and revisions as experience sheds more light. Remind your client to put himself in the picture, drawing his own image as he would like to see himself.

Steve, my client, who found himself the right job in New Mexico in Chapter 11, drew a picture of himself in exactly the environment he yearned for in his goals—the mountains with caves and a winding, but not tortuous, road leading through, suggesting challenge. There was a gorgeous sunset behind the mountains and large buildings on the lower reaches of the road, the "big place" where Steve worked.

---

results of their choice. Suggest your client survey the same people.

- Do you feel differently now that you have learned more? Share any new insights with your child.
- Try to help your client gain access to people knowledgeable about the occupation.
- Mention the logic of the match to your buddies, if, after thinking it over, you agree that it is logical.
- Ask gentle questions of your child/client when a mismatch appears evident.
- If your child remains determined, and you still don't think he's made the right choice, keep your counsel and voice only constructive and positive comments. To do otherwise may create an irreparable rift and set your child up for failure. It is consoling to know that virtually every important explorer, philosopher, scientist, or entrepreneur was considered crazy at the onset. Above all, don't close the door. Stay open and receptive to your child's adventures. For, after all, it is our role to bring up our children to do without us.

People stood on the sides of the road, some with arms out-stretched, representing the many whose stress he was reliev-ing. He drew himself, healthy and fit in his running shoes, halfway up the road. Alongside the road were signposts indi-cating Steve's objectives, and nestled in the mountains not too far from the large buildings below was a rustically charming home.

You can see that every person's drawing of his or her goals and objectives is a highly personal work of art. It is because it is so personal and specific that your client will be able to make it happen. Recently one of our clients returned to participate in a second course to "update" her planning process. Paula invited the other members of the group to spend our last day together at her "Italian villa" in the California hills. "You must see it," she said, "because twelve years ago, in the first course I took, I envisioned it exactly as it is." Paula, then a money manager in New York, had actually drawn a picture of herself in the hills of Tuscany overlooking the Mediterranean, where she rode horseback daily and from which she managed accounts for her investor clients.

As we arrived at her new home, we all gasped. It could have been a picture postcard of Tuscany, down to the olive trees overhanging her open windows and the blue Pacific spreading away in the distance. Paula's horse was stabled just down the hill. A shuttered corner of her living room concealed the modern communications equipment she used to work with customers around the country. It was a breath-taking replica of her original vision.

None of this takes place overnight. It requires persis-tence, discipline, and the identification of small, realistic, and rewarding steps along the way. It also requires making surveying a way of life. There will be some surveys which bring immediate gratification. Others require recasting and extended investigation. Your role as the parent/coach is to provide encouragement and perspective.

You will enrich your own life in the course of helping your client follow his dreams. It is inevitable that we learn from those we teach. Today, even though our firm has grown so much that we have a number of consultants on staff and much of my time is devoted to public speaking, designing corporate programs, and expanding directions for the company, I make a point of spending time in workshops with clients. It is I who learn and grow from these associations. Our clients remind me of the extraordinary power of this process. It is my hope, as time goes on, that you also will find your own life enhanced through application of these principles.

A Final Exercise

What opportunities we and our offspring have for leading distinguished lives! For further inspiration, here is the final activity: **"What I Am Grateful For."**

There are certain relationships, events, capacities, phenomena, and opportunities for which everyone feels gratitude. Ask your client to set aside some quiet time and list what these are. Allow plenty of time. Discuss your client's responses with him. How does what he has recognized help him now? How will he use or acknowledge that information in his goals and objectives? You, too, may enjoy engaging in this activity, writing down your own responses. It would be interesting, as well, to discuss your responses with your client. I'm given to wonder if I have ever told my own children how grateful I am for them.

RESOURCES

CONTENTS

FOR MORE INFORMATION . . .

Who am I? Where am I going? How do I get there? Now that you have explored with your client these three vital questions, you and your client may wish to look at more resources to help implement the answers.

We have evaluated much of the current material available to job seekers, and organized it according to the topics listed at left.

I. GENERAL CAREER INFORMATION

A Selection of General Career Books

The Career Decisions Planner, Joan Lloyd (John Wiley & Sons, 1992). Helps readers determine when to make a career move by asking many thought-provoking questions and analyzing relevant scenarios.

Careers and the College Grad, Gigi Ranno (Bob Adams, Inc., published annually). A resource guide aimed at undergraduates. Includes company profiles and contacts.

Choices: A Student Survival Guide for the 1990s, Bryna J. Fireside (Garrett Park Press, 1989). Directed toward high school students making decisions about college, part-time work, internships, volunteer work, etc. Asks such questions as "Who am I?", "What am I doing here?", "Am I having fun yet?"

The Complete Job-Search Handbook: All the Skills You Need to Know to Get Any Job and Have a Good Time Doing It, Howard E. Figler (Henry Holt & Co., 1988). The author identifies 20 skills necessary to target and land a job.

Discover What You're Best At, Barry and Linda Gale (Simon & Schuster, 1990). A test-oriented career aptitude system which aims to identify abilities and a career directory with descriptions of more than 1,100 careers. The goal is to help the reader select a career rather than settle for one.

Feel the Fear, and Do It Anyway, Susan Jeffers (Fawcett, 1988). Exceptionally useful in helping the reader overcome blocks to taking action.

Getting to the Right Job, Steve Cohen and Paulo de Oliveira (Workman Publishing, 1987). Particularly geared to the soon-to-be college graduate.

Guerrilla Tactics in the Job Market, Tom Jackson (Bantam Books, 1987). A compilation of 79 action-oriented tips for getting a job.

Job Power: The Young People's Job Finding Guide, Bernard Haldane, Jean Haldane, and Lowell Martin (Acropolis Books, 1980). Addresses the special issues faced by high school students in their job searches.

Joyce Lain Kennedy's Career Book, Joyce Lain Kennedy and Dr. Darryl Larramore (VGM Career Horizons, 1988). Presents the top 20 fields for liberal arts majors, including more than 300 job opportunities. Guides the reader through the process of career planning and job hunting.

Liberal Education and Careers Today, Howard Figler (Career Press, 1989). How liberal arts graduates can link their majors to employers' needs.

Making Vocational Choices: A Theory of Vocational Personalities and Work Environments, John L. Holland (Prentice Hall, 1985). John Holland has devised a "Self-Directed Search," or "SDS," to help readers pinpoint their areas of career interest and ability, which he calls their "Holland Codes." Companion works include the *Dictionary of Holland Codes,* the *Occupations Finder,* the *Alphabetized Occupations Finder,* and a self-marking test called *The Self-Directed Search.*

The New Quick Job-Hunting Map, Richard Nelson Bolles (Ten Speed Press, 1990). How to create a picture of an ideal job. Helps the reader identify the kind of work climate that will promote professional growth and satisfaction.

The 1993 What Color Is Your Parachute?, Richard Nelson Bolles (Ten Speed Press, 1993). A classic in the literature of life/work planning to which John Crystal was the major contributor. Richard Bolles covers the gamut of the job hunt—from defining skills that are enjoyable to use to where to use them, and how. Includes an extensive appendix, with information on alternative types of jobs and special problems.

The Three Boxes of Life, Richard Nelson Bolles (Ten Speed Press, 1981). Three boxes and how to get out of them—background piece to life/work planning.

The Smith College Guide, Elizabeth Tener (Plume, 1991). A job guide for the recent college graduate. Includes information on self-assessment, writing a resume, interviewing, and networking.

Where Do I Go From Here With My Life?, John C. Crystal and Richard N. Bolles (Ten Speed Press, 1974). The early classic in life/work planning. Crystal and Bolles devised a systematic, practical manual based on Crystal's process for analyzing capabilities and interests, philosophy of life, ideal job specifications, and more. Once the reader determines where he is going, the authors outline the way to conduct an active job search to get there.

Where to Start Career Planning, Carolyn Lloyd Lindquist and Pamela L. Feodoroff (Peterson's Guides, 1989). Lists and describes more than 2,000 career-planning sources used by Cornell University's Career Center. Includes books, periodicals, and audiovisual resources on topics such as study and work options, international careers, summer jobs, minority and women's issues.

Who's Hiring Who?, Richard Lathrop (Ten Speed Press, 1989). An excellent resource. Includes detailed information on how to write a successful resume or "qualifications brief."

Wishcraft: How to Get What You Really Want, Barbara Shur (Ballantine Books, 1983). A useful and encouraging book to accompany a job search.

Work in the New Economy,
Robert Wegmann, Robert Chap-
mann, and Miriam Johnson (JIST
Works, 1989). How readers can
most effectively conduct a job
search in the current economy.

Work With Passion, Nancy
Anderson (Carroll & Graf, 1984).
How to find your true calling and
apply it in the workplace. Includes
exercises to capture early memories, work skill grids, information
on contacts, the importance of
research.

**You Can Make It Without a
College Degree,** Roberta Roesch
(Prentice Hall, 1986). Practical
strategies for the nongraduate.

Books on Specific Careers

There is a wealth of information
available on every career in
your local library, college library,
career center, bookstore, and professional association libraries. The
following is a sampling of what is
available:

**From The Atlantic Richfield
Company (ARCO):**
   Airline Pilot
   Air Traffic Controller
   Armed Forces (Army, Navy, Air
   Force, Marines, Coast Guard)
   Case Worker
   Computer Programmer
   Analyst Trainee

   Correction Officer
   Post Office Clerk-Carrier

From VGM Career Horizons:
   Careers Encyclopedia
   Careers in Advertising
   Careers in Business
   Careers in Health Care
   Careers in Marketing

Guides to Corporate America

**Almanac of American
Employers: A Guide to
America's 500 Most
Successful Large
Corporations,** Jack W. Plunkett
(Contemporary Books, 1985).
Information on the 500 largest
publicly held companies in the
United States. Entries include
each company's type of business,
address, salaries, and benefits.
Companies are ranked according
to financial stability.

America's Corporate Families,
Dun's Marketing Service (Dun
and Bradstreet, Inc., 1987). Two
volumes. Volume I lists American
divisions and subsidiaries. Volume
II lists international divisions and
subsidiaries.

Companies That Care, Hal
Morgan and Kerry Tucker
(Simon & Schuster/Fireside,
1991). A guide to the most family-
friendly companies in America—

what they offer, and how they got that way. Includes information on what companies have the best leave policies, child-care facilities, elder-care assistance, flexible hours, and more.

Executive Jobs Unlimited, Carl R. Boll (Macmillan, 1979). How to successfully conduct a job hunt for an executive business position —still relevant.

The 50 Best Low-Investment, High-Profit Franchises, Robert Laurence Perry (Prentice Hall, 1990). A discussion of whether franchising is right for you, followed by information on the best franchising deals available by cost and proven track record. Includes hidden costs and warning signs to watch for.

Hot Tips, Sneaky Tricks and Last Ditch Tactics, Jeff B. Speck (The New Careers Center, Boulder, CO, 1989). Subtitled "An Insider's Guide to Getting Your First Corporate Job." An inside look into the recruiting process and how to use this information to land an interview and a job.

Inside Track, Ross and Kathryn Petras (Vintage Books, 1986). How to get into and succeed in America's most prestigious companies. Profiles of a wide variety of corporations, including information on salaries and "what it's really like to work there."

Management: Tasks, Responsibilities, Practices, Peter Drucker (Harper & Row, 1973). A classic resource for anyone considering the corporate world, where Peter Drucker is considered the management guru.

The National Directory of Corporate Training Programs, Ray Bard and Susan K. Elliott (The Stonesong Press, second edition, 1988). More than 1,000 opportunities to get recruited by the companies that launch fast-track careers in management, sales, finance, engineering, communications, and many other fields.

The 100 Best Companies to Sell For, Michael David Harkavy and the Philip Lief Group (John Wiley & Sons, 1989). For those looking for a career in sales, A to Z profiles of America's leading companies. Includes information on products and services offered by the companies, salary ranges and other benefits, corporate culture, qualifications needed, training offered, and opportunities available.

The 100 Best Companies to Work for in America, Robert Levering, Milton Moscowitz, and Michael Katz (Addison-Wesley, 1984). Descriptions of the companies, salary ranges and other benefits, opportunities available, and more.

YOUR LOCAL PUBLIC LIBRARY

S imple as this might sound, tapping the resources of your local library is often an excellent jumping-off point in a job search. Many libraries have designated Job Information Centers. They provide free information on occupations and careers, career planning, resume writing, interviewing techniques, planning a job search, and identifying potential employers.

The reference librarian will be able to guide your client to books, magazines, newspaper articles, and videos, helping him to identify or follow his field of interest. There are books—and often videos—on nearly every profession imaginable; often these resources have their own appendixes of publications and associations related to that interest.

Most public libraries participate in inter-library loan programs. If the resource you want is not available at your own library, ask the librarian to borrow it from another library for you.

Recommended Reference Books

W hile price tags of $20 and higher put many of these resources out of the reach of most of us, they are valuable tools for your career-planning process. Bring a pen and paper to your local bookstore and jot down the information you need from them. Or go back and talk to the reference librarian at your local or college library. Take your notebook or bring change for the Xerox machine—reference books usually don't circulate.

The Career Guide—Dun's Employment Opportunities Directory (Dun and Bradstreet Corp., published annually in November). Information on more than 5,000 companies that have 1,000 or more employees. Includes careers in computer science, management, sales, marketing, engineering, the sciences, mathematics, accounting, finance, liberal arts, and more. Entries usually include company's address, description, benefits, and a contact person.

Careers Encyclopedia, Craig T. Norback, editor (VGM Career Horizons, 1991). More than 180 detailed descriptions of careers, organized alphabetically. Includes salary information, qualifications, training, and more.

Dictionary of Occupational Titles (U.S. Department of Labor, current edition). Also known as *D.O.T.*, this government publication classifies occupations by type of work, required training, physical demands, and working conditions.

Dun and Bradstreet Million Dollar Directory (Dun and Bradstreet Corp., published annually in February). Information on 160,000 businesses that have a net worth of $500,000 or more. Companies covered include stock brokers, banks, industrial corporations, utilities, retailers, wholesalers, and insurance companies. Entries usually include company's address, names of executives, description, and educational data. Organized alphabetically according to company name.

Dun and Bradstreet Reference Book of Corporate Management (Dun and Bradstreet Corp., published annually in November). Information on some 200,000 directors, presidents, vice presidents and other managers in 12,000 credit, data processing, and personnel corporations. Entries usually include company's address, names of executives, description, and educational data. Organized alphabetically according to company name.

The Hidden Job Market (Peterson's Guides, current edition). A job seeker's guide to America's 2,000 little-known but fastest-growing high-tech companies.

Job Hunter's Sourcebook (Gale Research, Inc., current edition). An enormously useful source of company descriptions and job opportunities. Also includes extensive information on job-hunting.

Job Opportunities for Business and Liberal Arts Graduates (Peterson's Guides, 1993). Company descriptions, addresses, and contacts for business and liberal arts graduates.

Job Opportunities for Engineering, Science and Computer Graduates (Peterson's Guides, 1993). The title says it all.

Macmillan Directory of Leading Private Companies (Macmillan, published annually in March). Information on more than 6,400 privately-owned companies. Among the data included are companies' addresses, phone numbers, financial assets and liabilities, names and titles, number of employees, and U.S. and foreign offices.

MacRae's Blue Book 1993 (MacRae's Blue Book, Inc.,

Business Research Publications, published annually in March). Three volumes cover information on approximately 40,000 manufacturing firms. Volume I lists companies; volumes II and III list products.

Newsletters Directory (Gale Research, Inc., 1993). A large reference work, listing some 10,000 newsletters in various fields, published every two years.

Occupational Outlook Handbook (Compiled by the U.S. Department of Labor, published in May of even years). Detailed descriptions of some 250 occupations—covering more than 100 million jobs, or 86 percent of all the jobs in our economy. Describes working conditions, necessary training, job outlooks, earnings, related occupations, and sources to phone or write for additional information.

Standard and Poor's Register of Corporations, Directors and Executives (Standard and Poor's Corp., published annually in January). Two volumes. Volume I includes information on more than 50,000 corporations in the United States, with names and titles of more than 400,000 officials. Volume II contains 70,000 biographies of executives and directors.

Summer Jobs 1993 (Peterson's Guides, 1993). An annual publica-

tion listing summer activities and programs for those seeking careers in a wide variety of areas.

Summer Opportunities for Kids and Teenagers 1993 (Peterson's Guides, 1993). This annual publication also offers access to a video library of summer camps, and summer programs at American and European universities, independent schools, and colleges.

Where Can I Find Help With . . . (Ready Reference Press, current edition). A two-volume set subtitled "The Sourcebook of Career Services and Programs." Includes extensive resources for the young job hunter, such as testing services, resume services, job banks, job-referral sources, career-training programs, and more. Lists descriptions, addresses, and contacts in organizations.

Books on Interviewing and Resumes (see also Audiovisual Resources)

Resume references are included in this section so as to provide handy resources for you and your client, but the author urges you both not to rely on resumes to get the job.

How to Locate Jobs and Land Interviews, Albert L. French

(Career Press, current edition). Albert French identifies the "hidden" 80 percent of available jobs that are not advertised—and advises the reader on how to take an assertive approach and land a job. Topics covered include writing a "door-opening" cover letter and resume.

Resumes for Hard Times, Bob Weinstein (Simon & Schuster/Fireside, 1982). Subtitled "How to Make Yourself a Hot Property in a Cold Market." Includes information on how to size up your talents, how to assess the market, how to make your resume effective, and more. Charts, worksheets, questionnaires, sample resumes, layouts, and cover letters.

Resume Power, Tom Washington (Mount Vernon Press, 1985). An easy-to-understand, step-by-step guide to writing a resume. Answers typical resume questions and gives practical examples.

U.S. GOVERNMENT PUBLICATIONS

While government employment offices are not the panacea hoped for by many job seekers, the federal government does excel in offering a wealth of free publications about jobs and work. For information, write to the U.S. Department of Labor, Washington, DC 20212.

It also offers free reprints of articles and statistics on issues such as the growing diversity of earnings, work schedules (flextime), overtime work, people working two jobs, people working at home, and much more.

The U.S. Department of Labor publishes enormously useful reference works—most notably, *The Occupational Outlook Handbook* and the *Dictionary of Occupational Titles (D.O.T.)*. These are readily available in libraries and bookstores.

The U.S. Bureau of Labor Statistics provides information by telephone, on disk, on line, and through publications. Often these are available at no charge. Call 202-606-7828, or write the Bureau of Labor Statistics, Room 2860 Postal Square, 2 Massachusetts Avenue, Washington, DC 20212. These are good resources for background research but will not aid substantially in deciding on a career direction.

Resume Writing, Burdette E. Bostwick (John Wiley & Sons, 1990). Addresses key points such as what should go on a resume and what should stay off, how long it should be, and what kind of cover letter is best. Divides resumes into 10 different styles.

Who's Hiring Who?, Richard Lathrop (Ten Speed Press, 1989). An excellent resource. Gives detailed information on how to write a different sort of resume, or "qualifications brief."

A Guide to Professional Associations

Information about the career your client is interested in is available from the professional associations which serve them. They can often give you valuable data about necessary qualifications, working conditions, earnings, training, job outlook, and much more. The first two sources list associations, and they are followed by a small sampling of the many associations to which you can write.

Career Guide to Professional Associations (Garrett Park Press, current edition). Names and addresses of professional associations through which you can explore career possibilities.

The Encyclopedia of Associations (Gale Research, Inc., 1993). A three-volume guide to over 23,000 national and international organizations including trade, business and commercial, environmental, legal, governmental, educational, cultural, health, medical, sports, and more.

American Bankers Association
Reference Librarian
1120 Connecticut Avenue, N.W.
Washington, DC 20036

American Financial Services Association
Fourth Floor
1101 14th Street N.W.
Washington, DC 20005

American Marketing Association
250 South Wacker Drive
Chicago, IL 60606

American Medical Association
535 North Dearborn Street
Chicago, IL 60610

Associated Builders and Contractors
729 15th Street N.W.
Washington, DC 20005

The Educational Foundation of the National Restaurant Association
Suite 1400
250 South Wacker Drive
Chicago, IL 60606

Future Aviation Professionals of America
4959 Massachusetts Boulevard
Atlanta, GA 30337

**Institute for the Certification
of Computer Professionals**
2200 East Devon Avenue
Des Plains, IL 60018

**International Association of
Fire Fighters**
1750 New York Avenue N.W.
Washington, DC 20006

**National Association of
Accountants**
10 Paragon Drive
Montvale, NJ 07645

**National Association of
Broadcasters**
1771 N Street N.W.
Washington, DC 20036

**National Association of Social
Workers**
7981 Eastern Avenue
Silver Spring, MD 20910

**National Association of Trade
and Technical Schools**
2251 Wisconsin Avenue
Washington DC, 20007

**National Organization for
Human Service Education**
P.O. Box 6257
Fitchburg State College
Fitchburg, MA 01420

Newsletters, Newspapers, Magazines, and Journals

Career Opportunities News
Garrett Park Press
P.O. Box 190 C

Garrett Park, MD 20986-0190
Phone: 301-946-2553

Six issues each year cover topics
such as the current outlook in
various careers, resources for job
seekers, and special opportunities
for women and minorities.

Corporate Jobs Outlook!
Corporate Jobs Outlook
P.O. Drawer 100
Boerne, TX 78006

Publishes 100 reports each year
describing companies and their
compensation plans, advancement
opportunities, and more.

**Editorial Freelancers
Association Newsletter**
Editorial Freelancers Association
P.O. Box 2050
Madison Square Station
New York, NY 10159-2050
Phone: 212-677-3357
Fax: 212-777-8207

Includes rates surveys, new mar-
kets, profiles of freelancers, and
more. See an article in the
Sept.–Oct. 1991 issue "Your
Career: On Course or Dead in the
Water (And What You Can Do
About It)," which addresses spe-
cial concerns of freelancers.

**Financial World—America's
Top Growth Companies
Directory**
Financial World Partners
1328 Broadway
New York, NY 10001

Phone: 800-666-6639
Fax: 212-629-0021

Published annually in May. Information on companies which have a minimum growth rate of 5 percent over a 10-year period. Entries include companies' current and past ranking, sales and earnings growth rate, and other financial data.

Financial World—500 Fastest Growing Companies

Financial World Partners
1328 Broadway
New York, NY 10001
Phone: 800-666-6639
Fax: 212-629-0021

Published annually in August; however the name may change somewhat from year to year. List of 500 U.S. firms which have had the greatest growth in net earnings for the year.

Forbes—Up-and-Comers 200: Best Small Companies in America

Forbes, Inc.
60 Fifth Avenue
New York, NY 10011
Phone: 212-620-2200

Published annually in November. Lists 200 small companies considered to be the fastest growing, based on their five-year return on equity and other financial data.

Fortune Directory

Time, Inc.
Time and Life Building
Rockefeller Center
New York, NY 10020
Phone: 212-586-1212

Published annually in April. Information on the 500 largest U.S. industrial corporations, the 500 largest nonindustrial corporations, and the Service 500. Entries include companies' sales, assets, and other financial information. A similar directory of international corporations published in July.

The Inc. 100 Issue

The Goldhirsch Group
38 Commercial Wharf
Boston, MA 02110
Phone: 800-234-0999 or 617-248-8447

Published annually in May. Information on the 100 fastest growing publicly held U.S. companies in the manufacturing and service industries. Companies must have revenues greater than $100,000 but less than $25 million in order to be included.

The Inc. 500 Issue

The Goldhirsch Group
38 Commercial Wharf
Boston, MA 02110
Phone: 800-234-0999 or 617-248-8447

Published annually in December. Information on the 500 fastest growing privately held companies in manufacturing, service, retail, distribution, and construction. Entries are based on the companies' percentage increase in sales over the past five years.

Journal of Career Planning and Employment

College Placement Council, Inc.
62 Highland Avenue
Bethlehem, PA 18017
Phone: 215-868-1421

Four issues each year provide assistance to students in planning and carrying out a job search.

Kennedy's Career Strategist

1150 Wilmette Avenue
Wilmette, Il 60091
Phone: 800-729-1708

A monthly newsletter on career planning. Includes information on office politics, interviewing, resumes, and salaries.

Managing Your Career

Dow Jones and Co.
420 Lexington Avenue
New York, NY 10170
Phone: 212-808-6600

Provides job-hunting advice for college students. The college version of the National Business Employment Weekly.

National Business Employment Weekly

Dow Jones and Co.

420 Lexington Avenue
New York, NY 10170
Phone: 212-808-6792, or
800-JOB-HUNT

Job-hunting advice for all ages from the publishers of the Wall Street Journal.

Occupational Outlook Quarterly

Bureau of Labor Statistics
2 Massachusetts Avenue N.E.
Washington, DC 20212
Phone: 202-606-7828

Contains information and articles about a broad range of occupations.

U.S. Employment Opportunities: A Career News Service

Washington Research Associates
7500 East Arapaho Plaza
Suite 250
Englewood, CO 80112
Phone: 303-756-9038
FAX: 303-770-1945

An annual publication with quarterly updates. Information on more than 1,000 employment contacts in industries and professions including the federal government, the arts, banking, telecommunications, and education. Entries include companies' products or services, hiring practices, training programs and more.

Running a Family Business

Keeping the Family Business Healthy, John L. Ward (Jossey Bass, 1987). Gives academically sound, practical counsel on planning for a family business, including how to address personality differences.

Loyola University Family Business Center
P.O. Box 257608
Chicago, IL 60625-7608
Phone: 312-604-5505

A think tank and resource for families in business together.

Running a Family Business, Joseph R. Mancuso and Nat Shulman (Prentice Hall Press, 1991). How to avoid the pitfalls and maximize the profitability of a family business.

Audiovisual Resources

Apart from the Crowd
New Jersey Network
1573 Parkside Avenue
Trenton, NJ 08625
Phone: 609-530-5252

Videocassette in VHS. 30 minutes. A documentary featuring individuals who have left their former line of work and are making a living from their personal hobbies.

The Employment Interview
Southern School Media
1027 Broadway

Bowling Green, KY 42101
Phone: 502-781-1915

Videocassette in Beta or VHS. 35 minutes. Three different versions explore the interview process for high school, college, and adult education students.

Filmstrips for Career Choice and Job Search
Meridian Educational Corp.
236 Front Street
Bloomington, IL 61701
Phone: 309-827-5455

Set of 12 filmstrips showing people in the process of a job search and working at a variety of jobs. Available on videocassette as well.

How to Get a Job
BusinessWeek Careers
P.O. Box 5810
Norwalk, CT 06856-9960

Videocassette. 70 minutes. Career counselors and CEO's give tips on job search skills.

Interview Preparation
Cambridge Career Products
P.O. Box 2153
Charleston, WV 25328-2153
Phone: 304-744-9323

Videocassette in Beta or VHS. 30 minutes. How to successfully prepare for a job interview.

Job Seeking
Great Plains National
Instructional Television Library

University of Nebraska at Lincoln
P.O. Box 80669
Lincoln, NE 68501-0669
Phone: 800-228-4630

Videocassette in VHS. An eight-part series (15 minutes each) that covers the job search, including resumes and interviews.

Jobs: Seeking, Finding, Keeping

Agency for Instructional Technology
Box A
Bloomington, IN 47402
Phone: 800-457-4509

Videocassette in Beta or VHS. Series of 20-minute individually available tapes designed for high school students. Topics include: self-image; interests, aptitudes, and abilities; credentials; interview preparation; personal finances; and upward mobility.

Success in the Job Market

Great Plains National
Instructional Television Library
University of Nebraska at Lincoln
P.O. Box 80669
Lincoln, NE 68501-0669
Phone: 800-228-4630

Videocassette in Beta or VHS. Fifteen minutes. A series of six tapes specifically designed for the high school graduate who directly enters the work force upon graduation. Helps high

school seniors make informed decisions about the work world. Topics are: 1. Working at the Car Wash Blues. 2. Let Me Count the Ways I Know Me. 3. The Search. 4. Behind Closed Doors. 5. The Company. 6. Loving Me is Loving You.

Software

Career Design Software

P.O. Box 95624
Atlanta, GA 30347
Phone: 800-346-8007
Fax: 404-321-6474

Career Design Software, an extension of the New York-based Crystal-Barkley Corporation, offers a powerful and comprehensive career-development system. Career Design puts the methods outlined in this book at your fingertips. It is divided into three sections: "Who am I?", "What Do I Want?", and "How Do I Get There?"

"Who Am I?" helps job seekers and career changers identify their personal skills and preferred environment before starting a job search. "What Do I Want?", the heart of the program, allows users to define their interests, uncover their dreams and aspirations, develop precise goals for the areas of life that are personally important, and build a comprehensive plan of action for the future. "How Do I Get There?" teaches users how to attain their personal and professional goals. It includes: researching/targeting employers, preparing resumes and custom proposals, writing letters, communicating effectively during interviews, and negotiating compensation. Available on 3½" and 5¼" disks for use on an IBM or IBM-compatible PC.

Company Connections—The Cover Letter
Cambridge Career Products
P.O. Box 2153
Charleston, WV 25328-2153
Phone: 304-744-9323

Contains the names, addresses, and phone numbers of companies and professional associations in a variety of fields and guides the user through composing cover letters to them. Available for IBM and Apple computers on 3½" disks.

Compu-Job
Cambridge Career Products
P.O. Box 2153
Charleston, WV 25328-2153
Phone: 304-744-9323

A menu-driven program which guides the user through the job-search process. Sections include determining what career is right for you, where the openings are in your field of interest, and

interviewing. Available for IBM and Apple computers on 3½" disks.

850 Leading California Companies
Jamenair Ltd.
P.O. Box 241957
Los Angeles, CA 90024
Phone: 310-470-6688

Describes career opportunities in California. Available on 3½" and 5¼" disks for use with IBM or IBM-compatible PCs.

850 Leading USA Companies
Jamenair Ltd.
P.O. Box 241957
Los Angeles, CA 90024
Phone: 310-470-6688

Information on career opportunities in top companies throughout the states. Available on 3½" and 5¼" disks for use with IBM or IBM-compatible PCs.

Super Search Software
Jamenair Ltd.
P.O. Box 241957
Los Angeles, CA 90024
Phone: 310-470-6688

How to network, successfully represent past accomplishments, how to negotiate, and more. Available on 3½" or 5¼" disks for use with IBM and IBM-compatible computers.

On-Line Services

T hese are services that computer users can subscribe to.

Career Placement Registry
Career Placement Registry, Inc.
302 Swann Avenue
Alexandria, VA 22301
Phone: 800-368-3093
Fax: 703-683-0246

One file contains resumes of college seniors, recent graduates, and people with work experience seeking jobs. Used by both employers and prospective employees. Available on-line through DIALOG Information Services, Inc.

College Recruitment Database
Executive Telecom System, Inc.
College Park North
9585 Valparaiso Court
Indianapolis, IN 46268
Phone: 800-421-8884

Resumes of undergraduate and graduate students in all college disciplines. Available on-line through the Human Resource Information Network for the use of employers as well as prospective employees.

Corporate Jobs Outlook
Corporate Jobs Outlook, Inc.
P.O. Drawer 100

Boerne, TX 78006
Phone: 512-755-8810

Information on employment opportunities in 100 major firms, in areas including business, banking, insurance, computers, and retailing. Data on companies' growth plans, marketing strategies, advancement opportunities, and other career-related matters. Available on-line through NewsNet, Inc.

Moody's Corporate Profiles
Moody's Investors Service, Inc.
Dun and Bradstreet Corp.
99 Church Street
New York, NY 10007
Phone: 800-342-5647
Fax: 212-553-4700

Information on more than 5,000 publicly held companies. Includes such financial data as annual earnings, dividends per share, and stock-price history. Available on-line through DIALOG Information Services, Inc.

On-Line Hotline News Service
Information Intelligence, Inc.
P.O. Box 31098
Phoenix, AZ 85046
Phone: 800-228-9982

The file Joblines features all manner of job listings and resume services throughout North America and is updated periodically. Also available on CD ROM.

II. REGIONAL AND INTERNATIONAL RESOURCES

If you're thinking in terms of relocation or job change—as most Americans do 10 or more times in their lifetimes—be creative and do a little investigation on your own as outlined in Chapters 5 and 7 of the handbook dealing with surveying. Get in touch with state agencies and research local programs in colleges and universities. Write or call the local chamber of commerce and subscribe to the local newspaper. These will give you more of a feel for the new area.

As always, use your contacts. Do you know people who know people who live there? Get in touch with them! If you're a college graduate, contact your alumni office to see if there are fellow alumni living there.

Jobs by Region

The Job Bank Series (Bob Adams, Inc., 1992). These books have data on thousands of companies around the country. Includes descriptions of the companies, addresses, phone numbers, and contact persons. Information on areas of hiring activity, principal educational backgrounds sought, and fringe benefits offered.

Available for the following geographical areas: Atlanta, Boston, Chicago, Dallas-Ft. Worth, Denver, Detroit, Florida, Houston, Los Angeles, Minneapolis-St. Paul, New York, Ohio, Phoenix, Philadelphia, San Francisco, Seattle, St. Louis, Washington, D.C. To order, call 800-USA-JOBS. In Massachusetts, 617-767-8100.

The National Job Bank 1993, Carter Smith, Managing Editor (Bob Adams, Inc., 1992). Published annually and organized alphabetically by state, data on thousands of companies around the country. Provides descriptions of the companies, addresses, phone numbers, and contact persons. Includes information on areas of hiring activity, principal educational backgrounds sought, and fringe benefits offered.

Places Rated Almanac: Your Guide to Finding the Best Places to Live in America, Richard Boyer and David Savageau (Rand McNally & Co., 1989). This enormously helpful book offers information on 333 metropolitan areas around the nation. The authors rank and compare them according to such criteria as job outlook, cost of living, education, health, crime, infrastructure, transportation, climate, and the arts.

Suggestions for Career Exploration and Jobseeking (New York State Department of Labor, Division of Research and Statistics, NY-SOICC, Room 488, Building 12, State Office Building Campus, Albany, NY 12240. Phone: 518-457-6182). A free brochure about the New York job market that includes a list of state Job Service offices.

MAKING YOUR LOCAL COLLEGE A CAREER RESOURCE

There are more than 3,000 colleges and universities in our country, which makes it very likely that one is located near you. Many make their resources available to the surrounding community as well as to their own student population.

The libraries of colleges and universities usually have far more extensive career resources than local libraries—which is only logical, since most students attend college in anticipation of launching their careers. Personal contact is often helpful: if you can't find what you are looking for yourself, the reference librarian will usually be able to steer you in the right direction.

In addition to written material, videos and audio tapes are available as are software programs. Programs such as Myers-Briggs are intended to be used under the guidance of a trained professional, as they are only one piece of the career puzzle—not to be confused with the puzzle itself.

Alumni can continue to use the resources of their college or university throughout their lifetimes. In addition, alumni often provide a very valuable service to newcomers to the job hunting scene in their participation in mentor programs. As mentors, alumni make themselves available to graduates of their schools to provide information about different careers. Some mentors also offer internships or even entry-level positions in specific fields. Campus career services offices can often give guidance on how to tap into this valuable program.

College Career Services Open to the Public

Most colleges have counseling centers or career services offices where your client can continue an investigation of resources by speaking to career counselors and recruiters whether or not he is an alumnus. There he may read material on everything from different careers to company profiles to opportunities in the nonprofit sector. Have him look for the specialty journals in the career of possible interest.

A directory listing these offices is available: *Directory of Career Planning and Placement Offices,* published by the College Placement Council, Inc., 62 Highland Avenue, Bethlehem, PA 18107; phone: 215-868-1421.

Many colleges and universities open their counseling centers to the surrounding community as well as to their own student population. Their rates may be lower than those in the for-profit sector. Following is a selection of just a few of them by state. Note that while some of them specialize in serving women, they seve men as well.

In California:

San Jose State University
Re-Entry Advisory Program
San Jose, CA 95816
Phone: 408-924-6266

UCLA Extension Advisory Service
10995 Le Conte Avenue
Los Angeles, CA 90024
Phone: 213-748-2186

In Colorado:

Arapahoe Community College
Career Resource Center
5900 South Santa Fe Drive
Littleton, CO 80120
Phone: 303-797-5805

In Connecticut:

Fairfield University
Fairfield Adult and Educational Services
North Benson Road
Fairfield, CT 06032
Phone: 203-254-4000

In Illinois:

University of Illinois, Champaign-Urbana
Office for Women's Resources and Services
610 East John Street
Champaign, Il 61820
Phone: 217-333-1000

In Indiana:

Ball State University
Career Services, West Campus
Muncie, IN 47306
Phone: 317-285-1522

Indiana University
Continuing Studies
Owen Hall, Room 202
Bloomington, IN 47405

Phone: 812-855-0225
Offers occasional workshops
and consulting.

In Iowa:
University of Iowa
Business and Liberal Arts
Placement/Career Information
Services
24 Phillips Hall
Iowa City, IA 52242
Phone: 319-355-1023

In Maryland:
Goucher College
Goucher Center for
Continuing Studies
Towson, MD 21204
Phone: 410-337-6200

In Massachusetts:
Radcliffe College
Radcliffe Career Services
77 Brattle Street
Cambridge, MA 02138
Phone: 617-495-8631

In Michigan:
University of Michigan
Center for the Education of
Women
330 East Liberty
Ann Arbor, MI 48104-2289
Phone: 313-998-7080
Provides career guidance men
and women.

In Minnesota:
University of Minnesota
Minnesota Women's Center
5 Eddy Hall

Minneapolis, MN 55455
Phone: 612-625-9837
Open to men and women.

In Mississippi:
Mississippi State University
Career Services Center
P.O. Box P
Mississippi State, MS 39762
Phone: 601-325-3344

In Montana:
Montana State University
Women's Resource Center
15 Hamilton Hall
Bozeman, MT 59717
Phone: 406-994-3836
A resource for men and
women alike.

In New Jersey:
Fairleigh Dickinson University
Career Planning and
Placement
285 Madison Avenue
Madison, NJ 07940
Phone: 201-593-8945

In New York:
Hofstra University
Career Placement Center
240 Student Center
Hempstead, NY 11550
Phone: 516-463-6788

New York University
Center for Career and Life
Planning
719 Broadway, Third Floor
New York, NY 10003
Phone: 212-998-4730

In Ohio:
The University of Akron
Adult Resource Center
Akron, OH 44325-3102
Phone: 216-972-7448

In Pennsylvania:
Chatham College
Job Advisory Service
Woodland Road
Pittsburgh, PA 15232
Phone: 412-365-1100

In Utah:
University of Utah
Center for Adult Transition
1195 Annex Building
Salt Lake City, UT 84112
Phone: 801-581-3228

In Virginia:
Virginia Commonwealth University
University Advising Center
827 West Franklin Street
Richmond, VA 23284
Phone: 804-367-0100

In Washington:
University of Washington
Career/Life Planning
301 Lowe FH 30
Seattle, WA 98195
Phone: 206-543-2100

In Washington, DC:
George Washington University
Continuing Education for Women
20003 G Street N.W., Building E
Washington, DC 20009
Phone: 202-994-7000
Provides career guidance for men and women.

In Wyoming:
University of Wyoming
Counseling Center
P.O. Box 3035
Laramie, WY 82071
Phone: 307-766-4074

Career Counselors and Educational Consultants

There are many fine career and educational counselors and consultants beyond the ones I mention below. It was not possible to include all of them. Remember, however, that any organizaton that you approach should be investigated thoroughly before proceeding. Inquire about the specific background and approach of a counselor or consultant, area of expertise, and fee schedule. Also try to speak with others who have used their services.

A nonprofit organization called The Independent Educational Consultants Association lists members around the country who are dedicated to helping students identify and select appropriate schools, colleges, and educational programs. To obtain this list write or telephone:

The Independent Educational Consultants Association

P.O. Box 125
Forestdale, MA 02644-0125
Phone: 508-833-0670

Following is a selection of counselors and consultants around the country.

In California:
The Crystal-Barkley Corporation
152 Madison Avenue, 23rd Floor
New York, NY 10016
Phone: 212-889-8500 or
800-333-9003
Fax: 212-889-6715

The Crystal-Barkley Corporation has consultants in the Los Angeles area who are fully trained in the process on which this handbook is based. For more information, contact the headquarters in New York.

David Denman
619 East Blythedale Avenue
Mill Valley, CA 94941
Phone: 415-383-1834

Denman, an educational consultant, does troubleshooting and problem solving for young people from eighth grade through college. In his program, which he calls "Time Out," Denman organizes developmentally enriching opportunities for his clients, including internships, apprenticeships, and study-abroad programs. Recently, he placed two teenagers with the real Crocodile Dundee in Australia. According to Denman, "People graduate from college and haven't been anywhere but classrooms. I give them a taste of careers and people in the real world."

Virginia Dennehy
885 North San Antonio Road,
Suite A
Los Altos, CA 94022
Phone: 415-326-6115

Dennehy, a licensed psychologist, offers career and life-planning services to individuals and groups of all ages. She is also a speaker and a consultant. According to Dennehy, "There are plenty of jobs around for enterprising people who know how to get them. Whether the economy is expanding or contracting is not relevant to our process." She feels that there is a period of time when young people don't know what they want to do, and she assists them in defining their goals. She also is very knowledgeable about the Crystal-Barkley process and is well equipped to follow its principles in consulting.

In Connecticut:
Frankenberger Associates
88 Prospect Street
New Haven, CT 06511
Phone: 203-624-9397
Fax: 203-498-9296

The goal of Caryl Frankenberger and her associates is to provide families with a comprehensive and integrated set of services which address the academic, social, emotional, and career-planning needs of young people as they progress through the various phases of their schooling. According to Frankenberger, "We view career planning as life planning, and thus we identify clients' values, dreams, and goals as well as interests, abilities, and aptitudes." Their specialty is diagnosing learning disabilities, identifying each student's individual learning style, detailing a person's strengths and weaknesses, and using this information to make specific academic and/or placement recommendations.

In Illinois:

The Crystal-Barkley Corporation
152 Madison Avenue, 23rd Floor
New York, NY 10016
Phone: 800-333-9003
Fax: 212-889-6715

The Crystal-Barkley Corporation has consultants in the Chicago area who are fully trained in the process on which this handbook is based. For information, contact the headquarters in New York.

In Montana:

Donna Berkhof
Graphic Testimony

2301 Sundance Drive
Great Falls, MT 59404
Phone after 5 P.M.: 406-727-6134

As well as being a career counselor and tech prep coordinator for the Great Falls public schools, Berkhof has a private practice as a consultant in career counseling and program development. She says, "Clients focus on self-assessment, career decision making, and job-acquisition steps which include resume development, market analysis, interviewing, and identifying and researching targets."

Jennifer A. Carter, MPA
Directions for Career
Development
340 South Fifth Street West
Missoula, MT 59801
Phone: 406-728-7831

Carter, a career-development consultant, believes in teaching people how to manage a career for life. She emphasizes to her clients that until the economy shuts down 100 percent, there is always a job out there for them. She says, "The focus is you and it's your choice. Don't worry about the big picture."

In New York:

The Crystal-Barkley Corporation
Life/Work Design

John C. Crystal Center
152 Madison Avenue, 23rd Floor
New York, NY 10016
Phone: 212-889-8500 or
800-333-9003
Fax: 212-889-6715

This is the headquarters of the Crystal-Barkley Corporation which offers the proprietary process on which this handbook is based. Individual consulting, five-day courses, and interactive Career Design Software are options elected by clients of all ages. All consultation is provided by professionals personally trained by the author of this handbook.

Ruth E. Beltran Associates
210 East 68th Street, #1B
New York, NY 10021
Phone: 212-288-7547

"You must be much more aggressive in managing your career today," counsels Beltran. "There isn't externally provided security; you can't just leave it to fate." She works with young people, usually in their twenties, who are working but think that their job is not right for them.

To get closer to her clients' real interests, Beltran asks them questions such as "What did you like to do in school?" and "What did you fantasize about as a child?" Like many other career counselors we spoke to, Beltran says that young people are con-

fused about their values in their struggle with money versus quality-of-life issues.

Elizabeth Campbell
210 East 68th Street, #1B
New York, NY 10021
Phone: 212-772-1327

Campbell tells her clients, "Don't get externally focused about what you should do. The answers are in you." She helps people to touch their core values and find out "Who am I?" and how that translates into a fulfilling "World of Work" opportunity. Elizabeth's specialty is in working with people in their mid-twenties, especially dancers, who are seeking second careers.

In Ohio:

Barbara Hill
Hill & Hill Consulting, Inc.
393 Hawthorne N.E.
Warren, OH 44484
Phone: 616-352-6018

Hill does individual career counseling and also offers periodic five-day workshops in Chicago and in the Atlanta area. She tells young people, "Follow your dream; the money will follow." Since they are often jaded or depressed, Hill encourages new job hunters to forget about the expectations of others and keep working, keep networking, and stay motivated. "Don't look at trends," she advises. "Even a recession is not spread like peanut butter across the whole economy. If you want it enough, the job is out there for you. Volunteer or do an internship for six months; eventually you will get a job."

In Rhode Island:

Patricia Maslin-Ostrowski
3 Bliss Road
Newport, RI 02840
Phone: 401-849-7318

Maslin-Ostrowski advises her clients to first look inward and discover where their interests lie. She says, "The best approach is to look at the same interest from a variety of perspectives. If you'd like to work with animals, for example, you are not limited to being a veterinarian—you can be an advocate for animals, do research, write stories about them, draw them, or start a pet-sitting service. Be alert to the possibilities." Maslin-Ostrowski emphasizes the importance of talking to people who are already working in the fields in which you are interested.

In Texas:

Dan and Sharon Wiseman
Organizational Development Systems
450 N. Sam Houston Parkway East, Suite 250
Houston, TX 77060
Phone: 713-931-7243

The Wisemans help young people understand what their strengths are, so that they can spend their early years developing and honing them. They also offer clients opportunities to simulate working in various types of settings helping them learn what is required in today's workplace. According to Dan Wiseman, young people today are very success-motivated, put a lot of emphasis on material things, and want it all immediately. "They're going to have to put some time and effort into setting a goal and working towards it. They have to go to school and get experience through internships."

Chuck Freeman
Pastoral Education and Family Counseling Center
P.O. Box 49131
Austin, TX 78765
Phone: 512-472-5073

Freeman helps young people identify their purpose or calling in life. He says it is important for them to discern what they like to do, what they are talented at doing, and how to market those abilities. "A lot more creativity will be called for in the current marketplace. There are a lot of fears to be overcome, but young people must believe in what they're doing and have personal ownership in it. The rewards will be great," he says.

Testing Services

At Crystal-Barkley we are cautious about advocating testing services because of the tendency toward accepting results as absolute confirmation of direction. Tests, particularly those which measure aptitude, may be helpful in indicating fields to survey, but their results alone are not sufficient for decision making.

Johnson O'Connor Research Foundation

11 East 62nd Street
New York, NY 10021
Phone: 212-838-0550

The Johnson O'Connor Research Foundation administers a battery of tests to help people discover their aptitudes, so they may make more informed decisions about schooling and work. The foundation is headquartered in New York and has offices in cities throughout the country (see list at right).

Tests are administered to anyone age 14 or older, and may point out natural aptitudes or talents such as manual dexterity, spatial visualization, memory for numbers, and musical ability. Every career uses certain aptitudes, and the Foundation's view is that the career in which a person is most likely to be happy and successful is one which uses his or her natural aptitudes.

The Foundation stresses that aptitude testing is only one tool for individuals to use in career selection. It cannot tell you exactly what career to choose, nor does the Foundation provide general counseling services.

Suite 1023
3400 Peachtree Road, N.E.
Atlanta, GA 30326
Phone: 404-261-8013

347 Beacon Street
Boston, MA 02116
Phone: 617-536-0409

161 East Erie Street
Chicago, IL 60611
Phone: 312-787-9141

5525 MacArthur Boulevard
Suite 270
Irving, TX 75038
Phone: 214-550-9033

One Cherry Center, Suite 690
501 South Cherry Street
Denver, CO 80222
Phone: 303-388-5600

3200 Wilcrest, Suite 340
Houston, TX 77042
Phone: 713-783-3411

3345 Wilshire Boulevard
Suite 210
Los Angeles, CA 90010
Phone: 213-380-1947

The Monadnock, Suite 840
685 Market Street
San Francisco, CA 94105
Phone: 415-243-8074

1218 Third Avenue, Suite 900
Seattle, WA 98101
Phone: 206-623-4070

201 Maryland Avenue N.E.
Washington, DC 20002
Phone: 202-547-3922

**Consulting Psychologists
Press, Inc.**
P.O. Box 10096
Palo Alto, CA 94303-0979
Phone: 415-969-8901

The tests designed by the
Consulting Psychologists Press
are used by career counselors and
psychologists to help enable their
clients to achieve their goals.
Most tests require professional
training to administer, and so, if
your client wishes to take these
seek a qualified counselor in your
area to administer them. Among
the most well-known are the:

• Strong Campbell Interest
  Inventory
  A measure of interests—not of
  aptitude or intelligence—used
  as an aid in making educational
  and career decisions. Organized
  according to John Holland's
  occupational codes. (See "A
  Selection of General Career
  Books.")

• Myers-Briggs Type Indicator
  A widely used measure of personality dispositions and preferences. Can help in the choice of
  a major, compatible work or

educational settings, or an
occupation.

International Career Opportunities

**The Almanac of International
Jobs and Careers,** Krannich,
Carolyn R. and Ronald L., Ph.D.'s
(Impact Communications, 1991).
A comprehensive overview of
international employment oppor-
tunities.

**Directory of American Firms
Operating in Foreign
Countries** (World Trade Academy
Press, 1987). Names, addresses,
company descriptions, and more.

**How to Find an Overseas Job
with the U.S. Government** (By
mail, WorldWise Books, P.O. Box
3030, Oakton, VA 22124).
Overseas employment opportunities with 17 government agencies.

How to Get a Job in Europe,
Robert Sanborn, editor (Surrey
Books, 1991). A practical hand-
book. Surrey Books also has a
series on how to get a job in
Atlanta, Chicago, Dallas/Fort
Worth, Houston, Southern
California, New York, San
Francisco, Seattle/Portland, and
Washington, D.C.

International Careers, Arthur
H. Bell, Ph.D. (Bob Adams, Inc.,
1990). Asks the reader to look
internally before internationally—
focusing on who you are and what

EMPLOYMENT AGENCIES

Employment agencies are operated by state, federal, and local governments and private firms. We wish we had better news about these services. But as it stands, recent studies indicate that very few people actually get jobs through employment agencies. A private agency receives its fee from employers therefore they are working to fulfill employers' needs, not your client's. In fact, only about 5 percent of the people looking for positions through private employment agencies are successful in ob-taining them.

Government agencies rate a little higher on the scale, and some supply other services, such as job-search workshops. State employment agencies also develop occupational employment projections and other job market information. The *Occupational Outlook Handbook* of the U.S. Department of Labor provides the titles, addresses, and telephone numbers of state employment organizations for every state and territory of the United States.

you can do. Includes information on corporate jobs, government jobs, and opportunities in the nonprofit sector.

International Directory of Company Histories (Gale Research, Inc.). Five volumes published between 1988 and 1991. Information on 1,250 leading companies in the United States, Canada, Europe, and Japan. Entries include companies' addresses, phone numbers, descriptions, products or services, and branches and subsidiaries.

International Employment Hotline (WorldWise Books, Box 3030, Oakton, VA 22124; phone: 703-620-1972). A monthly newsletter of advice for those seeking international jobs. Includes addresses of international employers currently hiring U.S. citizens.

International Jobs, Eric Kocher (Addison-Wesley, 1989). A handbook of more than 500 career opportunities around the world.

III. LESS TRADITIONAL CAREERS AND VOLUNTEER WORK

Emerging and Alternative Career Resources

Alternative America (Alternative America, Cambridge, MA, current edition). A directory of more than 13,000 alternative, progressive organizations. Includes name, subject, and geographical indexes.

Careers Without College (Peterson's Guides, current edition). A series of books that describes jobs in high-growth fields that do not require a college degree. Each book covers necessary skills, responsibilities, and salary and career growth expectations. Fields covered include health care, fashion, computers, and music.

The Complete Guide to Environmental Careers, The CEIP Fund (Island Press, 1989). An introduction to environmental careers, such as forestry, park and recreation management, environmental planning, hazardous-waste management, land and water conservation, and solid-waste management. Suggests appropriate education, volunteer programs, and internships.

Creative Careers, Gary Blake and Robert Bly (John Wiley & Sons, 1985). Includes information on careers in travel, music, theater, movies, and television.

Great Careers: The Fourth of July Guide to Careers, Internships, and Volunteer Opportunities in the Non-Profit Center, Devon Smith, editor (Garrett Park Press, 1990). Includes careers in the arts, the environment, animal rights, working with the disabled, and much more. Explores international as well as domestic opportunities.

Off Beat Careers, Al Sacharov (Word of Mouth Press, 1985). Lots of ideas, with sources to contact for investigating unusual work.

Offbeat Corners: The Directory of Unusual Work, Al Sacharov (Ten Speed Press, 1988). A directory of more than 10,000 alternative groups and organizations, in fields ranging from ecology to the arts to women's issues. Includes name, subject, and geographical indexes.

Opportunities in Environmental Careers, Odom Fanning (VGM Career Horizons, 1991). Profiles, names, and numbers of organizations offering environmental career opportunities.

Rating America's Corporate Conscience: A Provocative Guide to the Companies Behind the Products, Steven D. Lydenburg, Alice Tepper Marlin, Sean O'Brien Strub, and the Council on Economic Priorities, (Addison-Wesley, 1986). Looks at corporations, and evaluates them according to their social responsibility.

"Trade and Technical Careers and Training" (National Association of Trade and Technical Schools). A free handbook on trade and technical careers and training. Lists accredited trade and technical schools. Provides career information. To obtain a copy write: National Association of Trade and Technical Schools, 2251 Wisconsin Avenue, Washington, DC 20007.

"Trade School Homework," Lynn Brenner (*The New York Times,* Section 4A, Jan. 5, 1992). According to the Career College Association, a group of 2,100 technical and business schools, the nation's 4,000 trade schools provide training for 130 occupations, from aviation mechanic to X-ray technician. This article provides the student with advice on how to choose the right trade school.

250 Home-Based Jobs, Scott C. Olsen (Atlantic Richfield Company, current edition). Describes home-based alternatives from aerobics instructor to tie resizer.

When 9 to 5 Isn't Enough, Marcia A. Perkins (Hay House, 1990). The message is not only to do what you love but love what you do. Perkins is a career consultant who presents seminars throughout the United States on "Charting Your Course for Success."

The Work at Home Sourcebook, Lynie Arden (Live Oak Publications, 1990). Gives the facts needed to find, apply for, and get work at home with companies ranging from accounting to creative writing, sales to word processing.

Books and Articles on Volunteering and Internships

Choices: A Student Survival Guide for the 1990s, Bryna J. Fireside (Garrett Park Press, 1989). Asks questions such as: Who am I? What am I doing here? Am I having fun yet? Aimed toward high school students making decisions about college, part-time work, internships, volunteer work, and other options.

International Directory for Youth Internships (Council on International and Public Affairs, 1990). Lists United Nations' agencies, and non-governmental organizations offering intern and volunteer opportunities. Entries include name of agency or organization, address, and job description.

Internships (The Career Press, 1990). A five-volume series on internships, ranging from advertising to the media to travel and more. Aimed toward college students who want to try out a career by working in or near a professional capacity for a summer or semester. Emphasizes deciding through this approach if the career is the right one for the student. Lists internships, describes typical workdays in each field, and includes appendixes of industry trade associations and publications.

National Directory of Arts Internships, Warren Christenson, editor (American Council for the Arts, 1991). Lists more than 900 host organizations offering more than 2,100 internship opportunities for art careers in arts management, dance, theater, music, literature, art/design, film/video, photography, and more.

"Soup-Kitchen Classroom," Vicki Goldberg (*The New York Times Magazine,* Sept. 27, 1992).

Rutgers University students volunteer (for college credit) in the community, working with the homeless and recovering addicts, in order to become more sensitive to community needs.

"To Fill Its Schools a Rural Town Opens Its Homes," Dirk Johnson (*The New York Times,* Sept. 30, 1992, page 8, Section B.) In a rural New Mexico town, students from the city have the opportunity to learn about a different way of life.

Volunteer USA, Andrew Carroll with Christopher Miller (Fawcett, 1991). A comprehensive guide to worthy causes searching for volunteers. Indexed by organization and region.

Volunteering and Government Service Programs

ACORN (Association of Community Organizations for Reform Now)
300 Flatbush Avenue
Brooklyn, NY 11217
Phone: 718-789-5600

A multi-racial membership organization of low income families working to gain power in their communities. Volunteers work as grass-roots organizers throughout the USA.

American Friends Service Committee
1501 Cherry Street
Philadelphia, PA 19102
Phone: 215-241-7000

An independent Quaker organization which sponsors summer service programs in Latin America.

The Peace Corps
199 K Street N.W.
Washington, DC 20526
Phone: 800-424-8580

The organization, whose name has come to be synonymous with volunteerism, entails a two year commitment to service in a third-world country.

Up With People
1 International Court
Broomfield, CO 80021
Phone: 303-460-7100

An international organization sponsoring young people from around the world who by song and dance build bridges between cultures. Tuition-based. Some scholarships available.

VISTA / ACTION
1100 Vermont Avenue N.W.
Washington, DC 20525
Phone: 800-424-8867

A nonprofit volunteer organization whose major goal is to increase the participation of the poor in community decision-making processes.

Federal Youth Service Programs
The Clinton administration is planning to institute national youth service programs. Currently envisioned are a "Summer of Service," in which teenagers will be ssigned to public works projects, and a tuition-reimbursement program through which college students will be able to pay back loans by working for a variety of social service and environmental organizations. For information, contact your senator or congressperson.

Guides to Getting Grants

If during surveying your client comes up with a project he's longing to do, but needs funding, these books may help.

Annual Register of Grant Support (Marquis Academic Media, Chicago, published annually). An up-to-date directory of more than 2,300 grant programs.

The Foundation Directory (The Foundation Center, New York, current edition). A reference volume listing more than 4,400 U.S. foundations.

Getting Yours: The Complete Guide to Government Money, Matthew Lesko (Viking Penguin, 1987). How to go about getting grants from the appropriate government agencies.

IV. TRENDS AND DEMOGRAPHICS

Forbes Magazine's Annual Report on American Industry

Every January, *Forbes* Magazine publishes a report on the performance of the various industry groups over the past year, and their outlook for the future. This can be a valuable guide in identifying industry trends.

In the January 4, 1993 issue of *Forbes* the performance of 1,209 companies is outlined. *Forbes* also identifies 21 "nimble" companies that are setting the pace for their industries. Nimble companies anticipate new markets and keep costs low. They avoid multiple layers of management and put a premium on quality and service. Following is a recap of *Forbes'* industry by industry outlook:

Aerospace and Defense
"Consolidation among defense suppliers seems finally to have begun in earnest."
In the Nimble 21: Loral Corp.

Business Services and Supplies
"The service industry is once again profiting as corporations let these cost-efficient suppliers do their dirty work."
In the Nimble 21: Automatic Data Processing

Capital Goods
"Business improved a bit for some makers of capital goods. That was good news, considering the industry's long slump."
In the Nimble 21: Emerson Electric Co.

Chemicals
"The chemical industry started to rebound in 1992. This year it should do even better."
In the Nimble 21: Rohm & Haas Co.

Computers and Communications
"For years, nimble PC clonemakers have nibbled away at IBM and other industry leaders. In 1992, the giants fought back."
In the Nimble 21: Advanced Micro Devices

Construction
"A wobbly economic recovery helped the construction industry turn the corner in 1992. This year's outlook for housing and highway building looks pretty good."
In the Nimble 21: Vulcan Materials

Consumer Durables
"The world turned upside down. GM imploded, Chrysler exploded and Japan eroded."
In the Nimble 21: Chrysler

Consumer Nondurables

"U.S. sales of household products and personal care products remained stagnant, but overseas markets continued to grow."
In the Nimble 21: Church & Dwight Co.

Electric Utilities

"At last the utility business is becoming competitive—thanks to the unregulated independent producers and weak demand growth."
In the Nimble 21: San Diego Gas & Electric

Energy

"The slump that began a decade ago didn't turn in 1992, and the year brings only a few hints of promise."
In the Nimble 21: Schlumberger, Ltd.

Entertainment and Information

"Movie companies, television networks, and publishers felt a mild recovery from the recession."
In the Nimble 21: Viacom, Inc.

Financial Services

"Banks and brokerage firms had a great year in 1992. Thank you, Alan Greenspan."
In the Nimble 21: NationsBank

Food Distributors

"Dining out hasn't lost its attraction in these lean times. In fact, restaurants that appealed to price sensitive customers were booming. But supermarkets and wholesalers struggled."
In the Nimble 21: Winn-Dixie

Food, Drink, and Tobacco

"As consumers brand loyalties weaken, these companies can no longer afford to be fat and happy."
In the Nimble 21: Dibrell Brothers

Forest Products and Packaging

"In 1992 the lumber business was great while the paper business was terrible. Expect more of the same this year."
In the Nimble 21: Louisiana-Pacific

Health

"Health care companies are scrambling to control the costs of their products and services—before Washington does it for them."
In the Nimble 21: Schering-Plough Corp.

Insurance

"Property insurers were battered by a string of calamities that made Hollywood disaster movies look tame."
In the Nimble 21: Cincinnatti Financial Corp.

Metals

"Metal prices remained depressed, which is good news on inflation but bad news for metal companies."

In the Nimble 21: Oregon Steel Mills

Retailing

"During the recession retailers and vendors got together and came up with better ways to manage inventory. The results should be bigger profits during the recovery." *In the Nimble 21:* Walgreen Co.

Transport

"In 1992 business was pretty bad for railroads and maritime companies. Truckers started to recover, but they will soon face government regulations." *In the Nimble 21:* Roadway Services, Inc.

Travel

"Carl Icahn is out. Can Al Checchi and Gary Wilson be far behind?" *In the Nimble 21:* Circus, Circus Enterprises

Books and Articles Forecasting the Job Market in the '90s

The Age of Unreason, Charles Handy (Harvard Business School Press, 1990). Extraordinarily wise commentary on where work and society are heading and what we can do to profit from the changes.

Careering and Re-Careering for the 1990's, Ronald Krannich (Consultants Bookstore, 1989). Information on current trends in the marketplace, how to identify opportunities, how to train or retrain for them, and how to land a job.

Careers for the '90's (Research and Education Association, 1991). Provides specific information on more than 250 jobs, including job descriptions, required education and training, earnings, working conditions, advancement opportunities, and outlook for the future.

Index of Employer Profiles (Career Research Systems, Inc., Fountain Valley, CA, published twice yearly, in March and September). A forecast of approximately 300 U.S. employers who expect to have management or professional opportunities in the following six months. Organized alphabetically and geographically.

Job Hunter's Source Book, Michelle LeCompte, editor (Gale Research Inc., 1991). Today's competitive job market has become increasingly complex. At any given time more than 7 million Americans are seeking employment. This useful guide profiles a wide variety of professions and occupations, and includes a job hunter's guide to the library and sources of job-hunting information.

"The Job Outlook for College Students to 2000" (U.S. Department of Labor, Bureau of Labor Statistics, *Occupational*

Outlook Quarterly, Summer 1990). On average, the U.S. Department of Labor expects about 92 percent of college graduates who enter the labor force over the 1988–2000 period to find college-level jobs.

"1993 Career Guide: Best Jobs for the Future" (*U.S. News & World Report,* Oct. 26, 1992). Success in the '90s requires a willingness to retool. Includes a regional salary survey and "hot tracks" in 20 professions, from accounting to wireless specialist.

Reinventing the Corporation, John Naisbitt (Warner Books, 1985). An intriguing look at what needs to occur within businesses and other organizations in order to prosper under contemporary conditions.

The Right Place at the Right Time: Finding a Job in the 1990s, Robert Wegmann and Robert Chapman (Ten Speed Press, 1990). How readers can most effectively conduct a job search in the current economy.

"Technology Without Borders Raises Big Questions for U.S.," Andrew Pollack (*The New York Times,* Jan. 1, 1992). A current trend in American companies is "the Global Lab," or the spreading of research and product development around the world, transcending national borders. This raises tough new questions for policy makers who want to preserve jobs for Americans.

Top Professions, Nicholas Basta (Peterson's Guides, current edition). The 100 most popular, dynamic, and profitable career opportunities for the 1990s and beyond. In-depth profiles of professions include information on salary and earning potential, current and projected number of professionals in the field, key entry-level positions, and contact numbers at professional associations.

"What's Ahead for America's 24 Key Industries" (*Business Week,* Jan. 11, 1993). "As confidence grows, it looks as if 1993 might be the year the economy finally shakes off the blues." Job prospects are looking up for college graduates. This article includes a 1993 outlook on manufacturing, high technology, natural resources, and finance.

"What's Ahead: 20 Predictions for 1993" (*U.S. News & World Report,* Jan. 6, 1992). Includes articles on the economic growth outlook for 1993, American banks and real estate loans, the federal debt, and the government's role in education, health, and safety.

V. ADDITIONAL RESOURCES

Books on Getting Organized

Balancing Career & Family, Marion Thomas (National Seminars Press, current edition). Overcoming the "Superwoman Syndrome." A handbook for balancing home and work and avoiding stress. Shatters the unreachable ideal of the perfect wife, mother, and career woman.

File . . . Don't Pile, Pat Dorff (St. Martin's Press, 1986). Systems of organization for every conceivable type of personal, business, and household paper.

The Job Search Organizer, John A. O'Brien (Miranda Associates, 1990). Handy workbook format to keep your client on track during a job search. Ideas adapt to a more inclusive notebook which your client may have set up already.

Solving the Work/Family Puzzle, Bonnie Michaels and Elizabeth McCarty (Business One Irwin, 1992). How to organize your life and eliminate unnecessary stress while balancing professional and personal responsibilities.

The Time Trap, Alec MacKenzie (AMACOM, 1990). A 20-year-old classic updated for the PC generation. This guide centers on "The Twenty Biggest Time Wasters" and how to avoid them.

Totally Organized, Bonnie McCullough (St. Martin's Press, 1986). How to organize your time and thoughts, using such down-to-earth methods as making lists and using notebooks.

Turn Chaos Into Cash, Jean Ross Peterson (Betterway Publications, 1989). A complete guide to organizing and managing your personal finances.

Books and Articles Specifically for Parents

Erasing the Guilt, Nancy S. Haug, M.S. and Nancy D. Wright, M.S., M.F.C.C. (Career Press, 1991). How to play an active role in your child's education—no matter how busy you are. This book offers guilt-free guidelines and practical, time-saving advice for parents who are concerned about laying firm foundations for their children's futures.

How to Help Your Child Choose The Right Career Objective, Frank Gruber, editor in Chief (The Research Institute of America, 1985). A pamphlet available in libraries and career centers designed to help you help your child thrive in the real world beyond school. It stresses acting as a role model for your child and helping him or her grow up with career awareness. Also mentioned are some pitfalls to avoid, such as concentrating too much on your child's test scores.

"Parent and Child: When Your Child Refuses to Follow Your Career Path," Lawrence Kutner (*The New York Times,* Oct. 31, 1991). A newspaper column advising parents what to do when their children's values and aspirations differ from their own.

Parenting: Ward and June Don't Live Here Anymore, Jim Dugger (National Seminars Press, current edition). This practical handbook is designed to help parents go beyond the stereotypes of what they *should* be, and be happy with the challenging—yet rewarding—experience of responsibly raising their own children. Also addresses the issue of how to help your children build lifetime values.

The Parents' Financial Survival Guide, Theodore E. Hughes and David Klein (The Body Press, 1987). Advice for parents on "achieving fiscal fitness," planning for the costs of school and college, helping your adult child, and more. Includes detailed information about such issues as life insurance policies and estate planning.

Guides for the College Bound

The Blue Chip Graduate, Bill Osher and Sioux Henley Campbell (Peachtree Publishers, 1987). A guide to landing the work your client wants, organized excellently for use during the college years.

College Home Videos
314 North 13th Street, #800
Philadelphia, PA 19107
800-248-7177

More than 125 official college videos provide a close-up look at colleges of interest. A chance to "visit" colleges at home if you are unable to do so in person.

Peterson's College Quest
A computer program to help the high school student—or college student seeking to transfer—select a college and search for financial aid. Order it through the *Guide to Four-Year Colleges* (next page) or see if your local or school library has it.

For the college selection: Your client identifies the qualities he is looking for in a college, choosing from hundreds available. The full data base is searched and a print-

COLLEGE VISITS

Mr. Robert Rummerfield
P.O. Box 21384
Charleston, SC 29413
Phone: 803-853-8149 or
800-944-2798

Robert Rummerfield, a former administrator at Johns Hopkins University, now arranges group visits for young people to colleges in the Mid-Atlantic and Southeast regions. He announces in the fall what colleges will be visited in the spring and in the spring, the fall itinerary. These trips are fully chaperoned, and visit four or five colleges in two or three days. They usually run no more than $300.

out shows colleges that match these needs.

For the financial-aid search: Your family's expected financial contribution is calculated and a personal report lists types of financial aid your client appears eligible for. This includes special cost and aid profiles of the colleges of interest.

Peterson's Guide to Four-Year Colleges (Peterson's Guides, updated annually). Detailed profiles of almost 2,000 colleges and universities, comparisons of entrance difficulty, financial-aid information, and Army ROTC section.

The Scholarship Book, Daniel J. Cassidy and Michael J. Alves (Prentice Hall, 1990). A comprehensive guide to private scholarships, grants, and loans for undergraduates.

Advocacy Organizations

For the Blind
Call the Job Opportunities for the Blind Program, at 800-638-7518.

For the Physically Challenged
President's Committee on Employment of the Handicapped
1111 20th Street N.W.
Room 636
Washington, DC 20036
Phone: 202-653-7518.

For Minorities
• League of United Latin American Citizens
National Educational Service Centers Inc.
400 First Street N.W.
Washington, DC 20001
Phone: 202-347-1652

- National Association for the Advancement of Colored People
  4805 Mount Hope Drive
  Baltimore, MD 21215-3297
  Phone: 303-358-8900

- National Urban League
  Employment Department
  500 East 62nd Street
  New York, NY 10021

For Women

- Catalyst
  250 Park Avenue South
  New York, NY 10003
  Phone: 212-777-8900
  Ask for their free career pamphlet, "Career Development Resources."

- U.S. Department of Labor
  Women's Bureau
  200 Constitution Ave. N.W.
  Washington, DC 20210
  Phone: 202-523-6652

- Wider Opportunities for Women
  1325 G Street N.W.
  Lower Level
  Washington, DC 20005
  Phone: 202-638-3143

Recommended Biographies and Autobiographies

The visions and dreams of those who came before us can inspire us to reach for our own ideals. Biographies and autobiographies portray the rich and memorable lives of a wide range of individuals, people who come alive to us in their genius and their failings. Often the stories are of scrappy kids who overcame their own difficult backgrounds to excel in careers of their choice. Whatever their stories, these people's joys and frustrations are inspiring to all seeking their way in life.

Blood Memory, Martha Graham (Doubleday, 1991). The autobiography of one of the most important and influential American artists. Martha Graham, a dancer, choreographer, and teacher, pioneered modern dance through her ability to conceive of dance differently, and created new forms of expression.

Boris Yeltsin: From Bolshevik to Democrat, John Morrison (Dutton, 1991). The story of Boris Yeltsin's life from his impoverished childhood in Russia's remote Ural Mountains to his triumph in the first direct elections ever held in Russia.

Eleanor: The Years Alone, Joseph P. Lash (W.W. Norton & Co., 1972). Following the death of her husband in 1945, President Franklin D. Roosevelt, Eleanor Roosevelt made her own controversial way. Her story shows what it takes to translate sympathy, vitality, and natural intellect into major influences on the quality of the national life.

Ellington: The Early Years, Mark Tucker (University of Illinois Press, 1991). Chronicles the youth of Edward Kennedy "Duke" Ellington, one of the twentieth century's most important musicians, whose distinctive style is rooted in Washington, DC's vital African-American community.

The First Woman Doctor, Rachel Baker (Julian Messner, Inc., 1944). Elizabeth Blackwell overcame the prejudice against women entering professions of the mid-1800s to become the first woman to practice medicine in America.

Frederick Law Olmstead: The Passion of a Public Artist, Melvin Kalfus (New York University Press, 1990). The story of the leader of the nineteenth-century urban-park movement, whose legacies include Central Park in Manhattan, Prospect Park in Brooklyn, and Franklin Park in Boston.

James Baldwin: Artist on Fire, W. J. Weatherby (Donald I. Fine, Inc., 1989). The story of James Baldwin, novelist, social thinker, and tireless crusader for civil rights.

Man of the House, Tip O'Neill with William Novak (Random House, 1987). Tip O'Neill chronicles his 50 years in public life, colorfully describing his rise from a humble childhood in Cambridge, Massachusetts (where the closest he ever got to Harvard was a summer job mowing the lawn) to speaker of the House of Representatives.

Marie Curie, Robert Reid (New American Library, 1974). A widely acclaimed biography of a great scientist, which brings to light the double standards women of accomplishment face and the difficulty of juggling a career and traditional female roles.

Margaret Bourke-White, Vicki Goldberg (Harper & Row, 1986). The story of the strong-willed woman who broke down the barriers against women entering the man's world of professional news photography and became one of the most important photojournalists of our time.

Margaret Mead: A Portrait, Edward Rice (Harper & Row, 1979). The saga of the controversial woman who contributed some of anthropology's most exciting fieldwork. At age 23, over the objections of her professors at Columbia University, Margaret Mead made the trip to the South Pacific which would later result in her classic work, *Coming of Age in Samoa.*

MOVIES AND HOW WE VIEW WORK/LIFE

Occasionally a movie comes along that has the power to change our perspective. Such films are useful as take-off points for conversations with our clients —they raise provocative questions on how lifestyles, values, and careers are shaped. They may be as serious and powerful as *Dead Poets Society* or as funny and off beat as *Tootsie.* You will run across many movies worth including in a discussion about life and work —for example, *Citizen Kane, It's a Wonderful Life, The Graduate* —in your video store, on TV, or at the theater.

My Life, Golda Meir (G.P. Putnam's, 1975). After a terror-shrouded childhood in Russia and a stormy adolescence in Milwaukee, Golda Meir went on to become the first woman to be prime minister of Israel. With commitment, courage, honesty, strength, and labor, she devoted her adult life to the birth and development of a nation.

A Sort of Life, Graham Greene (Simon & Schuster, 1971). One of the greatest authors of the twentieth century recalls his childhood, background, and the situations which formed him as a writer. Graham Greene's novels combine suspense with concerns about morality and spirituality.

West With the Night, Beryl Markham (North Point Press, 1983). An adventurer and philosopher, Beryl Markham, in 1942, was the first person to fly solo across the Atlantic from East to West. She describes how growing up in East Africa shaped her.

INDEX